RACE FOR THE PRESIDENCY

The American Assembly, *Columbia University*

RACE FOR
THE PRESIDENCY
THE MEDIA AND
THE NOMINATING PROCESS

Prentice-Hall, Inc., *Englewood Cliffs, New Jersey*

Library of Congress Cataloging in Publication Data
Main entry under title:

Race for the Presidency.

(A Spectrum Book)
At head of title: The American Assembly, Columbia
University.
"Advance reading for an American Assembly on Presi-
dential nominations and the media held at Seven Springs
Center, Mt. Kisco, New York, 1978."
Includes index.
1. Presidents—United States—Nomination—Congresses.
2. Mass media—Political aspects—United States—
Congresses. I. American Assembly.
JK521.R32   329'.01   78-11878
ISBN 0-13-750141-2
ISBN 0-13-750133-1 pbk.

10   9   8   7   6   5   4   3

PRENTICE-HALL INTERNATIONAL, INC. *(London)*
PRENTICE-HALL OF AUSTRALIA PTY. LIMITED *(Sydney)*
PRENTICE-HALL OF CANADA, LTD. *(Toronto)*
PRENTICE-HALL OF INDIA PRIVATE LIMITED *(New Delhi)*
PRENTICE-HALL OF JAPAN, INC. *(Tokyo)*
PRENTICE-HALL OF SOUTHEAST ASIA PTE. LTD. *(Singapore)*
WHITEHALL BOOKS LIMITED *(Wellington, New Zealand)*

Table of Contents

Preface

Long before the first state primary is held, presidential aspirants are reconnoitering the country, seeking visibility and backing and calculating their chances to become the party nominee months later—many months later.

But presidential hopefuls and their backers move in a mysterious way their wonders to perform. To most of the people who will eventually make their choice in the national election, the ways and means leading to the convention are remote and hard to fathom.

To Professor James David Barber of Duke University one thing seemed certain: reporters and news commentators played an outstanding role in presidential nominations. He concluded that a study of the nature and extent of this role would help to clear away some of the fog surrounding the complexities and in the end help us improve the process. "Thus far we Americans have been lucky," he said, "but there must be a better way to select our candidates."

Accordingly, Professor Barber assembled a group of academic authorities seasoned in the problems of research. And in a three-year project supported by the John and Mary R. Markle Foundation and The Ford Foundation, his team, through extensive personal interviews, long and patient perusal of newspaper and magazine files, and review of hour upon hour of television tape took a close look at the interaction between, on the one hand, television and newspeople and, on the other, the campaigners hustling coast to coast and border to border on behalf of their candidates. That interaction, the team found, has become the heart of the American presidential nominations system as the other major factors—e.g., parties and state and local bosses—seem to have withdrawn into the background.

The result of the study is this book. It comprised the advance reading for an American Assembly on Presidential Nominations and the Media held at Seven Springs Center, Mt. Kisco, New York, May 1978. The meeting brought together media specialists, campaign managers, and academicians to discuss changes in the presidential nominating process and in journalistic practices affecting it. (The report of the meeting is available from The American Assembly.) But the conclusions herein are significant for all of us and are offered not only to those professionally or peripherally engaged in campaigning but to those of us who ultimately decide who will go to the White House.

The opinions belong to the authors themselves and not to The American Assembly, a nonpartisan public affairs forum. Nor do the Ford and Markle Foundations, who generously funded the Seven Springs Assembly and the publication of this volume, necessarily support the views which follow.

Clifford C. Nelson
President
The American Assembly

Acknowledgments

Acknowledgment is gratefully made to the following for permission to reprint excerpts from works published by them:

St. Martin's Press, Inc. for quotations from *The Newscasters* by Ron Powers.

The New York Times for the quotation from R. W. Apple, "Democratic Chiefs Beginning to Rank Presidential Rivals," January 12, 1976. Copyright 1976 by the New York Times Company. Reprinted by permission.

Farrar, Straus & Giroux, Inc. and Candida Donadio and Associates, Inc. for the quotations from Michael J. Arlen, *The View from Highway 1* (New York: Farrar, Straus & Giroux, Inc., 1976). Copyright © 1974, 1975, 1976 by Michael J. Arlen. This material appeared originally in *The New Yorker.* Reprinted by permission of Farrar, Straus and Giroux, Inc. and Candida Donadio.

Oxford University Press for the quotations from Paul Fussell, *The Great War and Modern Memory* (New York: Oxford University Press, 1975).

Routledge and Kegan Paul, Ltd. for the quotations from H. S. N. McFarland, *Psychological Theory and Educational Practice.*

California Journal Press for the quotations from *Reporting: An Inside View* by Lou Cannon (Sacramento, Calif.: California Journal Press).

New Yorker for the quotation from "On the Campaign Trail with Mo Udall" by Elizabeth Drew, December 1, 1975 issue.

The Viking Press for the quotations from *Marathon* by Jules Witcover. Copyright © Jules Witcover 1977. All rights reserved. Reprinted by permission of Viking Penguin Inc.

Atheneum Publishers and Julian Bach Literary Agency, Inc. for the quotations from *The Making of the President, 1964* by Theodore H. White. Copyright © 1964 by Theodore H. White.

The New Republic for the quotation from an article by Robert Coles in the June 26, 1976 issue.

RACE FOR THE PRESIDENCY

James David Barber

Introduction

The old worry was that politicians dominate reporters, brandishing the sword of state; the new worry is that reporters dominate politicians, ruling the rulers with their pens. The worst of worries is the haunting fear that something has gone wrong with the way these characters dominate one another—and maybe the rest of us—as we puzzle over who ought to be President. We seem snagged on a paradox: thanks to the press, we know more than ever before about the candidates, certainly more than voters knew about Washington or Lincoln or the Roosevelts. Yet the modern Presidents who have come and gone since World War II would have to be placed, by any reasonable Dante, in mixed array among the circles of greatness and failure. We have been lucky, but these days there is much more riding on the throw of the dice than there ever was in the old-time village democracy.

That is the urgent challenge we address in these pages. We start with heavy handicaps. Groping for the journalist-politician nexus, we are none of the above: professors peering from outside at inside, in an age when every generalization is suspect. We have been trying that for several years now, and we have had a lot of help. With extraordinary openness and patience, presidential politicians and journalists gave us 222 long taped interviews. We collected what we could of the products of their interaction in 1975 and 1976—fifteen file drawers of clippings, more than 100 hours of television tape. The analytic labors were divided roughly as in the chapters below, though we met from time to time and all of us dealt with all of it. Arterton's vision focuses on the campaigners as they swim upstream in the media sea, first as a crowding school, then as a tight cluster pressing forward the winner-to-be. Matthews peers at the process from a high perspective: as the system-in-motion works its selective way, what operative criteria of

JAMES DAVID BARBER *is James B. Duke Professor of Political Science at Duke University.*

choice — likely to reappear next time and the time after that — are hardening around our presidential politics? Bicker views the nominating process from behind the television camera to see how the dynamics of modern network news organizations, with all their complex mix of function, help shape the process. Barber gazes (wonderingly at times) at the journalist as a literary person, a scientist, and an educator, and speculates as to how these cultural connections do and might direct the candidate-reporting enterprise. Then having mulled all that, alone and together, the assembled American conferers decided what to propose in the way of improvement.

Along this rocky road, we and the world lost Jeffrey L. Pressman. As in so many other realms of his life, Jeff gave us and this task his ardent labor, his shadow-piercing clarity of mind, his laughter, and his grace. We hold him in our memory as we write and speak, hoping the shine of his spirit shows a bit through these paragraphs and propositions.

Duke's Lawrence Goodwyn contributed sprightly interviews, and MIT's Edwin Diamond shared his triple vision (as teacher, newsman, and critic) with us amateurs.

Vanderbilt's Richard Pride did an insightful job selecting television materials for the research.

Our foundation mentors — from the first, Robert Goldmann of the Ford Foundation, at the last, Jean Firstenberg of the John and Mary Markle Foundation — thankfully would not stop with giving us money, instead got right into the act with their experienced wisdoms. The American Assembly's feisty bossman, Clifford Nelson, led us over crisis after crisis with his no uncertain terms.

On each of our campuses, we have said our thanks to the little bands of research assistants, secretaries, and bookkeepers whose thoughtfulness and diligence freed us to think our best; this is their book too.

So what will come of all this thinking? Gentle reader, that is up to you.

F. Christopher Arterton

1

Campaign Organizations Confront the Media-Political Environment

With the decline of political parties, the role of the mass media in the American electoral process has been enlarged. Newspapers, radio, news weeklies, and television have become the major source of information about election campaigns for the vast majority of American citizens. On the one hand, the corporate entities which comprise the communications media devote significant resources to news reporting and thus constitute the principal source of "objective news" about the campaign. On the other hand, these media either rent their services to campaign organizations in the form of political advertisements or donate them to campaigns as public service broadcasting or editorial statements (i.e., "Op. Ed." pieces). Thus, viewers, listeners, and readers—in the jargon of social science, those who "attend" the media—are provided with information of an overtly partisan nature transmitted through the media at the behest of candidates and their organizations or with information generated by organizations whose members subscribe to a journalistic creed of partisan neutrality. In either case, the prime means by which most voters derive their information about presidential campaigns are the mass media rather than through personal contacts with friends, family members, or work associates or by the direct efforts of political parties or candidate organizations.

The literature devoted to the relationship between print and broadcast media and American politics is still in its infancy. We do not have an abundance of careful studies of the role played by mass media in either the electoral or the governing process. The persistence of this vacuum is particularly surprising in view of the alarm frequently expressed concerning the potentials for media manipulation of an unwitting citizenry. The fact

F. CHRISTOPHER ARTERTON *is Assistant Professor of Political Science at Yale University.*

that these fears have proved largely undocumented cannot be taken as a conclusive demonstration that the media exert little influence upon our politics.

Drawing upon interviews with campaign managers and press secretaries from all the major 1976 presidential campaigns, this chapter will examine the perceived importance of news reporting organizations from the perspective of upper-level campaign decision-makers. The critical need which campaigners feel for making and shaping the news leads to a number of instances in which major aspects of campaign behavior are determined primarily by media considerations. And so, the inquiry is drawn to questions of what consequences the perceived importance of news reporting has for the conduct of presidential campaigns, and what can be done about those consequences.

To summarize the argument, our interviews repeatedly document the perception that the tasks of campaigning for the Presidency are so enormous that they cannot be accomplished without substantial reliance upon the news reporting process as a means of contacting and influencing voters. Beyond this, there are unique characteristics of the presidential nomination system which frequently make the perceptual environment in which candidates compete more important than the political realities. Since much of the perceptual environment is created/communicated by the news media, campaigners come to look upon the community of journalists as an alternative electorate in which they must conduct a persuasive campaign. The dominance of perception over concrete political support is particularly marked during the preprimary and early primary periods.The latitude of journalistic interpretation is also greatest at this time, when the indicators of growing or declining political support are at their poorest in predictive validity.

The result is a frequently noted overemphasis on the outcome of early primary and caucus states. If this media impact upon the nomination process is seen as undue, the solution lies not in searching for ways to reform campaign reporting, but in examining revisions to the political system which will diminish the importance of the early perceptual environment.

Campaigning through the Media

Political scientists studying the impact of listening to or reading reported news have been unable to document significant effects upon the attitudes, cognitions, or behavior of citizens. The effect may be there, but we have not been able to demonstrate it. In any case, political science findings notwithstanding, those who manage presidential campaigns operate on the conviction that what the media say about them will affect their candidates' votes on election day. The following quotes from our interviews impart some of the flavor of their campaigns' reliance upon the print and broadcast media.

> The television news organizations in this country are an enormously dominant force in primary elections. They're every Tuesday night, not only counting the votes, but, in some cases, setting the tone and, in almost all cases, reinforcing the tone of what the issues are that week. (Barry Jagoda, media advisor to Jimmy Carter)

> . . . the interpretation of the media [will be] that much more important than it was in '72, because I think that coming into the convention, if you're short of delegates, the real determining factor's going to be the psychological momentum the press creates. Is he the winner? Can he get the nomination? Is he acceptable? . . . and given that it's not going to be a clear and away winner, like no one's going to have enough, you know, an overwhelming number of delegates going into the convention, it makes that interpretation, that psychological momentum very important. (Frank Greer, press secretary to Fred Harris)

> You go into a place like New Hampshire and you've got two things in mind. Primarily is winning New Hampshire. Secondly is getting out the stories about your candidate and where he stands and all that to the rest of the country. . . . The more we have Ronald Reagan's name with the proper things in the papers, the better off we are, because it looks like he's moving around and it looks like he's active and it looks like he's campaigning. . . . (Franklyn Nofziger, press secretary to Ronald Reagan)

> Everywhere we go, we're on a media trip; I mean we're attempting to generate as much free television and print, as much free radio, as we can get. Any angle can play, whether it's his Congressional business or his campaign itself or the announcement of a state committee, anything that we can do that will generate a story everywhere we go. That's integral to the plans. (John Gabusi, campaign political Director for Morris Udall)

> You're really . . . running for President of the United States the way you would run for county school superintendent or state Senator or Governor or whatever, because . . . you're essentially going into a media market and trying to get all the good coverage you can there. And then you go to the next one and what happens in A has very little influence on what happens in B. . . . It's a very new audience, a new game, a new town, every day. . . . (Jody Powell, press secretary to Jimmy Carter.)

Political organization for electoral competition is primarily a communication process. Much of the business of campaigning involves contacting individuals, reaching them with persuasive messages. In the days when Americans were less geographically mobile and the reach of the corporate communications media less extensive, political parties served as preexisting, vertical, interpersonal links which could be mobilized on behalf of candidates during election campaigns. The difficulties of reaching voters during the campaign were eased by the maintenance of enduring political organizations.

In modern election campaigning, the functions served by the parties as ongoing networks of personal contacts can be achieved through use of different communication technologies: telephones, polling, direct mail, as well as the mass media. While these media require a good deal of expertise, they make superfluous the permanent organizations of party structures. Hence, they facilitate the emergence of ephemeral candidate organizations, i.e., campaigns.

That presidential candidate organizations should attempt to exploit the mass media is hardly surprising. The system under which we nominate and elect Presidents imposes a burden of rapid and repetitive communications with a diverse citizenry which temporary political organizations are simply incapable of achieving. It is natural for them to turn to the durable communication structures in order to campaign among a vast electorate. While an advertising program is almost always undertaken as a necessary component in the deployment of campaign resources, candidate organizations also attempt to load onto the media the costs of voter communication through the adoption of explicit strategies for dominating news coverage.

By the reasoning above, the media are important to campaigning at any level of our electoral system. Yet, there are certain factors unique to the presidential race in 1976 which heightened the strategic importance of the media for the contenders. These deserve some attention.

In the first place, journalists are forced by the economic realities of their organizations to make judgments as to the overall newsworthiness of the election contest in question. Quite obviously, the presidential race was deemed of greater importance than most other electoral campaigns and received consequently more coverage space. This is not to say coverage was unlimited; for while greater resources are ordinarily devoted to covering presidential politics, the amount of space available to even that campaign was a sharply limited portion of the total "news hole." Unlike many other campaigns, however, the presidential candidates did have a realistic opportunity to compete for national media coverage, although their prospects for coverage varied according to the degree to which they were seen as "serious" competitors.

Secondly, from the viewpoint of the campaigns, the large number of primaries complicated the task of campaigning for presidential nominations if only because of the sheer number of voters involved. The candidate organizations simply were not able to reach that large number of people and had to rely upon media to increase favorable name recognition. Initially, of course, the McGovern campaign (in 1972) and the Carter campaign began working in small states (Iowa and New Hampshire) where individual contact by the candidate or campaign operatives could reach enough voters to affect the election result. But that strategy of gaining votes could not be sustained in larger states or many more primaries. According to Joel McCleary, Carter's national finance director, "We had no structure after Florida; we had planned only for the short haul. After Florida, it was all NBC, CBS, and the *New York Times.*"

TABLE 1. Number of States Holding Presidential Primaries and Percent of Convention Delegates from Primary States Since 1912 by Party

	Democratic		Republican	
	Number of Primaries	Percent of Delegates	Number of Primaries	Percent of Delegates
1912	12	32.9	13	41.7
1916	20	53.5	20	58.9
1920	16	44.6	20	57.8
1924	14	35.5	17	45.3
1928	17	42.2	16	44.9
1932	16	40.0	14	37.7
1936	14	36.5	12	37.5
1940	13	35.8	13	38.8
1944	14	36.7	13	38.7
1948	14	36.3	12	36.0
1952	15	38.7	13	39.0
1956	19	42.7	19	44.8
1960	16	38.3	15	38.6
1964	17	45.7	17	45.6
1968	15	40.2	15	38.1
1972	22	65.3	21	56.8
1976	30	76.0	30	71.0

Source: Composed by the author from *Congressional Quarterly's Guide to U.S. Elections* and 1976 documents supplied by the Democratic National Committee.

Since 1968, the number of primaries has increased dramatically (Table 1). Because the percentage of convention delegates selected or apportioned by primary voters is now so large, candidates seriously seeking a presidential nomination either have to contest primaries or hope that the primaries produce a nomination deadlock, with a stalemated convention turning to them.

In 1976, most presidential candidates built their political strategy upon the demonstration effect of important primary victories. Campaign managers assumed that the increased number of primaries placed such a demand upon campaign resources that no one would be able to win the nomination outright, i.e., secure a convention majority in caucus or primary victories. They therefore counted upon the so-called "winnowing process" whereby candidates losing key primary battles would be forced to drop out of the contest. The strategy was to survive the primaries, enter the convention with a substantial block of delegates and the image of a winner, and walk away with the nomination on the first or second ballot.

Initially, all of the candidates except Wallace and Carter believed, therefore, they would win the nomination without entering the delegate selection process in every state. After the North Carolina primary—March 23, only one month after New Hampshire—the two Republican campaigns had to adjust their calculations to the developing struggle over every delegate. On the Democratic side—although most observers had not realized it by that point—the choice had become either a Carter victory in the primaries or an inconclusive primary season followed by a multiballot convention. In other words, no other Democratic candidate was entered in enough primaries to win the nomination before the convention.

As the number of primaries has expanded, the linkages between them have become more apparent, and the perceived role of media interpretation in making those linkages has increased. This argument was best expressed by John Sears, Reagan's campaign manager:

> When we only had four or five significant primaries ten years ago—that got any press attention anyway— . . . everybody knew New Hampshire was important but then you had a bunch of conventions and then you get to Wisconsin, and there was enough of a lag between the running of those two primaries—which usually were the most important—where people would sort of forget. . . . In a certain degree the Wisconsin primary would be run on its own. But that doesn't happen now [that] we have so many primaries, New Hampshire is still the most important; but once you get there, why everybody's writing that into the results in Florida because it happens so quickly. And as soon as that's over with, within a week afterwards, you're writing that into the minds of the people in Illinois.

> And this has raised the awareness of people as to how much of an important item the press is, and what they're doing. Previously people felt, "well the press, as long as we treat them fairly, and they look at us properly, why it's a matter of how well we do our other business." And now they begin to see that the press had a very great effect on the minds of the electorates as they move from place to place.

To be sure, victory in the New York primary may net the winning campaign a large number of delegates, but if commentary and reporting in the media convey the additional interpretation of progress in the race as a whole, then the victory pays larger dividends in terms of attracting support in subsequent primaries and weakening one's opponents. We shall return to this point below.

A third element enhancing the role of the media was provided by federal legislation. The 1976 presidential campaign was conducted under very different conditions for the financing of electoral politics, namely the 1974 amendments to the Federal Elections Campaign Act of 1971. In particular, two provisions of the act forced presidential campaigns to rely more heavily upon the media. First, the strict limits on the amount individuals could contribute to any one campaign ($1000) made raising money extremely difficult. In the preprimary period, for example, campaigners saw a direct relationship between the visibility and treatment they received in the national press and their ability to raise money. Typical was the lament of Fred Harris' press secretary:

> You're caught in a kind of vicious circle. In order to raise money, especially money from more than twenty states, then you have to have national media attention, not just good local media that Fred has been able to generate. . . .But in order to raise that kind of money dispersed among twenty states then you need national media exposure. You need it because people do judge by national media exposure as to whether the campaign is serious or not and, believe me, they hesitate before they give money. . . .They're going to wait until they see Fred's smiling face on national television.

The provision of federal subsidies to presidential campaigns at first appeared to make it more difficult for the stronger campaigns to overwhelm their opposition. The presumed effect of federal financing was to allow weaker candidates to remain in the race longer. In fact, subsidies barely compensated for the difficulties encountered in raising money under the contribution limits.

Second, limitations upon the amount of money campaigns could spend both in each state primary and over the entire nomination race placed a premium upon ways to pass the costs of communicating with the voters on to the corporately owned media. The fact that campaigns were limited in what they could spend and were also experiencing difficulty raising money led them to turn to the print and electronic media as a means of reaching voters, supporters, and uncommitted delegates.

Campaigning in the Media

In addition to the decline of political party structures, therefore, presidential campaigns were forced to turn to the mass media because of the complexity of their task and their inability to mobilize or employ other resources. Campaigners, aware of the level of resources committed by news reporting organizations to coverage of the presidential race, implemented, more or less explicitly, a news strategy to influence the coverage of their candidate. In so doing, they were interested not only in achieving a suitable volume of coverage, but they sought leverage over the content of news reports. Concerned with how the media would interpret campaign events, candidate managers and press secretaries came to view part of their function as conducting a persuasive campaign among the journalistic corps assigned to report upon the presidential race.

While assuredly campaigners at all levels believe that news reports will influence their ability to attract political support, the problem is more critical in presidential nomination races. The dynamics of presidential nominations accentuate the interpretive value of news reporting. Although the nomination is officially awarded by vote of convention delegates, presidential nominations are accomplished in a sequence of events stretching out over a six month period. Winning a presidential primary is, therefore, not like winning an election in which one individual secures a public office. Nor does a *presidential* primary resemble primaries held for other levels of public office (Governor, Senator, Congressman) in which one candidate emerges with the nomination as a tangible end product. There is a finality to the other electoral processes we experience: winning and losing are sharply distinguishable.

In presidential nominations, however, candidates acquire with each primary victory only a percentage (usually small) of the delegates needed for the nomination. To be understood clearly, winning a presidential primary must be set within the context of how the event contributes to the overall race. A given candidate's receiving only a bare majority of the votes may well indicate weaknesses which could be consequential in succeeding primaries; a narrow loss may demonstrate growing strength. Establishing the context within which the results of presidential primaries are to be understood is, in short, a matter of *interpretation*. Needless to say, the evidence needed to support that interpretation is difficult to obtain, thereby placing a premium upon the judgment of the individual or group of individuals who earn their living by making such interpretations, i.e., political journalists and practicing politicians.

Those who manage presidential campaigns uniformly believe that interpretations placed upon campaign events are frequently more important than the events themselves. In other words, the political contest is shaped primarily by the perceptual environment within which campaigns compete. Particularly in the early nomination stages, perceptions outweigh reality in terms of their political impact. Since journalists communicate these perceptions to voters and party activists and since part of the reporter's job is creating these interpretations, campaigners believe that journalists can and do affect whether their campaign is viewed as succeeding or failing, and that this perception in turn will determine their ability to mobilize political resources in the future: endorsements, volunteers, money, and hence, votes.

Both journalists and campaigners speak of the importance of "momentum," a vague conception that the campaign is expanding, gaining new supporters, and meeting (or, if possible, overachieving) its goals. In other words, in presidential nominations, because of the sequential nature of the process, the perceptual environment established by campaign reporting is seen as the meaningful substitute for political reality.

Reporters and political strategists, not surprisingly, often differ as to the nature of the race and the importance of a particular event to the general process. A passage from Jules Witcover's book *Marathon: The Pursuit of the Presidency, 1972—1976* in which he reacts to a frequently heard complaint illustrates the point:

> One unhappy Udall worker later stated in the *Washington Post* that the candidates themselves and the issues were lost in the efforts to draw press attention, and in the reporters' determination to draw significance from an insignificant exercise. "The reality of a presidential campaign," he wrote in a woeful misunderstanding of the dynamics of the system, "is the delegate count, but no significant number of delegates will be selected until March. . . ." The fact is that the reality in the early going of a presidential campaign is *not* the delegate count at all. The reality at the beginning stage is the psychological impact of the results—the perception by press, public, and contending politicians of what has happened.

Establishing "the psychological impact of the results—the perception by press, public, and contending politicians," however, is an exceedingly difficult judgment.

Consider, for example, a front page article in the *New York Times*, dated January 12, 1976, written by chief political correspondent R. W. Apple:

> A kind of rough standing among the candidates has suddenly started to emerge in the minds of political professionals around the country. . . . In the group from which the nominee is believed most likely to be selected are Senator Henry M. Jackson of Washington, Senator Birch Bayh of Indiana, former Gov. Jimmy Carter of Georgia and Senator Hubert Humphrey of Minnesota.
>
> In the second, candidates given a conceivable chance of being nominated, are former Ambassador Sargent Shriver, former Senator Fred R. Harris of Oklahoma and Morris K. Udall of Arizona. Some professionals think Mr. Udall belongs in the first category, but not many.
>
> In the third group, those most unlikely to be the nominee, are Senator Lloyd Bentsen of Texas, Gov. Milton Shapp of Pennsylvania, former Gov. Terry Sanford of North Carolina, Senator Frank Church of Idaho, Gov. George C. Wallace of Alabama and Senator Robert C. Byrd of West Virginia.
>
> Such early calculations are highly speculative. . . .

The illustration is not offered in order to criticize Apple's judgment—in fact as subsequent events revealed, his only error was in overrating Bayh's chances—but rather to point out that the criteria for asserting an emerging consensus among political professionals are not readily apparent. Apple refers to visits to twelve states and conversations with hundreds of politicians and activists as the basis for his article.

From the point of view of campaign operatives, this kind of rating has monumental consequences for their nomination prospects in two spheres: first, by facilitating or hampering their efforts to attract political support, and, second, by dictating the amount of news coverage they will subsequently receive. A subtle, reciprocal influence results from the pivotal role ascribed to campaign reporting by those who manage candidate organizations. On the one hand, beyond simply viewing the media as a convenient conduit to the electorate, campaign strategists are lead to attempting to influence the political judgments of the journalists themselves. Accordingly, the attitudes, beliefs, and behavior of the journalist corps become a milieu for political competition between presidential campaigns. On the other hand, campaigners accommodate their political strategies to the expected nature of campaign reporting. While their attempts to affect the judgments of newsmen are examined in the next chapter, strategic accommodation to those judgments — which, in my view, constitutes the most impressive evidence of media impact on presidential campaigning — is the focus of the remainder of this chapter.

Media Impact on Presidential Campaign Politics

The assertion that journalists exert an influence over the conduct of presidential campaigning does not imply that they intend such an impact or even that they could prevent the effects if they so desired. Whereas campaigns are quite open in their attempt to persuade journalists, the reverse influence relationship can be quite elusive. Anticipating the reactions of journalists, campaign decision-makers set their strategic plans and their daily behavior with a view toward how the press will report campaign events. The most direct influence of the media upon the campaign process derives primarily from the fact that campaign reporting is fairly predictable, and campaigners are able to design their activities taking these continuities into account.

On a superficial level, the building of campaign behavior around media considerations involves actions such as scheduling the campaign day so that events to be covered take place before deadlines; allowing a break in the schedule for filing stories; providing typewriters and telephones to facilitate the reporters' work; building into one's campaign organization a capacity to handle reporters' baggage and make their hotel and airline reservations; passing out schedules, advance texts of the candidate's major speeches, and other news releases containing reportable information; arranging private interviews with the candidate, family members, and staff personnel; and so on. In terms of organizational resources and candidate time, interactions with journalists comprise a substantial commitment of campaign effort. Much of what a presidential candidate organization actually does is related to its relations with the press, particularly those journalists who are assigned to travel with the candidate.

To a degree, this allocation is quite reasonable. For example, in his book *Political Campaign Management*, Arnold Steinberg argues that the value of the marginal advertising dollar must be weighed against the value of expending that dollar on staff work necessary for generating news coverage.

> Because visuals generate news coverage worth at least as much and probably more than commercials of equivalent time duration, the salaries of staff and related expenses to generate visuals must be measured by attaching a monetary worth to visual events.

He then goes on to estimate that the increased credibility that results from a news format makes that coverage worth at least one and a half times as much as the equivalent advertising time.

Beyond the mechanics of obtaining coverage, which, as noted above, may be taken as a rather trivial impact of news reporting on campaign behavior, campaigners frequently respond directly to criticism emanating from the corps of journalists. To present but a single prominent example, after Jimmy Carter was questioned by a reporter about his lack of a self-deprecating humor, for several days he worked humorous remarks about himself into his public appearances.

The influence of campaign journalism is felt on its most profound level, however, in the formulation of political strategies around media considerations. To the extent that they have control over the activities of their organizations, campaign managers plan with a view toward media interpretations as one facet of practically everything undertaken by the campaign. Major campaign decisions are rarely, however, based *solely* upon expected news reporting; media strategy and political strategy are intertwined as part of the same process. While few pure illustrations can be found in which campaign strategy was molded strictly by media considerations, the following case studies are instances in which the participants reported to us the supremacy of predicted news reporting in determining the campaign decisions. These examples extend to every arena in which campaigns must make strategic decisions: campaign organization, fund raising, the timing of decisions, scheduling, and the selection of key primary states.

CASE 1: SANFORD'S "LICENSE TO PRACTICE"

During 1975, a number of candidates began to build their political organizations around a replication of McGovern's effort in 1972. Like a number of others, Terry Sanford, the former Governor of North Carolina, decided to concentrate his efforts on a few early primaries (New Hampshire, Massachusetts, and North Carolina) and to rely upon his contacts in North Carolina to provide his financial base. Other funds were to be collected by building a financial arm into the primary organizations in states where he would make an effort. Thus, initial money would be raised only in three or four states and later the effort could be extended to the twenty states needed to qualify for federal matching funds.

By the summer of 1975, however, Sanford found his strategy running headlong into a perception among journalists that "qualification" constituted an important test of which candidates should be taken seriously. Since during the preprimary period, the amount of news space devoted to the coming presidential race is quite limited, judgments as to the newsworthiness of events of candidates can be quite consequential as to a candidate's ability to attract news coverage and, thereby, gain exposure to political activists and voters.

The Sanford staff and those of several other candidates had difficulty in obtaining coverage in the absence of meeting the qualifications for federal matching money. They reported being told specifically they would not be covered until they had qualified. As discussed by his press secretary, Paul Clancey, on July 7, 1975:

> That's definitely where the press corps has been known to influence the actions of the campaign, because we [or rather] Sanford maintained for a long time that he was not going to waste his energies on getting up political matching funds, and yet, it has become about the only game in town. . . . He had a major statement on defense spending last week and Udall got all the play because he could qualify in twenty states.

Jim Hightower, Harris' campaign manager, noted similar pressure upon his campaign, July 8, 1975:

> The press had decided that's the way they're going to certify who a candidate is, if you raise a hundred thousand dollars, which is ludicrous, number one, but it is a game they're playing. And not only are they trying to do it, but I think they've succeeded; I think we've got to go raise our $100,000 now.

John Gabusi, Udall's campaign manager, in an August 8, 1975 interview supported their view:

> The media start looking for the most simple benchmarks they can. For instance, they've all hopped on the idea that qualifying for matching funds means something more significant than in reality it may be. I mean, it really doesn't make any difference to our campaign or to Birch Bayh if they qualify on December 31st or July 1st because they still get the same amount of money on January 1, whatever it is. But, in the minds of the media, they have found a simple measuring tool that says "ah-ha, that makes them more significant because they can do it earlier."

The attention by news organizations to whether candidates had qualified or not took place despite the widespread recognition among campaigners that the test was meaningless as a real indicator of political strength. The sarcasm of Hightower's comment above was echoed by Sanford's campaign manager, Jean Westwood:

Everyone thinks that once you've got $100,000, you're viable. Well how far does $100,000 go in a national campaign? And you receive no matching money until the 1st of January no matter how much you raise.

Despite this interpretation of the political realities confronting the campaign, Governor Sanford decided he had to conform to those standards which would facilitate access to news coverage. At his press conference on July 2, 1975, describing qualifications as a "license to practice," he committed his organization to raising the necessary funds within one month, much to the surprise of his finance people. Raising money in twenty states instead of three or four necessitated an entirely different organizational structure, diverting resources away from the states in which he planned to make his early efforts. Staff members would have to be sent into nonessential states to set up "fund raisers" and Sanford's schedule would require him to spend less time in New Hampshire, Massachusetts, and North Carolina.

Not surprisingly, Sanford's switch in strategy did not receive a great deal of press coverage. In the July 3, 1975 *Washington Post*, David Broder, summarizing the press conferences of Sanford and Udall, referred to Sanford as "one of five candidates still struggling to cross that barrier [qualification]," and mentioned his hopes to qualify in July. A week and a half later, in the July 13 *New York Times*, Christopher Lydon quoted Sanford's "license to practice" in an article on the difficulties of raising money.

Sanford found qualifying harder than anticipated, perhaps because it does require an organizational commitment to raise money in each state. On October 23rd the *New York Times* carried a wire service report that Sanford had mentioned at a news conference that he had qualified in September, "but did not announce it then because he did not believe it important enough."

CASE 2: UDALL AND THE IOWA CAUCUSES

From their initial decision-making in early 1975 to November of that year, the Udall campaign planned to make their first solid effort in the New Hampshire primary under the assumption that, as in years past, the print and broadcast media would devote a great deal of attention to the build-up and results of that first primary. Campaigning in New Hampshire, Udall would attract considerable press coverage; winning New Hampshire (followed, hopefully, by a win in Massachusetts) would catapult him into the front runner status. It was a familiar route: "Our strategy," explained Stewart Udall, the candidate's brother, in a July 8 interview, "has to be a McGovern/ Jack Kennedy strategy in the key states, which are New Hampshire,

Massachusetts, and Wisconsin." Other interviews confirmed the same strategy; while Udall did have the beginning of an organization in Iowa, which was to hold precinct caucuses on January 19, the first major test was planned for New Hampshire.

Beginning on October 27, however, the national political reporters began to devote so much attention to the upcoming Iowa caucuses that it soon became apparent that the first big splash of the 1976 race would occur there, rather than in New Hampshire. R. W. Apple's piece in the October 27th *New York Times* not only put the spotlight for the first time on Carter's growing strength, but it also signaled the fact that the Iowa caucuses would be an important event from the perspective of news reporting organizations.

The significance of Apple's piece was enhanced by the clairvoyance of his reporting in 1972, interpreting the caucus results in Iowa as demonstrating unexpected McGovern strength. As in 1972, Iowa could be the first opportunity to observe which candidates were "emerging from the pack." According to Witcover in *Marathon:*

> The media's seizing upon Iowa, though it chose only 47 of 3008 delegates to the Democratic National Convention, was both understandable and defensible . . . in 1976, if there were going to be early signals, the fourth estate was going to be on the scene *en masse* to catch them.

All the attention caused the Udall campaign to reconsider its decision to stay out of Iowa. As frequently happens, the decision caused a split within the campaign. The efforts of key participants to explain their positions after the fact provide a unique opportunity to observe the importance of predicted media coverage in major political decisions. The campaign political director argued for making a major, albeit eleventh hour, effort in Iowa. His position was reinforced by a memo (quoted in *Marathon*) prepared by a key advisor after an exploratory trip into the state. The important passage of that memo read:

> • Iowa justifies the expense. It will be covered like the first primary always has been in the national press. If we can emerge as the clear liberal choice in Iowa, the payoffs in New Hampshire will be enormous.

Despite the argument by others in the campaign that it was by then too late to make a successful effort in Iowa, the political director's side finally won with the additional argument that even if they did not win Iowa, at least their presence there would keep the (liberal) front runner from emerging in the headlines until New Hampshire. The Udall campaign committed about $80,000 and, an even more precious resource, ten days of the candidate's time to the Iowa effort.

While it can never be ascertained whether this decision to switch resources away from the New Hampshire effort resulted in a poorer showing there, it certainly did not improve their New Hampshire campaign. With hindsight, Udall staffers admitted the preeminence of the media considerations in their mistaken venture:

> Iowa was regrettable in that we had not inclination or desire to devote resources and time and money to Iowa. But it became such a media event that I think some of our staff people — national staff and Iowa staff — panicked in the face of it, and we rushed in headlong. (Press secretary Robert Neumann)

> In 1975, the argument had been made in the press in the Spring of that year, that they were going to take another look somewhere besides New Hampshire. Well, I never believed that; I believed that the first election where people walked into booths and pulled the levers, that that was the beginning. . . . I just said we put all our marbles in New Hampshire and we start there. When I left the campaign in the middle of September . . . I didn't think we were going to make an effort there [in Iowa], and that had been the judgment of the campaign. The when other people who were then in campaign positions began to take the position that the press might do it [in Iowa]. . . . They reversed a decision that had been made and was there for a year. . . . The worse thing that happened was we took ten days away from the New Hampshire schedule, Mo's traveling time. (John Gabusi)

Their discovery that the media planned to cover the Iowa caucuses as extensively as they would the early primaries led Udall's advisors to conclude that they could not let the other candidates (principally Bayh and Carter) get the jump on them either in sheer amount of coverage or in favorable perceptions of political progress communicated by the media to New Hampshire voters. Needless to say, by·any standard this was a major campaign decision.

CASE 3: REAGAN AND SCHWEIKER

In the latest edition of *Presidential Elections,* Nelson W. Polsby and Aaron B. Wildavsky describe the condition of uncertainty which precedes convention balloting. To paraphrase their argument, delegates cannot be sure who other delegates will support and for how long, or what effects declaration or switches of support will have on other delegates, or who is going to win and when is the best time to get on that candidate's bandwagon so as to obtain a claim on the winner. A delegation's estimates are determined, in part, by what other delegates are going to do, which in turn may depend upon what still others are going to do or say they are going to do, and so on.

In the 1976 Republican race, much of the uncertainty which Polsby and Wildavsky describe had been eliminated by the continuous efforts of the major news reporting organizations to keep track of delegates' sympathies and commitments. The support claimed by the President Ford Committee as self-interested participants, inevitably ran well ahead of the estimates made by the networks and the *New York Times,* whose delegate counts were widely accepted as valid statements of the progress of the race. In the middle of

July, for example, the PFC claimed to have the needed number of delegates, while the media counts showed Ford not yet there, but closing in on the nomination.

Obviously the Reagan campaign was in a difficult position. To counter their deteriorating situation, John Sears arranged for Reagan to announce that Senator Richard Schweiker would be his choice for the vice presidential nomination. That announcement raised the possibility of broadened Reagan coalition, and meant, at a minimum, that delegates would have to be repolled to record any switches. As it turned out, the day of the Schweiker announcement, CBS News had been preparing a story for broadcast *that night*, projecting Ford the nominee on the basis of their delegate polls. Clearly the proposal of Schweiker as a running mate was a response to the political situation; but the timing of the announcement was related to necessity to forestall exactly such an occurrence in which one of the news reporting organizations would declare Ford the nominee. If that happened, the race would be over:

> We realized that something like that was going to happen fairly soon. There you have a clear situation where we had to try a defense; because if that had ever been broadcast over CBS one night, we would have had much less support than we ultimately had. (John Sears)

CASE 4: THE ROSE GARDEN STRATEGY

An incumbent President has a built-in advantage of being newsworthy in everything he does. The Presidency provides a forum from which the occupant can attempt to proselytize voters without giving the appearance of campaigning. The incumbent does not have to struggle to make the news; on the contrary, he has the luxury of deciding what kind of news he wants to make.

During the nomination campaign, Ford's advisors noticed a relationship between his national poll and ratings and the degree to which he was making news *as a candidate*:

> When he went out on the stump, his inexperience as a campaigner showed up. Throughout a day of five or six speeches, he would tend to get more strident and more partisan and harder on the attack, and when people began to see him this way on the evening news every night, his national approval ratings tapered off. Then, when he'd stay in the White House for three or four months, he'd come back a little bit in the national polling. (Robert Teeter, pollster for Ford)

A strategy book prepared for the general election campaign by Stuart Spencer and Robert Teeter recommended that Ford remain in the White House and make the news through presidential business. Contrasting campaigning in 1976 with the experience of 1948 (Ford liked to compare his political circumstances to those of Truman), the strategy book focused upon the consequential role of the media. According to Teeter:

> If Truman had to implement his '48 campaign today, he would probably lose because of TV. Truman was not that good on the stump (his speeches were awful!) and, while his "Give 'Em Hell, Harry" style was pleasing to relatively small crowds—who would only see it once—it probably would have quickly worn thin if seen nightly by millions in living color. (Witcover's *Marathon*)
>
> So this was the basis for the campaign strategy in the general election, the Rose Garden strategy. The President simply did better in communicating with the voters when he was perceived as President, not as a candidate for President. (*Campaign for President: The Managers Look at '76*, by Johnathan Moore and Janet Fraser)

While the briefing book emphasized the special role of television, roughly the same argument can be made for print reporting. Given a choice between making the front page of most newspapers by kissing a cowgirl, as happened during the Texas primary, versus greeting a foreign head of state at the White House, it is natural to see why Ford's advisors would lean toward the latter.

Normally, the candidate's time is one of the most precious resources available to a campaign. While Ford's advisors were persuading him not to campaign, their counterparts in the Carter organization were meticulously allocating his campaign days to key states according to an elaborate point system. Yet the Ford campaign decided to dispense with half the available days, because of the impact of campaign reporting.

An important difference exists between the first two case studies examined above and the latter two. The Reagan decision to select a running mate before the convention and the Ford plan to avoid campaign reporting were dictated simply by the fact that presidential campaigns are covered so extensively and intensively by the news media. On the other hand, the earlier campaign decisions are grounded in journalists' assumptions about the presidential race which determine campaign coverage both in substance and in allocation patterns. In the Sanford case, the assumption that qualification for federal matching funds was a reasonable criterion for separating serious from nonserious candidates imposed that standard upon the campaign. For Udall, the decision by many news reporting organizations to cover the Iowa caucuses in depth provided the stimulus for reevaluating the political strategy. The decision to allocate coverage to Iowa, of course, assumes that the Iowa results would be a valid indicator of progress in the national nomination race. The fact that it was the only barometer, or the first, does not, however, make it valid.

The dynamic element in an election campaign is rising or declining (or stagnating) political support. The task of a political reporter is complicated gravely by a lack of good indicators of candidate support. Some, like organizational strength, are difficult to measure. While amount of money or endorsements may be easier to observe, their value in generating electoral strength is open to question. In 1976, poll standing—frequently cited as the most reliable indicator—changed markedly over the course of both the prenomination and postnomination phases of the presidential campaign.

In the preprimary and early primary periods, therefore, the indicators of political support are at their poorest. At this time, however, the journalistic community is under considerable pressure to predict the nomination outcome as soon as possible. That pressure has at least four sources. Individual journalists build and maintain professional reputations for sagacity among their colleagues. News organizations compete to provide their readers, viewers, or listeners with rapid yet accurate reporting. A large field of candidates confronts media organizations with a difficult problem of assigning resources to provide coverage of everyone. Separating out those candidates with serious prospects for winning the nomination mitigates this problem; the earlier this can be achieved, the better. And, lastly, as campaigns gain political support, the candidate and upper-level staff become increasingly inaccessible. News reporting organizations, understandably, wish to assign reporters or correspondents to expanding campaigns while there still remain prospects for developing sources within the campaign and garnering a personal understanding of the candidate. Thus, both in the organizational planning for the reporting of news and in the substance of the early news reports, journalists undergo forces counter to the cautious treatment warranted by the inaccuracy of the available support indicators.

When the indices of political support are of weak predictive value, the professional judgments of journalists have, consequently, their widest latitude. As a result, interpretive commentary exerts its maximum impact on coverage patterns as well as the content of news reporting during the early stages of the nomination race. In other words, the strategic impact of the media upon the political environment within which presidential campaigns compete is greatest when the available indicators are weakest and require/permit the maximum in journalistic judgment and interpretation. Since communicating with voters and activists through news formats has become so central to campaigns, both in terms of substance and volume, the criteria by which newsmen conduct their own work—as, for example, their decision rules for separating serious from non-serious candidates—become standards to which campaigns must conform. In most cases, the significance of these benchmarks has become so widely shared by journalists and politicians alike through past experience that they are programed into the advance planning of campaign strategies. Few individuals of either profession question the arbitrary importance of the New Hampshire primary. It is, however, possible to see the pronounced impact when changes occur. In the two instances cited above, the fact that they involved indicators or standards not applied in the reporting of previous nomination races is hardly accidental.

While journalists *must* make these judgments in predicting future success and allotting coverage to candidates with serious prospects, they are unquestionably aware of, and uncomfortable with, the frailty of the data with which they must work, particularly during the long preprimary period. For example, the R. W. Apple piece quoted above, which ranked Democratic candidates in early January, continued (on the inside) as follows:

> Such early calculations are highly speculative. . . . Public opinion polls are of little utility until the electorates in various states get to know the candidates. So most of the judgments are based on instincts—instincts that may be thrown off this year by the unusual size of the field, by the new campaign financing laws and by the changes in the number and the order of primaries.

> But early calculations have a life of their own, because they are the backdrop against which politicians and the media tend to measure the performance of the various candidates in their early confrontations.

As a result, the early caucuses and primaries are seen as the first "hard news" stories of the presidential race, a perception which almost guarantees an inflated value placed on the results of these events. The assumption that these early delegate selection events have improved validity over indicators available during the preprimary season warrants skepticism. The unrepresentative nature of early contests is neglected because *finally* the contest has begun and there is, at last, hard news to report. This reasoning accounts, I believe, for the frequently remarked upon overabundance of coverage devoted to the initial primaries and caucuses and overestimation of the significance of these early results. For example, in a careful count of stories on the network evening news shows and in three daily newspapers during three months before the New Hampshire primary, political scientists Michael Robinson and Karen MacPhearson reported that fully 54 percent of the print stories and 60 percent of the broadcast time devoted to the 1976 presidential race dealt with the New Hampshire primary. A similar examination of coverage after New Hampshire by Thomas Patterson revealed that, after his early wins, Jimmy Carter dominated the news, receiving two to three times as much attention as that given any other candidates. The early delegate selection events themselves are given undue importance as yardsticks, and, consequently, the significance of their outcome is overstated.

Qualitatively, one could cite numerous examples in which the relevance of these first bits of "hard" data to the national political process was overestimated. After the Iowa caucuses, the *Miami Herald* awarded Carter the status of "front runner" with a story on January 21 headlined "Now Jimmy Carter's the Man to Beat." *Newsweek's* February 2nd analysis was only slightly more cautious:

> But the Iowa caucuses were serious business as well, the first event of the 1976 political calendar and an early litmus test of candidate credibility. And, when all the votes were counted, the caucuses had thrust a fresh new face into the *forefront* of Presidential *speculation:* Jimmy Carter. . . .

After the New Hampshire primary, NBC's Tom Pettit described Carter as "the man to beat," while *Time* on March 8 opined "his is the only campaign that holds real possibilities of breaking far ahead of the pack." Carter was on the cover of both major news weeklies: he appeared alone on the cover of *Newsweek* and was featured as a caricature astride a donkey being restrained by the other candidates on the *Time* cover. The clear cumulative impression of this news commentary is that Carter was breaking away and becoming the odds-on favorite for the nomination. Yet, after the New Hampshire primary, five states had selected or apportioned 145 delegates, or less than 5 percent of the total.

This reasoning can be labeled the "rush to judgment" argument: that is, the need to predict the nominee early and the lack of meaningful indicators during the preprimary period produces an overestimation of the importance of the first "hard news" (i.e., real delegate selection events) with the result that the overestimation becomes a self-fulfilling prophesy shaping subsequent delegate selection events. The rebuttal to this argument has been stated succinctly by Jules Witcover in the earlier citation. The importance of the initial events, according to the Witcover argument, derives from their "psychological impact" upon those actively involved in the nomination politics (candidates, campaigners, party activists, and party voters in subsequent primaries). News reporting merely records that psychological impact without itself contributing to it.

The "no-independent-impact" argument has two weak points. The first has been mentioned above: observing psychological impact is extremely difficult. The second is that if people hear about those results through the news which arrives with interpretation as to the meaningfulness of those results built-in, it is difficult to sustain the argument that the interpretation will be weighed separately from the "hard facts" (i.e., the actual results).

The results of early delegate selection events are not described as one candidate obtaining a small plurality in a multicandidate field in the first of a number of similar exercises. Instead, the sequential nature and diversity of the nomination process is too frequently neglected, even though the assumption that early primaries are representative of national sentiment is highly dubious. Yet, to aggravate the impact of these early interpretations, the behavior of the news reporting industry itself is directly determined by these perceptions, i.e., press coverage is thereafter directed disproportionately toward the winner.

Impact on Political Values

Where values embedded in the political process of selecting a presidential nominee run counter to those of news reporting, the former are often sacrificed. The examples described in case studies above are specific instances of yielding to journalistic values. On a systemic level, deference to journalistic values has also frequently implied the supplanting of political values. Since 1968, for example, the Democratic party has, through national rule changes, moved to optimize proportional representation in delegate selection systems. Yet, as Professor Patterson has pointed out, news reporting, by its overwhelming attention to winners, establishes a "winner-take-all" system.

Overemphasis on early results derives from interpretation of these events as valid indicators of national support, a tenuous assumption at best. Politically, the nomination race is a complex sequence of events in fifty states of great diversity. The structure of political competition, the local political culture, the type of primary, and the level of active campaigning are variables which complicate the generalizability of any one state to the national political process, particularly for small states early in the process. If historically diversity is a political value in the presidential nomination process, continuity is a dominant theme in reporters' interpretations which assume that one state's result is indicative of the national trend.

The "rush to judgment" runs counter to another important political goal. The delegate selection system is constructed so as to allow party activists opportunities to defer their choice for the nominee. In 1976 delegates were selected or apportioned toward the end of the primary calendar. In fact, 47 percent were apportioned during the last six weeks, between May 4 and June 8. In addition, the increasing percentage of delegates selected under proportional representation rules enhances the prospects that early events will fail to produce a determining result. Opportunities to defer judgment permit party leaders to observe a candidate's appeal in a variety of electoral settings and over several months of intense scrutiny.

If the results of primaries early in the process are interpreted as producing a front runner sustained by national popular support, however, an attempt to defer judgment until the convention—a "decision-making" or "brokered" convention depending upon one's viewpoint—runs the risk of being interpreted as an antidemocratic move. That the evidence of national popular support is from a few states voting in multicandidate fields is easy to overlook.

After listening to many of our respondents catalogue the impact of media commentary upon presidential campaigning, we asked what improvements they could envision. The best advice we received in response came from the manager of Udall's campaign, a campaign which, according to Peter Goldman of *Newsweek,* in a June 4, 1976 interview, had a justifiable complaint:

> It's possible that Udall has at least an arguable complaint about what's happened to him, you know with his wins and his inability to draw attention to himself and his positions and his continuing name recognition problem. So that . . . even after all this time, he's got to explain to people who he is, in some states . . . when Carter has . . . a couple of covers in each of the news magazines, he gets most of the air time—not most of it, but a good bit of it on the 11:30 primary night shows, and the "Today Show" and the "Evening News" the next day—and so the focus tends to be on the front runner, and I think some of the "also-rans" (Udall is the most conspicuous, I think) tend to get lost in the shuffle, and they may have a legitimate complaint.

In contrast to Goldman's perceptions, John Gabusi capsulized the perspective of campaigners:

> Maybe I'm too cynical, I mean, the fact of the matter is that you can make those kinds of criticisms but history proves that it doesn't make any difference; that's how they report it, that is how they've been reporting it, and that's how they will report it. It is bred in the nature of what the press is about. To say that they should not be what they are about, is to say well then they're not the press. Then you have government control of the press or you have somebody whose going to decide what they do, but no longer are they constituted the way they are, that's what it's about. They've got rating problems, they've got to hype things, they have to create conflicts to build interest. I mean, you have to do that, that's the business you're in. So I don't criticize them. They did precisely what we expect them to do.

While one may suggest improvements in campaign reporting, the recognition that one cannot—and should not—dictate the nature of campaign reporting leads to consideration of various *political* reforms of the nomination system which could operate to reduce the impact of journalistic interpretations.

A single national primary would abolish the sequential nature of nomination contests. The press, politicians, and public would not be confronted with "psychological impacts" of early results, although no doubt special groups within each party would form to award endorsements and these would be covered as legitimate campaign events. On the other hand, a national primary would probably reduce significantly the "openness" of the current nomination system. Candidates from outside established party circles or those with low levels of name recognition would be denied their present opportunities to concentrate those resources they do command on an initially smaller electorate. Thus, the sequential nature of our current system, with the resultant importance of perceptions and interpretations which journalists convey, does have a value in allowing weaker candidates some prospects for securing the nomination.

A regional primary system would incorporate the virtues of a sequential process leading to a national convention, while ensuring that the first event would be major enough to ease the difficulties of assuming representativeness.

Finally, some incremental steps may modify the relationship between campaign reporting and the realization of political values. Recently, for example, the Democratic party's Commission on Presidential Nominations and Party Structure (Winograd Commission) has recommended shortening the period within which delegates can be selected to thirteen weeks, from early March to early June. In other words, early caucus states and New Hampshire would be forced to move their delegate selection procedures into a shorter primary season. Assumedly, in a shorter delegate selection period, caucuses and primaries would cluster together, reducing the possibilities that any one state's results would receive overwhelming attention.

Any systemic modification short of a national primary cannot totally eliminate the propensity of political observers and journalists to focus on certain states, while ignoring others. For example, in the 1976 Democratic race, three states, California, New Jersey, and Ohio held primaries on the same day (June 8), but most attention was directed toward the Ohio contest. Likewise, on April 6, the significance of Senator Jackson's win in the New York primary was downplayed by a concentration on Wisconsin results. Among a range of early events, some state contests will always seem to be more critical and receive greater attention.

The three possibilities for change proposed here appear in reverse order of their likelihood of adoption. The actions of the Democratic party may indeed serve to narrow the period in which states may select delegates in 1980. The year 1976 saw the development of protoregional primaries in the Northeast, Northwest, and Border States. Very likely, the number of state primaries will continue to expand. A federal imposed regionalization, however, seems unlikely until the currently emerging system is perceived as no better than its predecessor. A national primary may well be the ultimate result, but also will probably only come about when experimentations with the other, less drastic, changes are widely perceived as unsuccessful.

F. Christopher Arterton

2

The Media Politics of Presidential Campaigns:

A Study of the Carter Nomination Drive

Relationships between presidential campaigns and news reporting organizations exhibit the characteristics of political influence; that is, actors on both sides are engaged in influencing each other in an effort to determine the news story for that given day. They are also maneuvering to expand their influence in future interactions.

One model by which the interaction of journalists and campaigners can be understood is that of adversarial relations as is captured by such titles as *Us and Them: How the Press Covered the 1972 Election* and *The Adversaries: Politics and the Press*. Campaign operatives seek to reach voters by manipulating the behavior of reporters and correspondents, while journalists are attempting to pry out of the campaign information about the strategy, organization, issue positions, and character of the candidate which the latter would prefer to keep from public view. Conflict between campaigners and journalists is quite real, but does not encompass the entirety of their interactions. While campaign-media relations are adversarial in part, they are also cooperative.

A symbiosis of the goals of journalists and those who manage presidential campaigns provides for a good deal of mutually beneficial interaction. On the one hand, news reporting organizations certainly define the presidential race as an important story which must be covered. Newspapers, magazines, radio and television stations, wire services, and networks, all wishing to bring their audiences information about the presidential campaign, are willing to expend considerable resources in news gathering and to devote a substantial portion of their "news hole" to presenting campaign events and commentary. Presidential candidate organizations, on the other hand, seek to use the news reporting process as a relatively inexpensive means of communicating with voters and political activists. Campaigns, therefore, are altogether happy to facilitate journalists in the conduct of their work.

Examining the relationship between the media and the incumbent Presidents, political scientists Michael Grossman and Francis Rourke describe the interactions as an exchange process in which reporters and officials each bring assets into a bargaining system through which the news is created. Both the White House press corps and the Presidency seek to alter in their favor the balance of trade between them: executive officials to confine the news to items favorable to them, reporters to broaden the range of potential news items.

A great deal of Grossman and Rourke's exchange model is adaptable to interaction during the campaign. But rather than adopt their terminology, I prefer to bring to this study language from the analysis of power relations. This approach focuses attention upon the political aspects of campaign-media interactions. Not surprisingly, those experienced in persuasive appeals for electoral support (campaigners) are sensitive to aspects of power and influence implicit in their relationship with journalists.

Although campaign personnel frequently use the word "control" when describing their impact upon "the free media," they really mean "influence." Campaigners recognize that the reported news is a result of many factors, most of which lie beyond their ability to affect.

Consideration of the power aspects of the relationship between press and politicians does not suppose, therefore, that campaigners can force journalists to write particular stories. Rather than attempting to influence directly the news product, campaigners search for circumstances in which they can narrow the range of available stories and interpretations, without incurring the costs of journalists' ire that might accompany overt penetration of the news reporting process. Candidates and their advisors are, for example, very aware of the consequences of political success for developing leverage over those journalists assigned to cover them.

Mutual influence relationships naturally involve a clash of perspectives which poses a difficult problem of empirical validation. One cannot accept as proof assertions by campaign operatives that they have succeeded in influencing the news coverage received by their candidate. Similarly, claims by journalists that their work is entirely unaffected by the conscious efforts of campaigners should not be taken at face value. The evidence offered below, therefore, includes opinions from both perspectives, a careful examination of the news product relating to some specific interactions and direct, independent observation by the author. Even so, the data is scanty and tentative, but it is the best available evidence which illuminates this consequential political process.

This chapter examines the evolving media politics of the Carter campaign. First, we consider the characteristics of campaign reporting which permit campaigns to orchestrate coverage. Next, we take up analytically the changes in the interactions between journalists and campaigns which begin in obscurity and grow, through electoral success, into major organizations. That developing relationship is then examined concretely in an interpreted chronology of the Carter campaign. I shall try to show how and why the campaign expanded its ability to circumscribe the news coverage it received. Finally, in 1976 all major campaigns experienced a "press crisis" at one time or another. Examining the "ethnic purity" and the *Playboy* stories illuminates the conditions under which these reversals occurred and the defensive strategies which campaigns employed against them.

It needs to be stated emphatically, in concluding this introduction, that the argument that campaigners often do succeed in influencing news reporting to their satisfaction should not be interpreted as a criticism of the professional competence of those individual journalists who covered the 1976 presidential campaign. In large part, as I will show, the campaign's growing influence is a function of institutional decisions by news reporting organizations and the expanding ability of the Carter campaign to dominate the political events which journalists seek to report.

Campaign Leverage in Media Politics

If the press and politicians interact in mutually supportive ways and if the press controls a precious resource for candidates (i.e., communications access to voters and activists), it is not immediately clear what resources campaign personnel bring to their media interaction which would allow them to gain any leverage whatsoever over the news product.

To begin that explanation, campaigners understand quite well the way in which journalists perform their job. In fact, of the twelve press secretaries we interviewed, eight had themselves come into politics from journalism. Campaign expertise in this area abounds, including written manuals on how to secure news coverage. Mostly, these materials describe the organizational demands of the news reporting process—deadlines of different media, the necessity of communication facilities, appropriate camera angles, the need for advance transcripts, and so on. Campaigners can use this information to facilitate (or impede) the flow of news about the campaign.

Beyond technical demands of the news reporting process, the media politics of campaigns involves accommodating to values which journalists bring to campaign reporting: the need to simplify and condense, their preference for the novel or unexpected, the attractiveness of conflict or a dramatic element, and the fascination with the "horse race" aspects to the election. Naturally, in seeking to shape news coverage, campaigners conform to these values in staging those events they would like reported.

The campaigner's accommodation to the news reporting process is, however, more complex than simply responding to the technical demand or the values inherent in modern journalism. Campaign personnel are aware that reporters and correspondents are themselves engaged in bureaucratic politics in their own organizations. The structure of news reporting offers opportunities for campaigners to aid, always subtly, the work of "our reporters" in competitive struggles with other reporters within a single media organization. For example, Jackson's campaign manager, Robert Keefe, described CBS's Leslie Stahl as "our best resource," because "she was as good at getting her stuff on CBS as anybody ever has been." The campaign staff sought wherever possible to help her do her work as in the campaign's interest.

Perceiving news reporting organizations as political systems, campaigners tend to view journalists assigned to them as something akin to ambassadors from media organizations to the campaign. For example, the Jackson campaign manager faced a difficult problem in how to convey to network news producers the campaign's strategic objectives in the Florida primary. Since delegates were elected in congressional districts, Keefe was attempting to carry the Miami districts while conceding the rest of the state to Wallace and Carter. He worried that statewide vote totals would be interpreted as a poor third-place showing for Jackson (which, in fact, they were). By Keefe's report, the campaign tried on several occasions to convince Stahl to see the primary from their viewpoint, hoping that she would both put that perception into her report the night of the primary and persuade her superiors at CBS to view the Jackson effort in that light. In this sense, correspondents and reporters come to be seen as the resident representatives of their news organizations. While like ambassadors, their loyalties to their organizations are deemed beyond subversion, they can, nonetheless, be utilized on occasion as an advocate of the campaign's viewpoint within their own political system.

On a third level, campaigners perceive the incentives of individual journalists as emanating from competition with their colleagues reporting the same story. Inevitably politicians seek to turn these incentives to their advantage, using the excuse of too many journalists to deny access to individual reporters, providing an exclusive leak, staging a photogenic but superficial event, making the candidate available to the reporter-correspondent at a time in which he is indisputably newsworthy for the front page or a live broadcast, and so on.

Finally, campaigners recognize that news reporting organizations are ultimately in competition with each other, if not financially then in terms of prestige within the journalistic community. Developing this into strategy, they seek opportunities, for example, to broker network competition into better coverage for their candidate by regulating access of the correspondents. While campaigns exhibit a tendency to cater to the needs of television correspondents, they also may arrange special events which advantage the print media. The degree to which the campaign attends to the needs of local versus national press may also be varied to the campaign's advantage.

In all these spheres—the demands of news reporting, the internal politics of media corporations, the reporter's incentives, the values brought to campaign reporting, and the existence of organizational competition— campaign managers seek to coordinate the interactions of campaign personnel with journalists to the candidate's benefit. While there exists a great deal of shared experience as to what a campaign can do in these areas to maximize its news objectives, there are no formal rules as to what a campaign *must* do. Thus, one campaign may organize "citizen press conferences" four or five times a day in which reporters are prohibited from asking questions, while another may schedule a daily press briefing. Reporters may complain about certain campaign practices or changes in their access to information. They have, however, little leverage to exercise on how the campaign conducts its news strategy. Ultimately, the campaigners hold the initiative because they control the actions and words of the candidate.

Campaigns do, however, vary widely in their ability to develop leverage over their news coverage. While in the final analysis these differences hinge upon the campaign's strength in the political arena, the actions of the news reporting organizations themselves frequently intervene to give the campaign the influence it desires. For those who work in media organizations, candidates vary in their perceived newsworthiness. To a large degree an individual's campaign for the Presidency is deemed worthy of news coverage based upon the seriousness of his electoral prospects. Thus the Reagan campaign was, from the time of his announcement, given extensive national coverage compared to any one of the Democratic contestants. Yet, other criteria apply as well. These may relate to a strong, but finite, block of support (Wallace) or prospects for denying the nomination to another (Brown) or high poll standings despite repeated denials of candidacy (Humphrey, Kennedy).

While newsworthiness is too vague a notion to attempt qualification, the demand for access to a given candidate by news reporters or the number of reporters assigned to cover the candidate on a more or less permanent basis or the comparative level of actual coverage could function as convenient substitutes for the notion. The Carter campaign was selected for this case study because the evolution of Carter from an unknown and unlikely candidate to the party's nominee is also a transition in perceived news-worthiness.

Using the standard of the size of the traveling press corps, the demand for access to Carter rose steadily during the first four months of 1976 and reached a plateau just after the Pennsylvania primary. By this time, he had crippled most of his early opponents (Bayh, Bentsen, Harris, Jackson, Sanford, Shapp, Shriver, Wallace, Udall) and was widely rated as the party's nominee unless he failed almost totally in subsequent primaries against late entrants Brown and Church.

Even for candidates deemed probable nominees, however, newsworthiness does not remain constant; it is also subject to short-term forces. Events such as primary victories may create brief periods in which a candidate is much in demand. The election night specials presented by the networks during the primary campaign, for example, heightened the "competition over the candidate's body." As we shall see in the case study presented below, Carter's advisors became aware very early of the possibilities of brokering media coverage during those occasions when his political successes made him the prime target of demands for access.

In general, the more campaigns are perceived as newsworthy—that is, the greater the demands for access to the candidate by journalists—the better able they become to influence the content of news about the campaign. Upon closer examination, however, the relationship proves to be disjunctive. Once a certain plateau in the size of the traveling press corps has been attained, most campaigns experience periods in which they lose almost all influence over the content of stories reported about their candidacy. Journalists covering the campaign collectively seize the initiative over content of the campaign's coverage. Reagan, Ford, and Carter each underwent these "press crises" in which, despite their best efforts to talk about something else, they found themselves responding repeatedly to reporters' inquiries on a single topic not of their choosing. These experiences are worthy of careful examination. They constitute important reversals from the normal campaign reporting, and, as will be argued more fully below, they appear to be partly a reaction by journalists to the norm of campaign dominance.

Dynamics in Media-Campaign Interaction

The initial position of a presidential campaign in its relations with media organizations depends heavily upon its political circumstances. To a limited degree, campaigns are able to exercise some choice in their news strategy; to a greater degree, their choices are constrained by their current nomination prospects. A number of the politicians who sought the Presidency in 1976 began their quest under conditions that demanded diligent efforts to achieve a meager amount of national coverage. With the exceptions of Wallace and Jackson, during the preprimary period all the Democratic candidates were basically in supplicant positions vis-à-vis the national news media. Two candidates, Carter and to a lesser extent, Harris, concluded, moreover, that their prospects were regarded as so low that seeking national media attention would not be even worth the effort involved. They developed a decentralized news strategy based on pursuing local press coverage in key states.

In developing his news strategy, Senator Jackson was able to exploit his important positions in the U. S. Senate to command media coverage from the Washington press corps on a range of topics. According to press secretary Brian Corcoran:

> The Senate is where the action is, not touring around the country. Bentsen and Carter have been running around, but they don't have one percent in the polls. You can't get known that way. . . . The place to get known is out of Washington. That's the media center of the U. S. That's where any newspaper worth its salt has a bureau. They have a 1,000-man press corps in Washington. We can get on "CBS Morning News," "A.M. America," and so forth. If we have something to say, we can go to the Senate press gallery.

In the Republican race, Ronald Reagan, seen as a credible candidate from the moment he announced, drew a large complement of political reporters in Florida and New Hampshire. Of course Ford possessed the advantage of the White House press corps and the capacity to dominate the news through his actions as incumbent.

During the preprimary period, candidate organizations are normally staffed by a few individuals, each fulfilling the rudiments of broad campaign responsibilities. As the campaign succeeds in developing political support, volunteers and staff are recruited at the national office and in the separate state-level branches. Gradually responsibilities are delegated to an expanding staff, and authority becomes increasingly stratified. At the same time, growing political support results in an increasing number of demands for access to the candidate and his upper-level staff by both politicians and journalists. The campaign director no longer answers his own telephone; instead he has the help of two or three layers of assistants whose duties include screening an increasing number of telephone calls. As a consequence of this rapid growth, the decision-making circles of the campaign become progressively more insulated and difficult for journalists to reach. The anecdotes of Jimmy Carter and Jody Powell traveling around New Hampshire with two reporters in a Volkswagen are legion; they contrast vividly with the access available to journalists after the New Hampshire primary when the campaign attracted enough of a press entourage to charter an aircraft.

When we first visited the Carter campaign in July 1975, the press section had just expanded to three full-time staff members: "an administrator, a writer, and a mouth." By our March 1976 visit, eight staff members aided by volunteers were necessary to respond to press inquiries, to write and produce press releases, and to make arrangements for the increasing number of journalists traveling with the candidate. During the general election campaign, twenty-five worked in the press section performing these functions.

Obviously, none of the other Democratic campaigns developed quite this dramatically. The Republican campaigns offered something of a contrast if only because they began at a comparatively high level of complexity and stratification. They experienced, accordingly, far less growth, but wound up with a comparable level of complexity.

The press corps traveling with successful campaigns likewise expands rapidly. During the preprimary period, few news reporting organizations assigned more than one or two correspondents or reporters to follow the race as a whole. Around the beginning of the year, the *New York Times* and the *Washington Post*, CBS and NBC, plus a number of other media organizations produced series of articles reporting on each of the candidates, providing an insight into their character, major themes, and political strategy. These series mark the real end of the preprimary period and the beginning of the primary campaign, a distinction based fundamentally upon media decision-making in the assignment of reporters to cover the race and the allotment of news space to carry their work. While the networks (and wire services) assigned film crews and correspondents to cover separate candidates in January, most print media opted for so-called "zone coverage," i.e., reporters were assigned to cover *all* the candidates in one state primary. The Republican coverage was an exception to this; the White House press corps traveled with the President, while most of the major regional and national dailies assigned a reporter to the Reagan campaign.

As the field of candidates narrowed rapidly after the New Hampshire primary, zone coverage was replaced by assignment to individual candidates, and what I shall refer to as "candidate coverage" began. After the Pennsylvania primary, most regionally and nationally important papers and the weekly news magazines had one reporter traveling more or less permanently with Carter. This pattern of assignment resulted in an increasing number of reporters traveling with the surviving candidates as their competitors withdrew. The Carter press entourage hit a plateau shortly after the Pennsylvania primary and remained there until late in the general election, when it expanded even further.

The advantages to a news organization of assigning a reporter or correspondent to cover a candidate for the duration of the campaign constitute a strong argument for "candidate coverage." Reporters develop much of their information by establishing regular contacts with a finite number of individuals occupying key campaign roles. Because growing candidate organizations become increasingly insulated at their top levels, journalists wish to develop sources within the campaign early while contact with these decision-makers remains possible. Personal acquaintances with the candidate and his top staff are assumed to be valuable resources for gaining insight into the campaign's activities. In addition, it is argued that reporters covering the same candidate develop familiarity with his public policy stands and are better able, therefore, to notice shifts of position. Administratively as well, candidate coverage offers certain conveniences to journalists and their organizations. Once the reporter joins the campaign, most arrangements for transportation, meals, accommodations, and communication back to his organization are taken care of by the campaign staff.

The disadvantages of permanently assigning one journalist to a campaign are less obvious, but they are, in my opinion, major. In the first place, permanently assigning a reporter or correspondent to cover one particular candidate constitutes an organizational commitment that that candidate will receive coverage. From that point on, the traveling journalist is busy filing stories, at least some of which must be broadcast or put in print. This proposition was most succinctly expressed in an interview by Irv Horowitz, Deputy National News Editor for the *New York Times:*

> A reporter gets more and more nervous when a story he has written has not been printed. After about three days they get pretty paranoid—we don't like him, we want to deprive him of his means of livelihood, etc. You can be sure of one thing. After not printing one or two stories written by a reporter, you just *have* to print the third!

Describing one day's efforts to present the news, Henry Rosenfeld of the *Washington Post* noted that separate stories on each candidate were a natural outgrowth of the assignment process:

> I question whether we really serve the reader by—having laid out the Democratic analysis in the primary round up—a separate story on the day's doings of four different candidates. I question the efficacy of that approach. It's inevitable [however] because we have four different staff reporters, each one anxious, after a very important [group of] primaries, to want to write something.

Finally, Bill Chesleigh, political editor of NBC-TV News, discussed the pressure that can build up within an organization once assignments have been handed out:

> . . . you do get a correspondent who will occasionally call and say, "Why hasn't my candidate been on this week? You've had three Carter spots and you've had none of my candidate." But he would say the same thing if he were not doing politics and doing general news, wondering why he's not getting on the air.

While not totally determinative, assignment patterns thus can influence coverage. Having made these commitments, media organizations lose considerable flexibility in their bargaining relationship with campaigners. Ultimately, of course, successful candidates deserve and will receive coverage. In the interims between primaries, however, a large volume of campaign news is heavily influenced by these organizational commitments.

Secondly, there exists an assumption in arranging coverage on a candidate-by-candidate basis that the essence of a presidential nomination and election is the activities of the individual candidates. While certainly these constitute a major part, they are but one aspect of the political process which leads to the selection of a President. Large aspects of campaign behavior, for example, certainly affect the final vote, yet fall outside of coverage organized around candidate travel (e.g., the slow construction of political organizations, the advertising campaign, and the raising and expending of campaign dollars). In addition, systemic trends, such as the development of support among important interest groups, or the growth or decline of strength in pivotal states or among big population groups, the development of stands on policy questions, and the changing acceptance by local and national party leaders are important election events not adequately observable by reporters traveling with candidates. Finally, candidate coverage leaves little possibility for comparative observation of the various contenders. While comparisons can be achieved through the editorial or production process, news reporting organizations function in the main by simply accepting or rejecting the work of reporters in the field. Syncretic analysis is simply organizationally difficult. Instead, the vast bulk of campaign coverage focuses upon the activities of the candidates qua individuals. Needless to say, what a candidate says or does are those aspects of the electoral process most, albeit not totally, under the control of the campaigns.

Third, the institutional problems of candidate coverage are magnified by difficulties encountered on a personal level by those journalists assigned to cover a single candidate over a lengthy period of time. Perpetually on the move, surrounded primarily by the candidate's staff and other journalists with the same assignment, reporters perceive all of their political information as polarized by the filtering question: "what does this mean for the electoral prospects of this candidate?" To argue that journalists come to view the race as a whole from the perspective of the candidate to whom they have been assigned is not to contend that they develop a bias in favor of that candidate. Rather, the argument simply makes recognition that the demands of the assigned job—to report upon the activities of a candidate and how they affect his prospects for election—over time come to blot out any comparative or systemic perspective.

The problem of perspective is not new. It was touched upon in *The Boys on the Bus: Riding with the Campaign Press Corps,* Timothy Crouse's critique of the campaign media in 1972. In fact, many of our respondents in major news reporting organizations echoed the concerns of David Jones, National News Editor for the *New York Times:*

...the experience of our political reporters is that when they get on that campaign plane, they get trapped; they're in a cocoon and it distorts their perception of everything that's happening in the campaign because they don't see the broader dimensions. ...

These dynamics are examined in the section which follows: a case study of the media politics of the Carter primary campaign. The analysis is offered as a partial documentation of the ability of campaigners to exploit the opportunities provided by candidate coverage. The influence Carter and his operatives were able to exercise on campaign reporting is not found so much in a direct effort to shape content; such attempts would surely have been counterproductive. Rather, they sought to orchestrate news coverage by taking advantage of the organizational decisions of media corporations and the consequently delimited individual perspectives of reporters assigned to cover their campaign on a continuing basis. As the campaign succeeded politically and an increasing number of reporters and correspondents were assigned to the campaign, the campaigners' leverage increased. Furthermore, an aspect of their growing political support was an expanding ability to shape the phenomena which journalists seek to report.

The Dynamics of Carter's Media Politics

Avoiding the tendency to attribute political success to the sheer genius of the principal campaign architects, we must begin this account with the recognition that Carter was aided in his relations with journalists by a good measure of luck. The most prominent example contributing to Carter's ability to maintain a perception of progress was the accidental fact that every significant primary loss was offset by a win, albeit in many cases an expected win, on the same day in another state (Massachusetts by Vermont; New York by Wisconsin; Nebraska by Connecticut; Maryland by Michigan; Oregon by Kentucky; Arkansas by Tennessee; Rhode Island by South Dakota; California and New Jersey by Ohio).

Furthermore, one could cite numerous examples in which campaign operatives tried to shape the coverage they received and failed. Despite repeated attempts, they never found a way to blunt the criticism that Carter's policy stands lacked specific details. Moore and Fraser in *Campaign for President: The Managers Look at '76* quote Jody Powell:

> There was no way on God's earth we could shake the fuzziness question in the general election, no matter what Carter did or said. He could have spent the whole campaign doing nothing but reading substantive speeches from morning to night and still have had that image in the national press.

Nevertheless, success in winning delegate votes did provide Carter's operatives with opportunities for influencing national news reporting—in particular, reports about the progress of the race or the "horse race" aspects.

One of the wisest early decisions made by the Carter staff was based on the recognition that they could not expect national press attention until they had shown some progress in the political sphere. Despite Hamilton Jordan's often quoted analysis in his 1972 strategy memo that "stories in the *New York Times* and *Washington Post* do not just happen, but have to be carefully planned and planted," the early campaign was based around an expectancy of little national coverage. Whereas Jackson could count on making the evening news occasionally and Udall could hope for it, the Carter candidacy was such a long shot that devoting major resources in striving for national press coverage would have been largely wasted effort.

Instead, Carter and his staff sought to maximize their exposure in states where they planned an early political effort. In other words, they decentralized their news strategy, putting their resources into the courting of local press and broadcast exposure. ". . . the *Des Moines Register* became more important [to us] than the *Washington Post*," Jody Powell recalled.

> When Jimmy goes anywhere, he does editorial board meetings. There is not, I don't think, a major paper in Florida that he has not sat down with the editorial board—the Miami papers, the St. Pete papers, the *Tampa Tribune*, the Jacksonville paper. We do that just as a standard part of the schedule. That's to meet with as many papers as there are.

While giving more attention to generating local news, Carter's operatives also left their opponents to compete for what little national coverage the major outlets were devoting to the presidential campaign during 1975.

Underlying their decentralized approach to news making was not so much an ingenious strategy for circumventing national political reporters, but a realistic appraisal of their possibilities of generating national news. Powell said on July 22, 1975:

> I would suspect that we concentrate more heavily on the local media than anybody else does, if for no other reason than . . . the national media . . . is not there for us. We've got to do the best we can . . . I have a feeling just from some of the candidates' schedules that I've seen, that even amongst folks like us who can't command the national media attention, that we're still placing more emphasis on the local media than they are.

As a specific example, in July of 1975 a considerable part of Carter's campaign schedule was devoted to seeking local media coverage:

> Jimmy's in Dallas tomorrow [July 23]. He's doing radio and TV news cuts in the morning, a half-hour segment for their morning show to be run the next day, editorial board [meetings] with the morning newspaper and the *Times Herald*, a luncheon speech, a speech to the AFL-CIO convention in the afternoon, a meeting with Democratic leaders after that, a half hour number on their statewide public

television network [show] called "Newsroom," and then a short meeting with political and money folks after that.

On a trip to the AFL-CIO convention, at least half of Carter's time was spent being interviewed by local journalists, despite the fact that the Texas primary was over nine months away.

Finally, the decision not to court the national media aggressively during the early stages dovetailed nicely with their desire to base the campaign in Atlanta. They recognized that their isolation from the national press would not be solved simply by making Carter more accessible to the Washington press corps. Hamilton Jordan told us on July 22, 1975:

> [Reporters] that cover Washington usually have covered the Congress or the White House. They generally have more of a knowledge of other presidential candidates that have Congressional backgrounds. . . . That is a built in disadvantage. I'm sure you could make a list of the 50 top press people in the nation's capitol, and I'm sure that most of them at some point in their career had interviewed Scoop Jackson or Mo Udall . . . . So there's that disadvantage that would not be overcome just by having our headquarters in Washington.

Atlanta was, of course, not as isolated as the Carter staff contended. The southern bureaus of most major news organizations are located there. Furthermore, the campaign had extensive contact with journalists headed through Atlanta to interview Wallace.

While admitting the handicaps which their lack of contact with the national press implied, Jordan also saw advantages in that the national press would expect less from them in terms of performance in the early primaries and caucuses.

> You're talking about continually overperforming in terms of arbitrary expectations they set for you. And they might set high expectations for us if we were up there [in D.C.] day in and day out, saying that we're going to do this and we're going to do that. Instead, they expect not much from us, and we, even to this point, have been able to overperform in terms of what they expect from us. And that's going to continue to be the case. It won't be obvious until the primaries begin and the caucuses begin.

Substantively, much of the early campaign contacts with the national press revolved around efforts to sound optimistic while not predicting that they would do very well in the early states. They were, of course, aided in their attempt to keep expectations low by the fact that few members of the national press corps took them very seriously (except, perhaps, as a threat to Wallace's southern strength).

Carter's media strategy, thus, was to avoid the temptation to predict specific primary victories as an inducement for attracting support, so that their achievements would come as a surprise to political observers, principally journalists. They believed, based upon an analysis of the McGovern campaign, that primary victories would be measured not as absolutes, but against expectations established by journalists and the campaigns themselves. According to Jordan:

> It has already been established in the minds of the national press that Mo Udall was going to do well in New Hampshire, that he should win New Hampshire. He has established that expectation. If he does not win New Hampshire, I think now by the measuring criteria that the press is going to apply, he will have underperformed. Well, we'd never talk about winning in New Hampshire. We never talk about winning anywhere. We talk about doing well. And so I think that the candidate and the campaign itself play a part in establishing this expectation with the media.

In sum, while many of their opponents—Jackson, Bayh, Udall, Shriver, and Sanford to name those I can be confident of—were pursuing national press attention, the Carter campaign, of necessity, turned their inability to attract serious interest by the Washington press corps into a strategic advantage.

The isolation of Carter from national media attention ended on October 27, 1975, when R.W. Apple reported that Carter held the lead in a straw poll taken in Ames, Iowa, by the *Des Moines Register* at a Jefferson-Jackson day dinner. Given Jordan's plans to keep expectations low, the decision to work for the best showing possible in the straw poll was a high-risk venture. He later remarked, "That early straw poll had a down-side; after that poll . . . we *had* to win in Iowa."

Nevertheless, the payoff of the Apple piece was acceptance by national journalists and expanding coverage. In *American Journal: The Events of 1976* Elizabeth Drew summarized the relationship this way:

> A story by R. W. Apple, Jr., in the *Times* last October, saying that Carter was doing well in Iowa was itself a political event, prompting other newspaper stories that Carter was doing well in Iowa, and then more news-magazine and television coverage for Carter than might otherwise have been his share.

Dick Duncan of *Time* recalled the effect of the Apple piece on other journalists as follows:

> When Jonny Apple kicked it all off and announced that Jimmy Carter from nowhere was going to carry the Iowa caucus . . . there was absolutely no doubt in my mind that . . . when Jonny Apple writes a story on the front page of the *New York Times* out of the blue, ordaining a new phenomenon, that that was the most important single event in the relationship between the media and Jimmy Carter.

Another of the journalists we interviewed, Peter Goldman of *Newsweek*, recalled that his magazine decided to give much greater attention to reporting the Iowa caucuses upon reading this Apple story and an equivalent piece by Jules Witcover in the *Washington Post.*

Breaking out of its isolation, the Carter campaign experienced a development in their relationships with journalists which began with this initial recognition by prestigious reporters that Carter's candidacy could no longer be dismissed lightly. From that point on, the campaign's influences over the content of its news coverage was enhanced by the repeated use of three resources. First, access to the candidate and top staff could be used to play upon competition among individual journalists and news reporting organizations. Second, Carter's physical location could be controlled so as to maximize coverage and to orient the traveling press corps toward certain events and away from others. And third, increasing political strength put into their hands the ability to stage political events in order to lead journalists to conclusions advantageous to the campaign. Note that the first two of these depend upon the decision of news media organizations to commit reporters to covering Carter on a continuing basis. After Carter's victory in the Pennsylvania primary, the expanded press corps traveling with the candidate guaranteed a sufficient level of coverage. Furthermore, the assignment of journalists offered an additional advantage in that the campaign could determine the physical location of those journalists assigned to Carter. As I shall show, the campaign used this advantage to highlight certain events and downplay others.

The third resource which allowed the Carter organization to influence campaign reporting indirectly was its political support in the electoral arena. Obviously, campaigns affect the process that journalists are trying to report. Less obvious, however, is the observation that campaigners will construct political events specifically for their results in campaign reporting.

The remainder of this section examines the use to which the Carter campaign put these three sources of influence over news content: journalistic competition, candidate location, and political control. The analysis will be confined to so-called "horse race issues": estimates of how the race is progressing, who is likely to be the nominee, what level of performance will be deemed evidence of expanding or shrinking political support, which events are most critical, and so on. There are several reasons for narrowing the focus of inquiry to these questions. In the first place, they lie at the heart of the political contest, the selection of a nominee. Second, campaigners believe that journalists' work in this area has an important impact on their ability to attract greater political support. The perceptual environment within which presidential campaigns compete is frequently more conse-quential than tangible events and the campaign reporter's task is to generate and convey notions about this perceptual environment. Third, discussion of how the race is progressing constitutes a substantial proportion of campaign reporting. Fourth, campaign goals in this area are more specific; they wish to convince journalists to put a given interpretation on a particular event, as, for example, to select one primary as a critical test of political strength. The issues are also more specific in that they are short-lived: after the event in question, the dialogue between politicians and journalists moves on to other questions. The influence relationships are thus more observable.

On the other hand, there are limitations to confining the scope of inquiry to these matters, which must be frankly admitted. Being specific perceptions which the campaign wants to establish, they are the most susceptible to influence. The development of a label like "fuzzy," by contrast, occurs slowly because it is linked to many different events and other beliefs about the candidate. Accordingly, perceptions at this level which find their way into journalistic commentary are a great deal more difficult to combat, requiring wholesale changes in the campaign's behavior. Thus, a considerable amount of journalists' opinion lay outside the scope of Carter's influence. As we shall note, however, when these become linked to horse race questions, the campaign can develop strategies for blunting criticisms in the news media.

Let us turn to some specific examples from Carter's news strategy in which the campaign did succeed in shaping coverage.

The Iowa caucuses were held the evening of January 19. Most national political reporters and contesting candidates were in Des Moines waiting for the results. Jimmy Carter was in New York waiting to broker those results into access to the morning network news programs. For later primaries the networks would report the results with live segments at 11:30 p.m. (EST). The Carter campaign discovered, however, that while important correspondents like CBS' Roger Mudd would be on hand in Iowa, reports would be taped for the morning and evening news shows the next day. Carter appeared on all three network morning shows, maximizing his exposure during that short time period when he was a genuine news item. At the beginning, therefore, the point of access to media exposure determined the location of the candidate. If live coverage would not come to Iowa, Carter would go to New York.

On New Hampshire primary night, the full news reporting apparatus of the networks had moved up to Manchester. For Carter's advisors political success meant that, to a certain degree, they could dictate to the networks and print reporters the conditions under which they would obtain access to Carter. Gerald Rafshoon, Carter's advertising manager:

> This was his first real national appearance and he was hot and new and fresh, and there wasn't much that the news organizations could do. They just had to take what they got on Carter that night.

With so many journalists on hand, they found themselves under great demand for interview time. Competition over access to Carter gave them, for the first time, the independence to tell one network that they would simply have to wait until Carter got around to them. Rafshoon recalled the scene with considerable glee:

> I got kind of a kick in New Hampshire listening to a guy from ABC arguing with Jody that he had been double-crossed. I can remember a year earlier if we could have a two minute shot on ABC, we'd have flown out of Georgia, gone up there, waited in the reception area, gotten his two minute thing, and flown back. . . [They said] "it's just going to kill us to see him with Cronkite before Reasoner, we're going to lose face". . . and, it was really, I guess a feeling of satisfaction that now it's a case of "rationing" his time to national media.

Competition also existed between the different media. The print reporters, of course, had to wait until after the networks were through for access to Carter. The campaign, however, had rented a hotel ballroom too small to accommodate all the press and political supporters. Being careful to maximize exposure, the press section of the campaign made sure reporters were admitted to the hall on a priority basis. Supporters and volunteers were kept outside.

By the Florida primary, the newsworthiness of Carter's victories was sufficient to merit a live interview in prime time. Carter's staff worked out an arrangement with CBS for Carter to be available early in the evening.

> Carter wants to be alone with his family on election night, and would be, but, of course, there's a lot of room for intrusion there. The night of the Florida primary, we told CBS that he would be watching [television] with his family. At 8:01 CBS News did an interrupt . . . with Cronkite interviewing Carter and there was no one in the hotel suite except his family . . . The networks have put him on live right along during the primary season, but, in order for that to happen, there has to be justifiable news reason. And, Carter sitting there watching the tube is a damn good reason. There's no better reason.

At the same time, these early political successes were followed by a gradual growth in the press corps traveling with the candidate. Not only does that mean that each campaign event will receive greater coverage, but also that newsmen will compete on a continuing basis with each other for the limited amount of private interview time with the candidate and his top level staff. In the fall, a casual conversation with Jody Powell could produce a half-hour car ride with Carter; increasingly, after New Hampshire written requests for interviews were required:

> At that point, it was not a matter of begging for additional coverage, it was trying to sort out the opportunities that you had and taking advantage of them, of the best ones.

Competition for access among the journalists assigned to cover Carter meant the campaign staff could establish and implement their priorities for allocating the candidate's time so as to maximize different varieties of news coverage. Because of the perceived credibility of television news and the degree to which Americans rely upon television for their political information, the campaign leaned toward facilitating network coverage when in competition with other media.

That competition dictated an organizational response from the campaign: recognizing the essential differences between print and electronic media, Jody Powell brought on Barry Jagoda to help him handle the technical demands of network journalism. Jagoda, who had worked as a producer at both NBC and CBS, described himself as:

> somebody who was involved in the decision-making process in television news, as opposed to being a reporter or researcher in television, of which there have been some people [involved in campaigns]: you know Ron Nessen was involved in that. But, I really understand how the bureaucracy works in television. I understand media politics extremely well; I'm a specialist at it.

Jagoda's presence produced an organizational differentiation within the campaign to deal more precisely with the differences between media.

> The attempt to work with the broadcast journalists was always handled by the press secretary of the other candidates. The point, I guess, was that there's no difference between Stan Cloud, Bill Plant, and Carl Leubsdorf; [they're] all doing the same thing—which is covering the news—[that] would be the generally accepted notion about reporters, although everybody knows that there's a different deadline situation, there are different mechanical functions. In my view, that's a simplistic understanding. . . .The differences between the people who are involved in magazine, periodical journalism and wire service journalism or daily journalism and *television* journalism are profound *because their decision-making processes are very different,* the assumptions are different. (emphasis added)

The relationship between Jagoda, who was designing the campaign's plans for making Carter available to network journalists, and his former colleagues was quite subtle. "I was never asked to stage anything," he recalled, "of course, then again I didn't need to be; I knew what they wanted." In terms of mutual influence, the campaign was advantaged by having someone who understood the technical demands of how networks put together their regular evening news and their election specials.

> When I call my friends at NBC and say, "Hey look it's Monday, and tomorrow's a primary night and we've got a half hour and let's figure out how we can use Carter and, you know, what are you going to do?" And somebody would say, "Well look, we're going to do an 'ethnic purity' segment in the last fifteen minutes, 'cause he screwed up on that last week." And I'd think about that for a while, and I'd say, "If we have Carter there in the first fifteen minutes then he'll get on live and talk about how nice it was to win. But if we have him there in the last fifteen minutes, he can do that too, and dominate the ethnic purity discussion." Now, that can be

construed to be media manipulation, . . . [but] it can also be construed as helping
to participate with the producers in the structure of their broadcast, so that the
broadcast would facilitate their own program objectives and goals.

During this period of increasing sophistication in dealing with national
journalists, the campaign operations also began to understand how Carter's
physical location could contribute to shaping the content of news coverage.

Carter's initial strategy had been to make major efforts in New Hampshire
and Florida, by-passing the Massachusetts primary. Upon their victory in
New Hampshire, however, Carter's advisors thought they had a chance to
win Massachusetts. Reluctant to divert Carter's schedule away from the
effort in Florida, they opted for a heavy investment in campaign advertising
to maximize votes in Massachusetts.

The results of the Massachusetts primary were a defeat of major
proportions for Carter, who a week earlier had been labeled "the man to
beat," by NBC's Tom Pettit. Carter placed fourth with 14 percent of the vote,
behind Jackson (23 percent), Udall (18 percent), and Wallace (17 percent).
Most press commentary, however, interpreted the loss mildly as "slowing
the Carter momentum." In general, journalists took a "wait-and-see"
approach to the Massachusetts defeat, perhaps because they would not have
to wait long. The Florida primary, which the Carter campaign had long been
billing as their critical test, was only a week away. An additional factor cited
by many was his lack of personal campaigning. For example, in the March
3rd *Washington Post* David Broder noted, "Carter spent only eight hours in
the state [in the last week] and concentrated his campaigning on the March
9 primary in Florida." In a similar vein, John Kifner wrote in a March 3rd
New York Times analysis, "He made only a single, brief appearance here in
what was for the other candidates a hectic week following the New
Hampshire primary." While no one thought that Carter had not tried to win
Massachusetts (most mentioned his advertising effort), the rather mild
treatment of his poor showing was bracketed by his lack of campaigning.
Not being there in person was somehow less than a full effort and, therefore,
at least partially excusable

Recall, moreover, that at this stage of the Democratic race, most news
reporting organizations were following "zone coverage," reporting on who
did what in Massachusetts rather than what each of the separate campaigns
did that week. Thus, reporters were better able to observe the Carter effort
in Massachusetts because they were covering *the event*. Traveling with the
candidate, the press would only have observed the one brief stopover and
been more likely to conclude that the campaign was making its significant
efforts elsewhere.

Once journalists were assigned to candidate coverage in significant
numbers, Carter campaigners could use the candidate's location to influence

coverage to their advantage. For example, six primaries were held on May 25, three on the West Coast (Oregon, Idaho, and Nevada), and three in southern border states (Kentucky, Tennessee, and Arkansas). Oregon was perceived as the state in which the outcome was uncertain; therefore most speculation hinged on how the candidates would fare in that state. The night of May 25 found Jimmy Carter in New York, in the eastern time zone. He was available for quotations after the southern primaries, but his schedule that day ended with bedtime at 11:01 p.m., just after the West Coast polls closed. Stories from the press traveling with him, emphasized the southern victories and mounting delegate tallies. For example, Witcover's front page analysis in the *Washington Post* was headlined "Carter Takes 2: Southern Strength"; Apple's equivalent piece appeared under the heading "Ford Tops Reagan in Kentucky Race; Carter is Victor." While these stories may be due to press deadlines of East Coast papers, the analysis by George Skelton on the front page of the *Los Angeles Times* was entitled "Carter is Easy Winner in 3 States in South." The article contained results from all six states, but the thrust of the piece was on the eastern victories.

Of course, Carter's efforts were not totally successful in obscuring his triple loss on the West Coast, but they did serve to deemphasize them. By morning Carter's comments could stress the combined results of the six primaries, and the necessity to "look at the overall national performance."

Two weeks later on June 8, delegates were selected on a single day in three primaries. California was generally conceded to its Governor Jerry Brown, although proportional representation meant that strong second and third place showings would net some delegates. In Ohio, Jimmy Carter was entered against Mo Udall, a candidate whom he had beaten twice before in major "head-to-head" contests. In New Jersey, Carter faced a combination of forces that constituted the major threats to his nomination: Jerry Brown, a candidate he had never defeated, backed by local party machines. By most objective assessments, New Jersey would appear the most critical test of the three. Based on polling data provided by Pat Caddell, the Carter campaign realized they were going to lose California and the New Jersey delegate race, but would safely win in Ohio. They, therefore, needed a means of emphasizing the Ohio primary.

One aspect of their strategy was to use Carter's traveling plans to highlight the significance of Ohio. During the last two weeks of campaigning, Carter spent two days campaigning in California, made appearances in New Jersey on four days, and was in Ohio on seven days. To highlight the eastern primary even further, the campaign cancelled a final trip to California and the whole day was given over to campaigning in Ohio, with a later evening appearance in New Jersey (the last of the nomination campaign). As Jon Margolis of the *Chicago Tribune* had noted in an earlier piece, the effect of these Carter last minute travels was to draw attention to the states in which he campaigned. Thus, during the week before the last three primaries, most analyses were describing Ohio as the critical background.

In case anyone missed the point, however, Carter provided an illustration of how a third resource—growing influence over other important actors in nomination politics—could be used to shape press commentary. The day of the three primaries, Carter called Mayor Daley of Chicago, who controlled eighty-six delegates nominally pledged to Illinois Senator Stevenson. In *Marathon* Witcover describes the call as follows:

> Carter laid it out cold: he was going to lose in California and New Jersey, but would win Ohio. Whether they cooked up together what happened next, or whether Daley acted strictly on his own, is not known; but the fact is that Daley took this prediction and used it in a way that it would all but force an interpretation that what happened in Ohio was the important thing; that California and New Jersey were side shows.

Daley held a press conference in which he said of Carter, "if he wins in Ohio, he'll walk in under his own power . . . " When asked how Ohio became the critical primary on June 8, Pat Caddell recalled:

> We orchestrated that. We were in trouble in New Jersey but we knew we were going to win in Ohio. Then Daley did it. Of course, we orchestrated that too! Jimmy called Daley and said, "We're going to lose New Jersey, but we'll win in Ohio."

Carter did very well in Ohio, just as he knew he would. His at-large delegate seats won 52 percent of the vote, and 126 delegates pledged to him were elected. Carter had been predicting he would add 200 delegates to his committed support, but this estimate had assumed a better showing in New Jersey. Yet, the size of his Ohio win brought him 218 delegates for the day.

With Daley's endorsement virtually assured, the pieces began to fall quickly into place. The three networks carried statements by his Ohio opponents saying they thought Carter would now receive the nomination, an opinion generally supported by the broadcast journalists. That night Jerry Brown kept insisting, however, in live network interviews from Los Angeles, that his victories meant that the nomination was not secured for Carter. In fact, Brown was quite startled to learn just before his interview with Cronkite that Carter seemed to have the nomination sewed up, as the dialogue in Figure 1 indicates. Mickey Kantor, Brown's campaign manager, recalled their surprise at how fast the support went to Carter:

> We felt we had two weeks to four weeks to effect all this. Things were moving so fast for us. We were concentrating on Oregon, Nevada, Rhode Island, New Jersey, California and how the media was viewing this situation. *And then the media turned on the Ohio victory* so quickly, it was like being hit in the face with a bucket of cold water. *(Marathon)*

Fig. 1. Richard Wagner (RW) of CBS News Sets up Live Interview with Jerry Brown (JB), Los Angeles Bureau, June 8, 1976, 9:10 p.m. (EST)

(Brown enters small room filled with television equipment and sits in one of two chairs, facing Wagner.)

JB: What are you showing?

RW: Sevareid said he didn't see how Carter could be stopped.

JB: Jesus, he lost two out of three tonight!

RW: Well, say that! Look, here's how it will go. Walter will start the interview. He'll say . . . well, with Church, he said —

JB: (interrupting) What did Church say?

RW: He thought it would be hard to stop Carter . . . .

JB: What about Udall, what did he say?

RW: He said it was all over. It's all up to you now. Daley said today, "If Carter wins in Ohio, he has it, and nobody can get it who hasn't run in the primaries." He knocked Hubert right out of the saddle.

PRODUCER: We're coming on.

RW: Look, I may never get a chance to ask a question; Walter may do it all . . . .

CBS STAFFER: When it's his show, he runs it.

BROWN STAFFER: Jerry, your hair's falling down.

PRODUCER: Okay, here we come.

(Cronkite asks a long question from election central in New York, not heard in room.)

JB: Well, we're feeling awfully good. We're encouraged by New Jersey, We won two out of three through tonight and . . . .

Once the nomination victory had been proclaimed over the networks, reality began rapidly to catch up with projections. Early the next morning, George Wallace called Carter to say he was releasing his delegates and urging them to vote for Carter. Daley, having started the bandwagon by helping to focus journalists on a primary he knew in advance Carter would win, made his endorsement official, and Jackson called to say he would shortly release his delegates. Twenty-four hours later, Carter had a convention majority.

Carter's control over the July convention has been widely acknowledged.

Most observers have noted that convention events were staged so that they would make the best impression upon television audiences. The resources mobilized by the Carter campaign were the same. Knowing the news reporting organizations were committed to giving the convention maximum coverage, they were able to use access to the candidate and his staff, Carter's location, and, most importantly, their influence with other politicians in order to stage a convention that was interesting (who would be Vice President?), dramatic (Carter's acceptance speech), and harmonious. Principally, they sought to orchestrate events so as to lead journalists and, hence, their audiences to the conclusion that the party was united behind the Carter candidacy. They largely succeeded.

"Press Crises": Reaction to Orchestration

In the analysis of the ability of the Carter campaign to influence news reporting, I have concentrated on the horse race aspect of nomination. While a great deal of campaign reporting dealt with these competitive aspects, analyses of issues and character were certainly available. At the beginning of the year, for example, several news corporations produced a special series treating the broad outlines of each candidate's program and background. In these matters Carter was less able to generate advantageous coverage as the campaign wore on. Initially, Carter's personal life received abundant coverage for the many unusual aspects of his background and members of his family. Late in the primaries, reporters began to worry about characteristics which might be hidden behind his reserve and smile: his impatience, lack of self-deprecating humor, vindictiveness, anger at criticism, and so on.

On policy questions, Carter never gave the press very many details of his programs. His troubles on this front began shortly after the primary season opened, with the Brill piece in *Harpers* and his abortion stand during the Iowa caucuses. Steven Brill's "Jimmy Carter's Pathetic Lies" appeared in *Harpers* in February 1976. The *Boston Globe* in reprinting the article quoted *Harpers'* editor, Lewis Lapham, as saying that over 100 newspapers had asked for permission to excerpt the article. In February, Scoop Jackson pinned the label "fuzzy" on his programs, a perception which grew into a major problem in the late primaries and general election.

As these criticisms of Carter began to build up, they became less amenable to influence because they were extensively linked to multiple campaign events and beliefs about the candidate. On occasion, however, perceptions at this level become connected to specific events, creating an immediate crisis for the campaign. Carter's advisors experienced at least two of these "press crises."

For a political campaign, press crises are periods in which the candidate and campaign operatives undergo persistent questioning from journalists relating to a single topic. Most of the news coverage of the campaign during these short periods is related to that issue, which is defined by the press corps. Campaigners are on the defensive; they have lost most of their initiative over the content of the news. The questioning of Reagan's plan to allow states to take over $90 billion of federal programs or of Ford's position on the domination of Eastern Europe by the Soviet Union are good examples of these crises. For Carter, his statement about preserving the ethnic purity of neighborhoods and his interview published in *Playboy* each produced days of campaigning dominated by reporters repeatedly asking the candidate to clarify his position.

These crises are not, however, unrelated to the horse race issues. All of these four episodes share a common trait in that the candidate's position can be directly tied to his electoral possibilities: Reagan's plan raised the prospect of curtailing government programs desired by important segments of the electorate; Ford's statement threatened his appeal to voters of Eastern European ancestry; the ethnic purity concept jeopardized Carter's support among black voters (a key component of his coalition), and his remarks in *Playboy* were seen as offending Texans and raising questions among those whose primary affinity to Carter was based on religious conservatism.

Press crises involved broader questions of a candidate's policies and character. Reagan's transfer proposal capsulized his conservatism and provided a link to Goldwater's highly unsuccessful campaign. Questions of Ford's competence and his detente policies were raised anew by his statement during the second debate. Carter's southern background and the possibilities of latent racism were implicit in the questioning of his ethnic purity stand. His propriety, judgment, and religiosity became questionable during the *Playboy* crisis.

Campaigns, therefore, tend to lose most of their influence over daily reporting once an event establishes a negative link between major aspects of a candidate's character or policies and his electoral prospects. When that occurs, reporters have found a means which makes the broader questions of personality or policy more reportable and germane. The electoral link, thus, is critical in giving visibility to deeper questions.

The Carter campaigners were convinced that a major aspect of these crises was the reaction of journalists to the amount of influence over content normally exercised by the campaign. Carter's advisors agreed that many reporters did not care particularly about his policies toward open housing and ethnic neighborhoods, but wished merely to use the matter as a means of testing how well the candidate could handle himself under fire. Jody Powell:

I really think in some ways the best thing we did to get it over with . . . was to meet it head on and just . . . open it to the press, you know, let them ask their questions, hostile or otherwise, [and] demonstrate that he could handle it and that sort of thing. I think that's what the press is looking for . . . [that is] they're a lot more interested in how, whether he could handle the problem than they were in whether he was a racist or not.

Charlotte Scott, Carter's Pennsylvania press secretary:

> They were looking for something, in the first place. Everything had been going so smoothly; he'd been winning; there had been no mistakes; he was the ideal candidate; he was picking up support; and, all of a sudden, there was a chance, something to level in on. There hadn't been an opportunity beforehand . . . Everyone made a living off it for two weeks.

In other words, when asked to explain the occurrence of these press crises, campaigners think first not of the substantive issue, but of the political relationship between the press corps and the candidate. They see the crisis as arising in their mutual influence relationship as a reaction to the candidate's exercising the initiative in almost every encounter.

In a sense, the campaign argument would lead to the conclusion that sooner or later Carter was bound to develop a major press problem. The fact that it happened so early, before Pennsylvania, is itself a reflection of the perceived likelihood of his prospects. That is, a candidate has to attain a certain plateau of status before the dynamics for a press crisis are in place. It requires, for one thing, a press corps traveling with the candidate of sufficient size to keep press conferences focused on the one issue, despite the candidate's attempt to talk about something else. For another, a crisis of this proportion necessitates that decision-makers in news organizations believe that the candidate is important enough to merit all the coverage.

The attention given to the *Playboy* interview cannot, however, be explained by the same logic. Yet, when asked about that exchange, Carter's advisors offered other explanations that were also essentially political. Jordan argued that the press was overcompensating for having handed Carter the nomination during the summer months.

> They were trying to protect themselves because they'd gone overboard during the summer. They had already started writing pieces about who was going to be in Carter's cabinet. To some extent, it looked to me like a rationalization just in case Carter didn't win for all the stories they had written during the summer. They really went overboard during the summer.

Rafshoon believed that the problem originated in the intertwining of Carter's future and the careers of the journalists covering him. By the time of the general election, they had become so linked that journalists reacted strongly when they perceived Carter making unnecessary mistakes.

> I think this is subconscious, but if you notice, the people that covered Jimmy are now moving into the White House. Something I found out on the airplane. The reason some of our guys, the people covering us, started attacking Jimmy was they

were kind of pissed at him. They were mad; like he was ruining their future. "We're all in this together, we've been covering this guy for two years and now he's going to blow it for us."

In assessing their relations with the media during the general election, the conclusion of Carter's advisors was that, "unfortunately, the free media got out of our control." In fact, the events of the fall campaign were a series of one press crisis after another for each campaign. Why should campaigns have such problems during the fall?

The general election campaign is distinguished from the nomination race in that there were no concrete events during the fall for campaigners and press to construct standards around. From the journalists' vantage point there was less hard news to report (except perhaps the periodic polls). In the absence of successes to write about, they naturally turned to the mistakes of both campaigns. Again, establishing the link to the election outcome was an important motivation in selecting campaign news to report.

Campaigners, on the other hand, were left without specific standards to compete against (except the final result). The lack of concrete horse race events made it difficult for campaigners to focus the press on specific issues of their choosing. They had, furthermore, little means of convincing journalists that they would eventually be successful, and, therefore, they lacked the means of building campaign momentum around journalists' interpretations.

With this background, it is little wonder that both politicians and journalists cooperated on turning the four debates into pseudoprimaries that could be "won" or "lost" by the contenders. Both sides felt more at home with that conception of the race. They gave the campaigns the appearance of standards which they could attempt to manipulate to their advantage (was a tie really a win, after all?). For the journalists, the debates provided a focal point around which they could write about the horse race aspects of success and progress.

Summary: Candidate Coverage and Media Politics

The media and campaigns need each other: journalists define presidential politics as an important story to be reported fully; campaigners want to reach voters through the news reporting process. When news organizations commit themselves to reporting the activities of a specific candidate, they lose a great deal of their flexibility in their relationship with that campaign. From that point on, the campaign can count on a regular flow of news rather than having to seek out coverage. As a number of journalists are assigned to the campaign, they are able to use competition among journalists to the advantage of their candidate.

Of course, the nature of campaign reporting defers much of the initiative in the relationship to candidates. They are expected to take public positions and engage in other behaviors which the news media can report. A great deal of campaign reporting, however, involves not the policy positions or activities of the candidate, but a discussion of standards which campaigners ought to meet: their progress, or lack thereof, in the race; and their prospects for electoral victory. In these matters, campaigns develop an increasing ability to narrow political reporting as the campaign develops political strength.

There are, however, two important exceptions to the general propositions that campaigns can develop influence in their political relations with journalists. First, they find it difficult to combat labels or images which slowly become affixed to their policy stands ("radical," "conservative," "fuzzy,") or their personalities ("dull," "vindictive," "lightweight"). Second, occasionally during the campaign, reporters collectively seize the initiative in defining the important news: campaigns are unable to dominate the agenda of reported news because the press is collectively focused upon a single issue which is disadvantageous to the campaign. These press crises may, in fact, be a reaction to the persistent attempts of campaigners to narrow the range of reportable events. Whether a reaction or not, few journalists would hold up the coverage of the $90 billion transfer plan or the Eastern Europe gaff or the ethnic purity statement or the *Playboy* interview as the most shining examples of campaign journalism in 1976.

The influence campaigns are able to exert over coverage grows during the campaign as a result of political success. Winning candidates are increasingly able to coordinate political events. They frequently do so in such a way as to lead journalists to conclusions that advantage the campaign. Growing influence in the political community provides campaigners with the means of shaping the phenomena which journalists are attempting to report. In designing their activities to affect the reported news, campaigners operate under the assumption that a given analysis by journalists will produce an intended result in the political domain.

Beyond the use of political muscle, campaign staff members are also able to develop leverage over news coverage due to the assignment pattern of major media corporations. News media primarily report election politics by focusing upon the activities of the contesting candidates. Once a journalist has been assigned permanently to a campaign, his or her presence has several implications from the campaign point of view. The reporter serves as a vertical guarantee that the candidates' activities will be reported. Rather than arranging flashy, single events to draw reporters to the campaign, the organization can act as a regular dispenser of reportable news. A great deal of campaign effort goes into selectively facilitating the reporter's work. Of course, campaign staffers hope that if stories they wish reported are made readily available while other possible stories are hindered, the traveling journalists will keep themselves occupied with the former.

In addition, campaigners perceive that the news produced each day is heavily influenced by the internal politics of news reporting organizations. In a bureaucratic struggle between "our reporters" and those covering other candidates, they may find opportunities for surreptitiously influencing that political process to facilitate the work of journalists covering them.

There exists, furthermore, a natural tendency for journalists covering the one particular candidate over a long period of time to become heavily influenced by the perspective of that campaign. This is not to suggest they lose their journalistic objectivity and become advocates of that candidacy. Rather, since almost all of the information they receive about the election comes through their interactions with campaign personnel, journalists naturally become focused upon events in terms of how they affect that one campaign. The broader perspective is usually absent. For example, several instances were examined in which the Carter campaign was able to shape the general contours of reported news simply by careful attention to the physical location of their candidate.

Finally, with expanding demands for access to the candidate and upper-level staff, campaigners are able to utilize journalistic competition to their own advantage. Campaign priorities between media, such as a preference for television or even a particular network, may be facilitated through control of access. Individual journalists can be put in the position of competing with their colleagues for information rationed by campaigners. The demand for access varies through time: it increases as a campaign develops political strength and becomes particularly intense in periods immediately following events such as primary victories.

The conclusion reached from careful attention to campaign news reporting in 1976 and interviews with campaigners and journalists is that the liabilities of candidate coverage outweigh the benefits. Examining interactions between campaigners and journalists as a political relationship leads to the conclusion that candidate coverage passes over to campaigns too much of the initiative of what constitutes the news of the day. More resources ought to be devoted by news reporting organizations to covering other aspects of the election process. For example, journalists ought to be assigned to cover primaries rather than candidates even in the later stages of the nomination process.

There are obvious reasons why decision makers in news media organizations desire to have a correspondent-reporter with each major candidate at all times. While involving greater administrative inconveniences, the regular rotation of reporters on a two or three week basis would preserve the necessary independence of judgment. It would also necessitate a greater degree of cooperation and information sharing among colleagues in the same media organization, yielding a better comparative perspective within the organization.

On the other hand, despite the added burden of deciding and implementing the rotation schedule, the disadvantages of rotation are not great. Campaigns need news coverage; campaigners are much more troubled by a lack of coverage than by negative coverage. Accordingly, rotation of journalists would not entail an enormous loss of sources within the campaign organization. If journalists feel they need to develop an in-depth personal understanding of the candidate, they should be assigned to travel with the candidate early during the preprimary period.

Many factors contribute to the content of reported news: the timing and nature of events, the structure of the news reporting organization, the unique combination of skills and values of the reporting journalist, to name a few. This chapter has focused upon the interactions between journalists and the campaigners they are assigned to cover, from the viewpoint of the latter. Campaigners conceive of their relationships with journalists as partly political, and they attempt to develop those resources which will allow them to influence the journalists' behavior. While ultimately their major resource lies in developing strength in the political domain, an important source of influence derives in the coverage decisions of news reporting organizations, namely the decision to assign permanently a reporter-correspondent to a given campaign. Rotation of reporters would preserve a greater degree of independence for journalists in their political relations with campaigns.

Donald R. Matthews

3

"Winnowing":

The News Media and the
1976 Presidential Nominations

The news media have become a part of national political campaigns. Contemporary television is obtrusive. Campaigns have had to adjust to the needs of the medium. National political campaigns have become little more than a series of performances calculated to attract the attention of television news cameras and their audiences. But the change in the political role of news gathering organizations can not be ascribed solely to this new technology. The long-run decline in the effectiveness of party organization, combined with recent efforts to "democratize" nominating procedures, have also fueled this development. No longer do party officials and associated elites meet in nominating conventions to choose a presidential candidate from among their own numbers. Today rank and file voters are directly and indirectly involved in the choice. Party officials have lost most of their control over nominations and self-starting presidential aspirants contest in open arenas for control over national convention delegates and their votes. The news media are the main way the actors in this dispersed and prolonged drama communicate with one another and with those who prefer to stand aside and watch. A struggle over the content of political news has become the core of presidential nominating politics.

None of these generalizations are likely to surprise the readers of this book. But the new political role of the news media raises problems for journalists and politicians—and those of us who spend our time studying them—for which we have no adequate answers. *How does the enhanced*

DONALD R. MATTHEWS is *Professor of Political Science at the University of Washington. Professor Matthews wishes to acknowledge Louise White and William Haltom for their research assistance on this chapter.*

importance of newspeople and news organizations — their values, organizational needs and technologies — affect presidential nominations? Specifically, how and how much did the media affect the nominations of Jimmy Carter and Gerald Ford in 1976?

Some Preliminary Distinctions

Most discussions of the political effects of the news media are overly simple, either too benign or too lurid. The news media are depicted either as all powerful political forces or as neutral observers merely reflecting reality. It does not help much to say that neither of these views is entirely correct nor entirely wrong. The news media are very powerful but there are limits on (and other contenders for) this power. If the news media really dominated our political life as some allege, Jimmy Carter would not be President of the United States today. Nor, in all probability, would Gerald Ford or Richard Nixon or Lyndon Johnson or Harry Truman or Franklin Roosevelt have been President in the past. Thus while the news media inevitably shape "reality," this distortion need not invariably favor the media's preferences between political parties, candidates, or policies.

If we are to make any headway in this inquiry we must begin by drawing a few clarifying distinctions. First of all, we must distinguish between *causes* and *covariation*. Winning candidates for presidential nominations, for example, attract more space on the nation's front pages than losing ones — but is this *cause* (the greater exposure results in victory) or *covariation* (winners are more newsworthy than losers and would win anyway)? The effects of the media may be either *manifest* or *latent*. If the news media had self-consciously and intentionally set out to "sell" Jimmy Carter to the American people as President, their success would have been a manifest effect. This was clearly not the case. But the news media, in their pursuit of large audiences and "good reporting" may have depicted the events of 1976 so as to lead to Carter's nomination — a latent effect. A third and final distinction may also help: media effects can be felt either on the *process* or the *outcome* of presidential nominations. It is rather easy to demonstrate how the news media affect the strategies, behaviors, and style of presidential nominating contests, that is, the process of collective choice. But the more important question is outcomes — what kind of persons are chosen as presidential nominees? This chapter tries to look at the results of news media coverage (cause-effect relationships), whether they are intended or not (manifest or latent), on who wins (outcomes).

This concern directs our attention primarily toward the early stages of the nominating process. Causes must precede effects. And the early stages of the nominating process are so unstructured and ambiguous that the press then enjoys maximum discretion in defining the situation. "I can't wait until next January," one of the nation's leading political journalists said in late 1975, "then I'll *know* what I should be writing about." Paradoxically, the media's greatest opportunities to affect outcomes are when most of the audience are paying the least attention. (See Figure 1.)

Fig. 1. *Hypothetical Relationship Between Phase of Campaign and Media Effects*

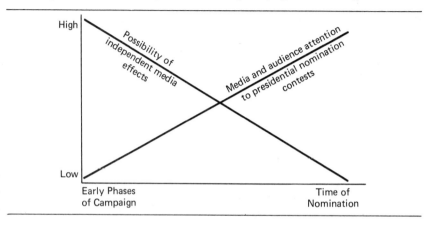

This by no means implies that the media play no significant role in presidential nominations. Rather it means that those newspeople who report upon the early stages of presidential nominating politics (reporters specializing in national politics) and the news organizations who employ them (a half dozen elite newspapers, the news magazines, the wire services and newspaper editors, and the broadcasting networks) have most of whatever independent media power there is.

The Lessons of '72

Presidential nominations occur at four-year intervals. Their predictability allows ambitious politicians to begin their assaults on the Presidency years ahead of time. They occur frequently enough that one round of presidential nominating politics provides the foundation for the next four years of maneuvering, and the participants in the current round of presidential nominations—candidates, managers, activists, the press—draw "lessons" from four years before.

But the cycle is slow. Few people are personally active in more than a handful of presidential nominations. Generalizations about how they work are based on very small "Ns." And so much can change in four years that conventional wisdom can be outdated even before it is applied.

Nonetheless, the "lessons" of 1972 were pretty clear to the political specialists in the news media, and these "lessons" had some effects in 1976.

DON'T PREDICT THE WRONG WINNER AGAIN

In 1971 and 1972, political pundits nearly to a man had predicted that Senator Ed Muskie of Maine would be the Democratic nominee. His campaign's collapse after a lackluster showing in the early primaries was a source of considerable embarrassment to the political reporters whose stories had informally "elected" him. They were to be extra careful not to make the same mistake again four years later. Besides, our reporter-informants told us in 1975, political reporting placed much too much emphasis on winning and losing anyway. 1976 seemed to be the year to rise above the imagery of the sports page and to write and talk about more important things.

DON'T COUNT ANYBODY OUT

In 1972 the news organizations had ruled Senator George McGovern out of contention before the primaries.

Most of the reporting on the preprimary stage of presidential nominating contests is done by reporters based in Washington, D.C. And they "knew" firsthand that McGovern was a run-of-the-mill Senator who inexplicably wanted to become President. Despite McGovern's appeal to antiwar protesters on college campuses and in middle-class suburbs, the Senator from South Dakota scarcely surfaced in national opinion polls. He seemed to have no chance to develop the stature or attract the resources necessary for a nationwide campaign. Hence, he was dismissed as a "lightweight."

The mistake in 1972 had been to overlook the possibility that McGovern could convert vehement opposition to the Vietnam War into enough money and an amateur campaign organization which could win low-turnout political contests such as presidential primaries and precinct caucuses. McGovern's miraculous string of primary victories and subsequent nomination was explained primarily by time-specific factors—the Vietnam War and the organizational savvy of McGovern and his youthful aides. The latter explanation became less plausible after McGovern's heroically inept general election campaign. But the winding down of the war in Southeast Asia seemed to make a McGovern-style victory by a long-shot candidate unlikely in 1976—there was no other issue capable of mobilizing amateur campaigners on the horizon. Nonetheless, the news media were still reluctant to eliminate entirely *any* possible winners in 1976, including a number of possibilities who neither campaigned nor admitted they were candidates.

DON'T LET "THEM" CONTROL THE NEWS

Every modern day campaign for high political office is (among other things) a struggle for control over the content of the news. Campaigners try to get the press and broadcast media to carry their campaign appeals to supporters; the news media try to carry interesting and accurate and useful political information to their audience. Neither side can achieve its goals without the cooperation of the other. Yet there is much manipulation and conflict, and the news organizations do not always prevail. The "news" which the media carry is not always to their own liking.

In the 1972 general election campaign, for example, President Richard Nixon had escaped close press scrutiny simply by not campaigning. Press attention had focused by default upon the inept McGovern. The Watergate break-in occurred during the campaign; still, Nixon won reelection in a landslide. There was a self-conscious concern in 1976 that an incumbent President not be allowed to use the White House to dominate the news in this fashion again.

But the problem is broader than how to cover an incumbent President running for reelection. Campaign reporting traditionally consists of reporters following individual candidates around the country, reporting on where the candidates went, what they said, how the audience reacted, and the like. The ease with which national political campaigns can coopt or otherwise manipulate a traveling pack of reporters was irreverently described by Timothy Crouse in his *The Boys on the Bus* based on the 1972 campaign. While the tone of the book was unappreciated by many of its subjects, most political reporters seemed to agree with its basic thesis. The "lesson" was clear enough—the news media must not allow themselves to be captured and exploited by the candidates this time.

BEYOND THE HORSE RACE

The deep thinkers among the press corps and broadcast networks—urged on by their academic friends and critics—set out in 1976 to do a better job covering political issues and presidential character and qualifications than they had four years before. Four years before, a massively flawed President had been reelected by a landslide: how could and should the news organizations do a better job in assessing and depicting the character and qualifications of the contenders? The treatment of "issues" in 1972 was unsatisfactory as well. Nixon managed to avoid talking about them; McGovern did talk. But the media had not paid much attention to McGovern's policy statements until the California primary—when it turned out that some of what McGovern had been saying made little sense. By then McGovern's nomination was virtually assured: would it have been if Democratic primary voters had known more about McGovern's issue positions earlier in the game? No one will ever know. But a better job on "issues" was in most reporters' minds as the 1976 round of presidential nominating politics began.

So many things about presidential politics had changed by 1976 that some of the lessons of 1972 quickly proved irrelevant.

The trauma of Watergate had resulted in a new President with no previous national campaign experience pitted against one of the nation's most formidable and experienced campaigners—concern over an incumbent bias in the news seemed a lot less appropriate with Gerald Ford in residence at 1600 Pennsylvania Avenue. The worry over premature predictions eroded as the number of Democratic contenders grew to more than a dozen; somehow that number had to be reduced quickly if the news media were to do a halfway decent job of reporting on the Democrats. (The sagging economy and hence tighter budgets and shrinking news holes made the problem worse.) Then, too, the formal rules of the game had changed a lot since 1972. The number of presidential primaries had increased from twenty-three to thirty—at which 73 percent of Democratic convention delegates and 68 percent of the Republicans were to be popularly elected. The Democrats had banned "winner-take-all" primaries, and required candidates for convention seats to reveal their presidential preferences. And the nominating campaigns were to be partially funded by tax dollars for the first time; along with the federal dollars came strict limitations on expenditures and elaborate reporting procedures.

All these changes over four years meant that the game was to be significantly different in 1976. How it was to differ and who would benefit from the changes was not clear.

Predicting Outcomes

The "people who brought you Ed Muskie as President" were wary of predictions in 1976. But this conflicted sharply with the need to do something about the extraordinarily large list of Democratic contenders (and possible contenders). Somehow they needed to be sorted out in order to write interesting and dramatic stories. One basis of classification was expected performance—"serious candidates" versus "lightweights." Other classification schemes were used as well—especially "liberal-conservative" and "insider-outsider" distinctions—but predicted performance was by far the most important of these criteria since early predictions can become self-fulfilling prophecies. "Serious" candidates receive more press attention than "lightweights"; this publicity can lead to improved name recognition, higher poll standings, and the availability of more resources, which in turn leads to still more favorable predictions of performance.

Even when they prove to be grossly wrong, the press' early predictions can have major consequences. The history of both parties' nominations in 1976 illustrates this latter point.

THE "BROKERED CONVENTION" SCENARIO

During 1974 and 1975 few political reporters believed that *any* of the growing list of active Democratic candidates could win the nomination in 1976. The polls showed Senator Edward Kennedy, Senator Hubert Humphrey, and Governor George Wallace to be the most popular leaders in the party. Senator Kennedy had withdrawn from consideration and Humphrey had sworn not to campaign for the nomination. If taken literally—and as time passed, more and more people did—that left Governor Wallace the only Democratic possibility with a sizable national following. And Wallace, despite serious questions about his health, was actively raising money and developing a grass roots organization in anticipation of what was expected to be an aggressive campaign.

But, virtually all reporters were convinced that Wallace would not win. Rather it seemed probable that he would go into the convention with about a third of the delegates. The dozen or more other candidates would divide up the remaining delegates so that no one could attract the 50 percent-plus-one votes needed to win, and the convention would deadlock. Ultimately the party would be forced to turn to an established leader not actively seeking the nomination—probably Hubert Humphrey. The overwhelming play which this scenario received in 1975 in the *Washington Post* and *New York Times* can be seen in Table 1.

TABLE 1. Direct Reference to Candidate Nomination by Process in the *Washington Post* and *New York Times* in 1975

Candidate Nominated & Process	Jan.-April	May-Aug.	Sept.-Dec.	All Year
Humphrey drafted	4	9	29	42
Kennedy drafted	9	9	6	23
Muskie drafted	2	3	2	7
Other nonactive candidates drafted	0	2	6	8
Brokered outcome; no candidate named	2	8	6	16
Wallace nominated	2	3	1	6
Other active candidates nominated	1	5	12	18

This scenario had many advantages for the media, especially during the early stages of the nominating process. It made sense out of a complex situation without declaring any active candidate the front runner. It did not eliminate anyone—except Wallace, and it actually overestimated the Alabama Governor's strength. For while Wallace had more money and better organization than ever before, the fire was gone, a casualty of an assassin's bullet and the cooling of racial conflict. This overestimation of Wallace, of course, resulted in Carter receiving more credit than he deserved for his narrow victory over Wallace in Florida.

Interestingly, the brokered convention scenario persisted even after it became apparent that George Wallace was a great deal weaker than he seemed in 1974 and 1975 and despite Senator Humphrey's refusal actively to campaign in the primaries. The Humphrey noncandidacy was kept very much alive by the CBS-*New York Times* postelection surveys and other polls which showed that Humphrey would have done well if he had been on the ballot in the early primaries:

1.   Humphrey would have received 24 percent of the vote in Massachusetts if he had been on the ballot. Jackson received only 23 percent without that competition.(*New York Times*, March 4, 1976.)
2.   "The *Times*-CBS Poll showed that almost one-third of Florida Democrats would have voted for Humphrey had he been on the ballot." (*New York Times*, March 10, 1976.)
3.   "About 40 percent of those who voted [in Illinois] for all Democratic candidates except Mr. Wallace said they would have voted for Senator Hubert H. Humphrey of Minnesota had his name been on the preferential ballot. Had he campaigned here, the figure might have been larger." (*New York Times*, March 17, 1976.)

This process of making Humphrey the beneficiary of primaries in which he did not run gradually altered the brokered convention scenario into a stop-Carter-with-Humphrey story as the ex-Georgia Governor pulled away from all the other active contenders.

THE FORD CAN'T BE SERIOUS SCENARIO

Several misjudgments in the coverage of the preprimary stage of the Republican contest seem to have had important effects on the ultimate renomination of President Ford.

Ironically, one such error was a widespread and systematic underestimation of Ford as a campaigner. Partly this resulted from Gerald Ford's pre-White House reputation in the Washington community as a clean cut, reliable boob. Brilliant, witty, clever, quotable he was not—as House Minority Leader or as President. His early efforts at organizing a national campaign looked amateurish to experienced observers. "Any President with Ron

Nessen as his press secretary and Bo Callaway as his campaign manager can't be serious about running for reelection." Rumors about Mrs. Ford's health added to widespread speculation that the President might not run for reelection at all.

All this led to Ford entering the primary season with very little expected from him. Ford's narrow "victory" over Governor Ronald Reagan in New Hampshire would have been interpreted as a defeat if almost any other President had been involved. Reagan attracted a larger share of the New Hampshire voters than McCarthy in 1968 or McGovern in 1972 and yet, unlike them, was *not* declared a "winner."

The media coverage of the Republican contest tended to assume that the early primaries would be crucial, as they proved to be for the Democrats. Yet Ford's early victories did not lead to the irresistible momentum that Carter's early wins did, despite the news media's best efforts. The main reason for this probably was the important differences in the situation within the two parties in 1976. On the Democratic side there were many candidates—in this kind of situation people choose among candidates on the basis of personal preferences *plus* estimates of their probable chances of victory. It makes little sense to most people to back a first choice if he has no chance of winning. Jimmy Carter was not the first choice of many people outside his home state of Georgia, but as the prospects of his success increased (and of other candidates diminished) his following multiplied very rapidly as the persons for whom he was a second or third choice abandoned their fading first preference candidates to join his bandwagon. But the Republican contest was a two-way race. In such a situation reasonable people support their first choices without regard to who will win or lose, and the early leader's margin is not magnified by the same kind of bandwagon effects which prevail in multiple candidate situations.

Declaring Winners and Losers

Who wins—or loses—a presidential primary is frequently unclear. Getting the most votes or electing the most pledged delegates are not automatically interpreted as "victories." And it is possible in some states for a candidate to get the most votes without winning the most delegates, or vice versa. More often than not, winning a presidential primary means doing better than expected; losing means disappointing expectations. The media find a winner in these curious contests by arriving at a rough consensus on how candidates should do and then measuring the vote and delegate outcomes by this rubbery yardstick. This "numbers game" is a big part of primary election reporting—how many votes and/or delegates must candidate "X" win before he can be said to have "won" (or "lost")? Without such "analysis" the raw facts and figures of presidential primaries would be virtually meaningless to most Americans.

SETTING EXPECTATIONS

But how are these expectations arrived at? What kinds of evidence are used? Obviously the candidates have an interest in keeping expectations about their performance low enough to make it possible to exceed them while not discouraging their own following. But "winners" must succeed in doing this in a competitive situation in which others are following the same strategy. Reporters are not usually misled by all this preelection day gloom. But they must look beyond the campaigns to local political experts and other reporters for help in setting these expectations.

The *bases* upon which expectations of performance are set can be several. In 1976 few of the active campaigners had run for the nomination before, hence *historical experience* was not widely used as the basis of expectations. The most important exception was George Wallace's strong showing in Florida in 1972 which contributed to excessively high expectations four years later under quite different circumstances. These changed conditions—Wallace's health, the lack of busing issue, the existence of a "respectable" southerner on the ballot in 1976—were all discussed in the preprimary and postprimary analyses. But Wallace's 42 percent vote in 1972 still remained the standard by which his 1976 performance was judged. *Preprimary polls* seemed to have affected expectations on many occasions—Ford's showing in New Hampshire and Florida, Reagan's in North Carolina were viewed as "victories" partly because they did better on election day than in the polls. *Geographical propinquity* is frequently used as a basis for setting expectations. Candidates are not only expected to run strongly in their own states but also in states nearby (e.g., Bentzen in Oklahoma, Brown in Nevada, Udall in Wisconsin, etc.). Finally, *cost-benefit calculations* are often utilized—how well a candidate does considering his investment of time, energy, money in the state. This approach is mostly used to explain away relatively poor showings in gaining votes and delegates, but occasionally is used to discount an arithmetic victory (e.g., Jackson's in New York). Obviously which of these bases are used to judge the performance of which candidates can make a difference.

THE GREAT NEW HAMPSHIRE OVERKILL

The interest of news organizations in predicting outcomes—preferably earlier than the competition—leads to a special interest in the first formal steps in the presidential nominating process early in the presidential year. Political reporters who were having trouble getting their work printed in 1975 ("Only my mother can find my stories back among the shipping news") suddenly start to get some stories on the front page. The number of reporters assigned to political stories increases. Television camera crews show up at more and more occasions. There is a brief surge of media attention focused heavily on one of the nation's smallest and least typical states, New Hampshire (Table 2).

TABLE 2.   Number of Television Network News Stories on Early Primaries, 1976*

Primary State	Date	Number of Stories	Number of Delegates	Number of Stories per Delegate
New Hampshire	Feb. 24	100	38	2.63
Massachusetts	Mar. 2	52	147	.35
Vermont	Mar. 2	6	30	.20
Florida	Mar. 9	50	147	.34
Illinois	Mar. 15	38	270	.15
North Carolina	Mar. 23	19	115	.17
New York	Apr. 6	30	428	.07
Wisconsin	Apr. 6	42	113	.37

Source: Michael J. Robinson, "Television News and the Presidential Nominating Process: The Case of Spring," unpublished manuscript, 1976.

*Note: All three network's nightly news stories combined, weekdays only.

Presidential primaries are made to order for television news. They are predictable and hence relatively easy to cover on camera. They combine human interest, conflict, drama, and uncertainty. New Hampshire's small size, nearness to the metropolitan centers of the East Coast, and New England landscape and culture make it an especially attractive subject for national television. The fact that it is also the first presidential primary makes it nearly irresistible. In 1976 the three national television networks presented 100 stories on the New Hampshire primary or exactly 2.63 stories per delegate selected there! None of the other early primaries received half as much attention from television. While the print media did not overdo New Hampshire as extravagantly as NBC, CBS, and ABC, they were not too far behind in the great New Hampshire overkill of 1976.

The consequences of the media infatuation with the New Hampshire primary are obvious—"winners" of that contest receive far more favorable publicity and a far greater boost toward the Presidency than the "winners" of other primaries. A week after New Hampshire, for example, Senator Jackson won the Massachusetts primary by a very solid margin. While this clear victory temporarily improved his perceived chances for the Presidency, it did not generate the kind of momentum in subsequent primary states that a New Hampshire triumph usually does.

New Hampshire overkill favored Carter and Ford in 1976. It is unlikely that either could have won their party's nomination without it. Carter's entire strategy was based on keeping expectations (read: media expectations) low while winning the Iowa caucuses in January, the New Hampshire primary in February, and Florida primary in March. He had been quietly cultivating these three states for several years. His carefully nurtured strength in these states, combined with the fact that he was little known anywhere else (except, of course, in his home state of Georgia) gave his early victories a shock value that made them especially newsworthy to a novelty-prone press. A few national political reporters, most particularly R. W. Apple, Jr. of the *New York Times,* revealed Carter's strategy and growing strength in late 1975, and this resulted in his being cast in the unexpected role of front runner in the New Hampshire Democratic primary. But he managed to edge Morris Udall by 4,300 votes and to be declared the victor nonetheless.

$90 Billion, Ethnic Purity, and Other "Issues"

The media's preoccupation with who is winning and who is losing presidential campaigns leaves little time or space to devote to issues. Traditionally, journalists blame politicians for the lack of attention paid to public policy debate in campaign reporting. Certainly they did in 1976. Thus John Chancellor, speaking to a group of editors, complained that he had not seen "a campaign so lacking in a discussion of real issues in twenty years of covering national politics." Howard K. Smith (presumably not to be outdone by another network) agreed that "this is the first presidential [election] since Al Smith was beaten for allegedly aiming to put the Pope in the White House that has been almost entirely fluff."

And yet, practically every one of the more than a dozen active candidates for the two major party nominations issued a series of "position papers" or "issue statements" early in his campaign. (Jimmy Carter released twelve such statements between the date of his formal announcement and the New Hampshire primary.) Most of the candidates in 1976 had served in the U. S. Senate for many years where they had repeatedly taken recorded positions on most domestic and foreign policy issues. And candidates for presidential nominations talk about political issues at almost every street rally or coffee klatch or businessmen's lunch they attend. These presentations may be long on rhetoric and short on substance but it still can be said that the presidential aspirants talked much *more* about public policy and issues in 1976 than the media did.

One reason for this is the division of labor with the press corps. The tone and style of presidential campaign reporting tends to be set by reporters who specialize in politics all the time—the Germonds, the Broders, the Witcovers, the Apples, and their equivalents outside Washington, D.C. Political reporters tend to be fascinated by the process, the mechanics of politics. They are not particularly interested in, or knowledgeable about, policy issues. Issues tend to be covered by other reporters—specialists on economics or foreign policy or what have you—in the relatively large news organizations where full-time political reporters work.

Thus of the large quantity of low grade, highly repetitive talk about political issues which went on during the nominating battles of 1976, the media selected out a small fraction as newsworthy. A few of these items became headline stories, and may have had some effects on the ultimate outcome of both races.

WHAT STATEMENTS ON ISSUES ARE NEWS?

Judging from recent experience, a candidate's statement on public issues is most likely to be reported if it represents a *change* in the candidate's position or if the statement is *inconsistent* with other positions the candidate holds at the same time or if the candidate supports a line of actions which is obviously *impractical.*

The traveling press hears candidates give the same speech over and over again. This standard speech quickly loses news value to them unless it is altered in some way. Those who have not heard the same speech many times before might interpret the same speech quite differently. Jules Witcover in *Marathon: The Pursuit of the Presidency* describes this phenomenon when Governor Reagan switched the emphasis of his standard speech from domestic to foreign policy after the New Hampshire primary.

> . . . national reporters traveling with Reagan, on the alert for anything new in Reagan's speech, zeroed in on his new foreign policy material woven into the standard speech. But the local reporters, many of them hearing Reagan for the first time, plucked out his best, and oldest, lines and wrote about them as if they had just come out of the cellophane. . .

Reporters place a premium on internal consistency. "A politician can get away with a great deal," one of the best reporters in the business said a few years ago, "so long as he is consistent." A candidate for the Presidency who takes inconsistent positions can expect rough treatment—as such recent casualties of presidential politics as George Romney or Barry Goldwater can testify. Impractical or impossible policy proposals are pounced on by all with glee—the best example is George McGovern's demi-grant proposals in 1972.

The press corps mostly ignores campaign talk about policy issues unless it appears likely that this talk will affect electoral outcomes. The political consequences of issues are what matter to them. The merits (and demerits) of policy proposals are largely ignored.

WHOSE STATEMENTS ON ISSUES ARE NEWS?

The press pays more attention to the issue positions of some aspirants for presidential nominations than others.

Anything a President of the United States says about public policy is likely to attract attention—even if it is said in the midst of a campaign situation. Incumbent Presidents usually campaign by being "presidential." Thus the distinction between President and candidate is often hard to draw. Reagan, as the only active opponent of a sitting President, received a lot more media attention than any of the Democratic competitors as the media sought to achieve some parity with Ford, but the incumbent's advantages still remained awesome.

The news media also pay more and more critical attention to the issue statements and policy positions of candidates as their chances for the nomination improve. At first, presidential aspirants and their managers have to try very hard to get political reporters to pay any attention to them. The relatively personal and intimate relationship between candidates and the few reporters who are covering them changes as the primaries begin. If the candidate does well, the number of news organizations covering the candidate increases daily until a small army of reporters and television technicians are following him everywhere—the relationships between the campaigners and the press become more distant, critical, and confrontational. Most of the time, the candidate is able to keep control over the traveling band—indeed that's one reason why candidates travel so much—but if he makes a mistake someone is likely to catch it and get it published.

But the greater attention to the policy component of the leading candidates' campaigns is more than just a response to changing personal relationships. More importantly, it is part of the more detailed and searching scrutiny a politician undergoes as he draws closer and closer to the Presidency. The press (as well as the rest of us) does not apply the same standards of adequacy to an ex-Governor of Georgia running for President with a 4 percent rating in the latest Gallup Poll and the same men with a better than even chance of being nominated by the majority party for the highest office in the land.

This escalation of standards of evaluation, combined with some increased media attention to issues, can be so sudden as to be unnerving, particularly for a fast-rising "outside" candidate like McGovern in 1972 and Carter in 1976. Policy statements which were greeted with yawns when they were issued months ago come in for close attention for the first time. Positions which were overlooked or tolerated then are criticized when looked at as pronouncements of a potential President.

THE "FUZZINESS" ISSUE

As the press began to look closely at Jimmy Carter's issue positions—and given his early successes, this came early in 1976—they were confronted with unusual complexity and ambiguity. Unlike most of the other candidates, Carter was personally unknown; he had no long period of service in

Washington or a long list of public policy positions or a clear ideological position. There was little Hubert Humphrey or Henry Jackson could do to alter their public images. But Carter's unfamiliarity allowed him to try to convey a fresh approach to politics, stressing personal qualities—trustworthiness, morality, compassion, technical ability, efficiency, love, practicality. He sought to avoid being stereotyped into traditional political categories. According to Carl Leubsdorf's 1976 article in *The Annals,* reporters noted that "he had a way of stating issues so that he drew support from those with opposing views . . . he often refused to state things in a precise way that would give reporters a sharp, easy quote." The *Wall Street Journal* on February 23, 1976, eloquently stated the press' confusion when it referred to Carter after New Hampshire as "a moderately liberal conservative."

Carter's approach to issues drove many a reporter up the wall. Attacks on Carter's "fuzziness" became a central theme of the campaign—begun by the press, then picked up and used by his opponents. One of the advantages of the charge was its own imprecision—it could mean duplicity, vagueness, lying, ambiguity, inconsistency, dishonesty, and more. The "fuzziness" of the "fuzziness story" made it difficult to answer.

THE "ETHNIC PURITY" ISSUE

The brouhaha over Jimmy Carter's remarks on "ethnic purity" illustrates the way in which issue controversies tend to arise and to be resolved in presidential nominating campaigns.

The candidate first used the phrase in a private interview with Sam Roberts of the *New York Daily News* about federal housing policy. Witcover in *Marathon* describes the exchange:

ROBERTS:"Well, can a black central city survive surrounded by all white neighborhoods?"

CARTER:"Yes, my next-door neighbor is black. It hasn't hurt us—provided you give people the freedom to decide for themselves where to live. But to artificially inject another racial group in a community? I see nothing wrong with ethnic purity being maintained. I would not force racial integration of a neighborhood by governmental action. But I would not permit discrimination against a family moving into the neighborhood."

Roberts presented the quote without comment in the sixteenth paragraph of a nineteen-paragraph story which appeared on page 134 of the Sunday *News.*

Two days later a CBS reporter asked for a clarification of the quote at a press conference in Indianapolis. In his response, Carter did not say what he meant by "ethnic purity" but reiterated his opposition to government programs which would "inject black families into a white neighborhood" and support for freedom of movement into and out of neighborhoods. In the course of his explanation he used some new language—"alien groups" and "black intrusions"—which his auditors found more than a little newsworthy.

The stories written on the basis of this news conference converted the matter into a major national controversy. At first, these stories had two thrusts: a) Carter's policy stand on racially integrating housing and b) Carter's use of such potentially insulting phrases as "artificial" integration, "alien groups," "black intrusion," and "ethnic purity." The story was picked up and spread further by Morris Udall, by black leaders, and numerous syndicated columnists. In the process, the criticism shifted away from Carter's policy ideas to his language. In a few days Carter apologized for "careless" and "improper" choice of words and the story quickly receded from view. An opportunity to discuss the substance of a complex policy issue had been lost by its reduction to the single phrase "ethnic purity."

THE $90 BILLION BLUNDER

In September of 1975 ex-Governor Reagan of California in a speech to the Executive Club of Chicago proposed that a number of federal programs (costing $82.4 billion in the 1976 federal budget) be transferred to the states. The speech was routinely reported in the *Chicago Tribune* and largely forgotten. Two months later Reagan announced his candidacy and the transfer of programs scheme was referred to in a few columns and articles in the national press. Since the proposal seemed altogether consistent with Reagan's thoroughgoing conservative images, it just wasn't very newsworthy.

But two things happened to the idea which converted it into "news." First, Reagan began to redefine the idea from one calling for a simple transfer of programs between governmental levels to a way of cutting the federal budget. And President Ford attacked the idea on the grounds that the states would be forced to raise taxes—especially the state of New Hampshire where the first confrontation between the two candidates was soon to occur. Media coverage of the story thereafter took off. It became a running story for several months.

Reagan was never able to explain how huge tax savings could be made at the federal level without cutting back on popular but expensive programs (social security, medicare) and without forcing the states to increase their taxes. Running stories must have shorthand labels—"ethnic purity," "$90 billion"—or they cannot last. Unfortunately for Reagan, the shorthand label of this running story made it difficult for him to redefine the issue by scaling down the magnitude of his dollar claims—the issue was "the $90 billion" issue.

Thus Reagan began his formal campaign in New Hampshire very much on the defensive, having given the Ford campaign an ideal issue in a state with neither a sales nor an income tax.

Given the way the news media cover issues in presidential campaigns, it's not surprising that campaigners come to see issues as highly dangerous. A member of Carter's staff said, "The issues can never help you, but they can sure kill you."

Creating Drama and Suspense

THE DEMOCRATIC CONTEST

As the plausability of the "brokered convention" scenario faded in late March and April, the Democratic contest was in grave danger of becoming a dramaturgical bomb. After a breathtaking surge upward following his early "victories," Carter's poll ratings had stabilized at about 30 percent—essentially the same as Humphrey's (Figure 2). The poll standings of all the other Democratic contenders were either steady at around 5 percent or sharply declining (Wallace and Jackson). Not many delegates were selected yet, but Carter was getting about a third of those which were (Table 3) and was gradually pulling away from the others (Figure 3). Humphrey, of course, as an inactive candidate had no officially pledged delegates. With no campaign organization, no campaign funds, and the deadline for filing in most primaries either past or fast approaching, his chances of signing up many pledged delegates were nearly zero. The Carter organization, as judged by expenditures, was steaming along, especially when compared to the other Democratic campaigns (Figure 4). Given these facts, and Carter's stunning successes in Pennsylvania, his nomination seemed virtually assured.

Wave II—consisting of the late-starting candidacies of Governor Jerry Brown of California and Senator Frank Church of Idaho—saved the story by providing an element of uncertainty and suspense in the Democrats' nominating picture. A suspension of disbelief is helpful in enjoying most theatrical productions; it was essential in order to take the second wave seriously. But most of the media did.

Jerry Brown proved to be excellent copy—a "new face" with a unique style and a vague anti-Washington message. He was a novelty, much as "Jimmy who?" had been just a few months before. Brown's campaign in Maryland was staged for the national media (it was too late for his supporters to file in the delegate races), and the media outdid themselves. On the *Washington Post* the Maryland campaign was covered by metropolitan staff reporters, and Jules Witcover (of the national staff) dryly remarks that they treated Brown's campaign as "the Second Coming."

TABLE 3.   Percent of Selected Delegates Pledged to Democratic Candidates by Dates in 1976

Date	Carter	Jackson	Udall	Wallace	Church	Brown	Others	Uncommitted	Total
March 2	25	21	18	21	—	—	12	3	100 (145)
March 17	31	14	6	15	—	—	28	6	100 (401)
March 24	34	11	5	17	—	—	22	11	100 (493)
March 31	34	11	5	17	—	—	22	11	100 (493)
April 6	27	21	16	11	—	—	11	14	100 (855)
April 13	28	19	14	11	—	—	12	16	100 (925)
April 21	28	19	14	11	—	—	12	16	100 (931)
April 28	28	13	11	9	—	—	21	18	100 (1,184)
May 5	36	13	11	9	1	—	14	17	100 (1,523)
May 12	36	13	11	9	1	—	13	17	100 (1,577)
May 19	38	12	14	7	2	—	10	18	100 (1,904)
May 26	38	11	13	7	3	1	10	18	100 (2,278)
June 2	38	11	13	7	3	1	9	18	100 (2,330)
June 9	39	9	11	6	2	8	7	18	100 (2,891)

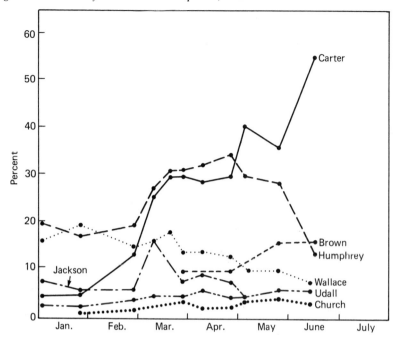

Fig. 2. First Choice of Democrats in Gallup Polls, 1976

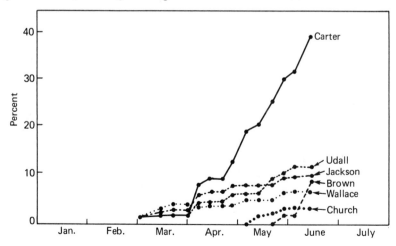

Fig. 3. Percent of All Delegates Pledged to Democratic Candidates, 1976

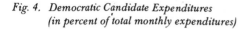

Fig. 4. Democratic Candidate Expenditures
(in percent of total monthly expenditures)

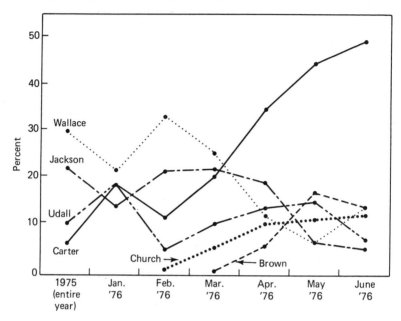

Not to be outdone, the *New York Times* Washington bureau overplayed the story, too. It was far too late in the game to be interested in purely symbolic victories—delegates were the main game now, and neither Brown nor Church had a chance to collect enough of these to stop Carter, either alone or in combination.

The overplaying of these last minute challenges to Carter was the result of a felt need for more drama and suspense. The emphasis on prediction in American political journalism can lead to a bored and inattentive audience, especially as the capacity to make reliable predictions increases. Once all the predictions have been made, why stay tuned in? The only good reason is that the prediction may be wrong. But the story has been altered. Now the suspense is over the accuracy of the prediction rather than the outcome of the event. This is the structure of election night shows—an early prediction based upon limited returns followed by a prolonged and anticlimactic reaffirmation of the prediction. Once the brokered convention scenario was abandoned, the story of the Democratic presidential nomination of 1976 roughly followed that script.

THE REPUBLICAN CONTEST*

According to William Keech in a paper presented to the 1976 American Political Science Association Meetings, once Governor Reagan weathered his disastrous showing in the early primaries, he proved to be "the strongest challenger to an incumbent President since former President Roosevelt ran against President Taft in 1912." While never able to match Ford's popularity among rank-and-file Republicans once the campaign formally commenced (Figure 5), he was able to stay close to the President in the Gallup Polls until the very end (Figure 6). The contest for delegates was essentially a toss-up from the end of April until the final machinations at the Kansas City convention. Uncertainty there was aplenty without the news media trying to create any more.

This does not mean that the media did not affect the Republican outcome—it did. But these impacts helped make for a close race rather than a bandwagon victory.

Fig. 5. First Choice of Republicans in Gallup Polls, 1976

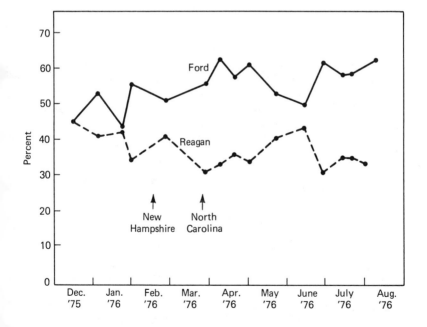

Fig. 6. Percent of All Delegates Pledged to Ford & Reagan, 1976

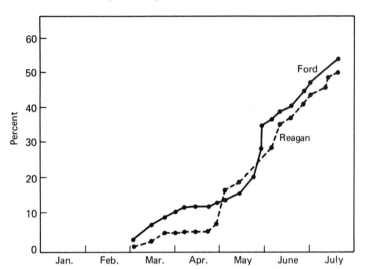

Some Conclusions

I have sought to suggest some ways in which the news media contributed to the presidential nomination of Jimmy Carter by the Democrats and Gerald Ford by the Republicans in 1976. Sorting out causes from mere covariation is not easy, and the evidence is often thin. But I think a reasonable, if preliminary, case has been made that news organizations and newspeople had major independent effects on the presidential nominating politics of that year. These impacts were mostly unintended consequences of the press and broadcast industries covering the story as they thought it should be covered at the time. Hindsight shows that mistakes were made and that some of those had political consequences. But the media have even greater political significance when they do their job well.

THE ISSUE OF MEDIA POWER

Americans are rightly suspicious of concentrated political power. Thus the findings of this analysis, as anecdotal and arguable as they are, should be disturbing. A small—and shrinking—number of private, profit-seeking news organizations are affecting the nation's choice of Presidents in ways which even they do not understand.

"The media," of course, are not so monolithic as this chapter seems to imply. I have had to talk about "the media" as if there were no differences between newspapers and television and news magazines and wire services, between national and local organizations, or within each of these categories. There is some diversity within the news media but there is also much concentration of control and even more voluntary cue-taking. The political power of a handful of elite reporters and newspapers, two wire services, and three broadcast networks is sobering. Clearly public policy should seek to encourage more diversity and competition within the news industry, more professionalization of journalism, more continuous and informed criticism of news media performance. None of these typically American palliatives, in the amounts one can reasonably expect in the near future, will do a great deal by itself. Perhaps doses of all three might make a discernible difference.

The chances are that the news media will remain powerful actors in the presidential nominating game from now on. This may not be an altogether bad thing. American Presidents are not chosen by peers who personally know them and their strengths and weaknesses well—as are most leaders in the private sector or as prime ministers are in parliamentary systems. Ultimately American Presidents are chosen by a mass electorate which knows them only faintly at second hand. A preliminary screening of potential Presidents by persons who know the candidates intimately through extended personal exposure (rather than through hyped-up campaign imagery) may be quite desirable. Today that "screening" is informally and imperfectly performed mostly by political reporters. In the past, this function was performed by established political party leaders and large campaign contributors. It is not self-evident to me that these groups were any wiser or more dedicated to the commonweal than the press.

WHAT KIND OF CANDIDATES WIN?

The contemporary organization, technology, and practices of the news media, when combined with the current rules of the major parties, seem to favor certain types of presidential aspirants over others.

The renomination of Gerald Ford was a near ultimate test of the power of incumbency. Ford was our first nonelected President; he had taken over the White House in the wake of a political scandal of unprecedented proportions. An inexperienced and indifferent national campaigner, he defeated the strongest challenger to an incumbent President in more than half a century. The news media have helped create an office whose incumbent is virtually unbeatable in nominating contests.

And certainly 1976 demonstrated that a little-known outsider can win— despite all the advantages of the long-established, Washington-based presidential aspirants. Carter's victory was the result of many factors in addition to the coverage his campaign received from the news media. But we can expect other Jimmy Carters—overambitious, underemployed, underfinanced outsiders—to try to pull off the same media-induced "miracle" in the party out of power every four years from now on. Whether they will succeed is highly uncertain. 1980 and beyond may prove as different from 1976 as 1976 was from 1972.

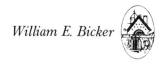

William E. Bicker

4

Network Television News
and the 1976 Presidential Primaries:

A Look from the Networks' Side of the Camera

Network television news coverage had a major influence on the preconvention activity of the 1976 presidential campaign. Social scientists have already studied and will no doubt continue to study and debate the effects of television news coverage on individual voting decisions, on support for candidates, and on other factors important in determining who stays in and who leaves the race for the Presidency. However, there was no debate about the importance of network television news among serious candidates and their strategists.

The purpose of this chapter is to examine news coverage of the 1976 preconvention presidential selection process from the perspective of the people and organization who are, collectively, network television news. The focus here is not on the content of the programs as they were broadcast and seen by the country during the first six months of 1976, but instead on the individuals who planned them, and the structure and process by which they developed the materials broadcast over the networks during this period. From this perspective, five questions will be considered. What was the situation the networks faced in 1976? On the basis of its structure and organization, how was the news-gathering potential of the networks mobilized to prepare for the 1976 election? How did the networks plan and then implement the plans to cover this period? What were the intended and

WILLIAM E. BICKER *is Director of the State Data Program at the University of California, Berkeley. Professor Bicker wishes to acknowledge Barbara Buswell and Eric Smith for their research assistance on this chapter, and Irene Baldwin, Mary Louise Groom, and Maureen McMullen for other assistance.*

unintended results of this planning process? What were the effects on the fortunes of those in the contest?

Achieving a full and accurate description of the intense activity of network television news covering the presidential race during the first six months of 1976 in the few pages allotted here is, perhaps, no less a fantasy than getting a full and accurate summary of all the major events of the day in the nation and the world summarized in thirty minutes each day Monday through Friday. It would, one might say, be a most naive author who would conclude such a chapter with the comment, "Well, that's the way it is," and an even more foolish reader who believed it. This discussion will, I hope, serve instead to highlight some aspects of the coverage of the 1976 election from the perspective of the networks, and thereby provide some points of departure for understanding the powerful, but still very young and evolving social institution which is network television news in America.

The Environment: Change for the Future, Criticism of the Past, and the Current Internal Situations

Network news approached the 1976 election in an environment of concern about change in the future and criticism of the past. Their own organization and mode of operation were also an important part of this environment. Therefore, it is important to examine these segments of the environment which set the stage for their plans and their execution of those plans.

POLITICAL CHANGE–NEW RULES FOR THE NOMINATION PROCESS,
NEW TASKS FOR THE NETWORKS

The process of reform has made it difficult to mark the beginning and end of particular presidential elections in the past decade. The 1976 presidential election season saw changes still under way in party regulations in 1975. Certainly by 1976 the nomination process could be seen as having undergone two rounds of major reform following the 1968 and 1972 elections. Party and government leaders reflected the discontent of the nation as 1976 approached. Rules were changed; states changed the dates of their primaries and began jockeying for position in 1975. When interviewing for this project began, executives in each of the three major commercial network news divisions had clear apprehensions about their coverage of the 1976 campaign.

Their concern was based on the changes in the primary process from 1964 to 1976 which presented the network television news teams with a host of problems. Just between 1972 and 1976 the number of primary states had swollen from twenty-three to thirty. The elections would take place during a time period lasting from the 24th of February in New Hampshire to the 8th of June in California, New Jersey, and Ohio. This sixteen week period left only three Tuesdays in which there was not a primary election in one of the thirty states (see Table I). The number and geographic spread of the primary elections alone created logistical problems for the networks as well as the candidates.

The change in the distribution of power over delegate votes, and hence the outcome of the nomination, was even more important than the logistical problems caused by the growth of primaries. Prior to the major reforms of the late 60s and early 70s, primaries had not been a major source of delegates to the national party conventions. After all the rules had been changed in 1976, however, 70 percent of the delegates to the national conventions were selected in the primaries. The power to nominate had shifted from the political activists and professional politicians to the voters in the primary states. This created a new situation, and was a source of great concern for the networks.

Regulation of the campaign process and funding procedures, each a product of new federal law, coupled with changes in the rules of the parties, added new complexities to the problems of providing adequate news coverage. Just as important was the problem of the absence of a clear "front runner." Neither Edward Kennedy or Hubert Humphrey was in the race. Their absence, coupled with the new rules, opened the way for an extraordinarily large field of Democratic contenders, in all, thirteen or more candidates. On the Republican side, there was a nonelected incumbent who would be challenged by a representative of the dominant right wing of his party. This meant that not only could there be a large number of contestants in every primary on the Democratic ticket, but there would probably also be major contests on the Republican side as well. Thus the networks, along with other news gathering and disseminating organizations, would be denied the luxury of dealing with single party contests in most of the primary states as they had in the past.

The new rules and regulations made it difficult for the networks to use their normal means of determining whom to cover. McGovern had shown that the old means of assessing the seriousness and therefore newsworthiness of a candidate by his position in the polls, or "clear claim" on the nomination would no longer be adequate in this environment. The federal financing laws raised doubt in particular about one of the means that had been employed for establishing a candidate's credentials—his ability to raise money. Not only did the newsmen have to learn the new rules and adjust to them, but they had to explain them to the public as well. Many political events in the campaign season took on meaning only when the new rules of the game were understood (e.g., the qualification of a candidate for federal funding by raising sufficient funds in small amounts in twenty different states).

TABLE 1.   1976 Convention Votes

Date	State	Democratic Number	Democratic Percent	Republican Number	Republican Percent
Feb. 24	N.H.	17	.74	21	1.31
Mar. 2	Mass.	104	4.55	43	2.68
	Vt.	12	.52	18	1.12
Mar. 9	Fla.	81	3.54	66	4.11
Mar. 16	Ill.	169	7.39	101	6.30
Mar. 23	N.C.	61	2.67	54	3.37
Mar. 30	—	—	—	—	—
Apr. 6	N.Y.	274	11.98	154	9.60
	Wisc.	68	2.97	45	2.81
Apr. 13	—	—	—	—	—
Apr. 20	—	—	—	—	—
Apr. 27	Penn.	178	7.78	103	6.42
May 1	Texas	130	5.68	100	6.23
May 4	Ala.	35	1.53	37	2.31
	D.C.	17	.74	14	.87
	Ga.	50	2.19	48	2.99
	Ind.	75	3.28	54	3.37
May 11	Neb.	23	1.01	25	1.56
	W.V.	33	1.44	28	1.75
May 18	Md.	53	2.32	43	2.68
	Mich.	133	5.81	84	5.24
May 25	Ark.	26	1.14	27	1.68
	Idaho	16	.70	21	1.31
	Ken.	46	2.01	37	2.31
	Nev.	11	.48	18	1.12
	Ore.	34	1.49	30	1.87
	Tenn.	46	2.01	43	2.68
June 1	Mont.	17	.74	20	1.25
	R.I.	22	.96	19	1.18
	S.D.	17	.74	20	1.25
June 8	Cal.	280	12.24	167	10.41
	N.J.	108	4.72	67	4.18
	Ohio	152	6.64	97	6.05
Total Delegates Selected in Primary Process		2,288	100%	1,604	100%
Percentage of Total Convention Votes		76%		71%	

During the "break" between the Democratic and Republican national conventions in the summer of 1976, one senior CBS producer looked back and reviewed the past sixteen months with both relief and conviction:

> In terms of looking at about how many people we'd need, how many people we're going to have to be covering, and then obviously the budget related to all of that, I was right on the mark about everything, and it is not because I was smart—It was because I was frightened. I could see by March [of 1975]... 1976 is going to be one of the most complex years we've ever done, and we've got to coordinate things or else we're really going to be blowing money, because we'd be just scrambling, because we're going to have candidates coming out of the woodwork, and more primaries than we've tried to deal with before, and it's going to be an awful snarl unless we do some good planning, some really good planning.
>
> I projected our budget and all of our planning with the thoughts that we could have as many as ten Democratic candidates going right up to the wire, all the way through. It was a fright budget, trying to take the maximum horror I could think of of how much we'd have to do. It turned out perfectly because people dropped away and it didn't work out that way all the time. I was keeping a firm grip on what we were doing and how we were using our people and facilities all of the time, so we ended up in our budget, without any sudden, "Oh my God—we didn't allow for X happening", just because there was some pad in there, because I had built into it my maximum fright.

This statement differs from those made by executives at the other two networks only in its degree of candor.

CRITICISM AND CONCERN OVER THE COVERAGE OF PAST ELECTIONS

Dealing with the changes alone would have been a significant challenge, but there was also the area of the problems with coverage of previous presidential races that had to be at least considered. Television, particularly network news, had been the subject of substantial criticism during the years preceding the 1976 presidential primary season. In part this was due to the misperception of the source of the message, the media, with its content. In large part, however, many of the criticisms of television news and its coverage of presidential elections was borne out by the concerns voiced by the leaders of the media itself. Executives, producers, writers, and correspondents alike joined in agreeing that things had to be done better than they had been in the past. Few of the outside critics were more concerned or articulate than those in the media in general, and in television news in particular.

It is, therefore, difficult to pin down the origin of particular concerns and criticisms—to separate outside criticism from the concerns and self-criticism found within the networks themselves regarding previous coverage of the presidential nomination and election process.

Few people from network television interviewed in this project would cite *Boys on the Bus* or others who pointed out the deficiencies in previous campaign coverage. However, the litany of failures to cover the issues, the attention given to the "media events," the personalities and activities of campaign personnel, and the machinations and power plays within campaign organizations were voiced both inside and outside network headquarters in a remarkably similar fashion. Perhaps the major difference was the personal degree of concern expressed by those involved in the production of network television news; they saw the problems as ones faced by *their* medium and *their* profession.

Regardless of their origins, the concerns of network executives, producers, and correspondents at the beginning and throughout the process of selecting a nominee for President of the United States were focused on not repeating the mistakes of the past. These included the following items in particular.

Television news coverage had been criticized for viewing the candidates as the candidates wished themselves to be viewed, i.e., for allowing the candidates to manipulate their coverage. For instance, the media allowed Richard Nixon to campaign on the basis of ending the war in Vietnam with his "secret plan" without ever seriously asking what that plan might be or raising questions about its existence. In 1972, the media allowed Nixon to campaign for reelection from the Rose Garden and the Oval Office, never raising questions about his stewardship. Other media-wise politicians capitalized on the logistical problems and capabilities of television, and made it almost impossible for the media to get beyond anything other than that which the candidates wished the viewers to know. Correspondents were criticized severely for accepting what they were given and asking no questions.

In 1972 George McGovern was not taken seriously until it was too late—another example where both those in the networks and outside agreed that coverage was lacking. The criteria by which the networks selected the set of candidates with reasonable chances of attaining the nomination clearly had failed. Since the extent of coverage a candidate receives affects his or her chances of being nominated, errors in decisions of whom to cover may have significant impacts on the elections. This was a criticism which the networks took particularly seriously.

Another criticism was that the networks spent too much time talking to one another and to professional politicians, and not enough time paying attention to the interests, needs, and desires of the electorate who would ultimately decide among the candidates. Rather than look at public opinion on an issue, the correspondents interviewed Governors, Senators, Mayors, and other political activists. The critics argued that the general public was being ignored. The relevance of their criticisms was heightened by the increase in the number of primaries in 1976, and the correspondingly greater importance of the voters in the candidate selection process.

Probably the most widely heard criticism was that instead of covering the issues in the campaign, the networks focused on the personalities of the campaign managers and other aspects of the campaign organizations—the so-called "Teddy White stories." Related to the networks' failure to take McGovern seriously was the failure to examine his positions on the issues until his nomination was virtually assured. Only at the end of the primary season, when Hubert Humphrey, McGovern's last remaining opponent, questioned McGovern's issue positions did the networks finally turn to the issues. The subsequent hubbub when the nation became aware of McGovern's negative income tax proposal foretold McGovern's overwhelming defeat at the hands of Richard Nixon the following November.

While the changes in the primary process may have initiated the changes in the manner in which the networks covered the elections, the criticisms of past coverage certainly influenced those changes. In planning for the 1976 elections, the networks faced a vastly different situation from that of 1972 and 1968. As they planned to adjust to the new situation of 1976, they attempted to respond to their critics as well. The result was a massive response to vastly changed circumstances in the networks.

The NBC, CBS, and ABC planning processes for coverage of the 1976 presidential election were conducted in an atmosphere of concern over the failures of the past and apprehension about the uncertainties of the future. The 1976 election year was so different from previous election years that no one felt confident that they understood it. Unlike the situation in previous years, the networks were facing a complex, little understood election year which differed in many major aspects from the previous elections. The past, in short, could not be used as a sure guide for the future.

THE ATMOSPHERE AND ORGANIZATION OF THE NETWORKS

The external factors, such as changes in the political process and the concerns over problems with past performance which were shared by those inside as well as outside the networks, were seen by correspondents, staff, and executives from their own organizational perspective. Therefore, to complete this overview of important factors to the network news organizations covering the 1976 preconvention race, the internal organization, structure, and atmosphere of the organizations themselves must be considered.

Here it must be emphasized that a lack of space allows for only a sketchy discussion of this very important subject. Edward J. Epstein's *News from Nowhere* provides a somewhat dated overview of the area but is still the only treatment of any length of network television news.

Pressure is an everyday fact of life in network news. The competition between organizations and within each organization is intense. The egos which provide the strength to present live, frequently unscripted analyses of events for millions of viewers also can produce tense situations for each other as well as for those in charge of insuring that adequate facilities are available behind the scenes. The stakes are always high for the networks, production units within the networks, and the individuals. All of this seems to reach its peak in the coverage of a race for the Presidency. One NBC producer summed it up in these words:

> Do I have any feelings for the competition? Well, yes, there's a lot of pressure on everybody to be first, to be competitive. You could call the conventions and the presidential elections the network olympics. The olympics of news, and the primaries are the preliminaries.

The presidential race is seen by those in network news as presenting an opportunity to affect a lasting change in viewing habits for the evening news show. This is no doubt based on the experience of 1960 when the NBC team of Huntley and Brinkley, through their success in covering the Republican and Democratic conventions of that year, replaced the "CBS Evening News" as number one in the ratings and remained on top for more than six years. Achieving the number one status for the flagship or evening news broadcast is important not only to the news division, but is of clear importance to the network itself. The importance to the network derives not only from the income generated by the news division, of which the evening news is the prime source, but also has consequences for the network's relationship in general with its affiliates, which in turn have direct bearing on the overall income of the network and all of its broadcasts.

A complicating factor in 1976 in particular was the question of how to cover the thirteen weeks of primary elections during the spring. This raised major questions concerning an interruption of the entertainment line-up for those Tuesday evenings by broadcasts or even announcements of winners, which might disrupt viewer loyalty for a particular night's entertainment line-up. Prior to 1972, this was not a problem. The electoral activity of 1968 and before was sporadic in the late winter and spring, when entertainment revenues for the networks are high. The concentrated activity of the conventions and general election campaign took place primarily during the summer and early fall, when entertainment programs were being rerun or tested before a smaller viewing audience.

What follows is a very brief discussion of the economy of the networks and the news operations, an examination of the three networks' relative strategic positions in terms of entertainment and news, and how this affected their approach to the primaries. Next, the network news' organizational pattern for coverage of the primary elections will be examined. Finally, the formats and styles of the basic news outlets of the networks will be compared. All of the above are factors involved in internal decision-making regarding the length, time, and character of coverage for the 1976 preconvention activities.

Network news is a product not only of the professional dictates of news judgment, but of corporate structure as well. The three major television networks are large, profit-making corporate entities. NBC is itself the major profit-making subsidiary of its parent corporation, RCA, and was begun with the initial intention of providing a means to increase the sale of RCA's radio receiving and transmitting equipment.

Each network is organized into major production divisions for its television broadcasts. These include entertainment and sports as well as news. Each division is headed by a president, who is a vice president of the network. Each division has control over its personnel and makes decisions based on the parameters provided by the networks. The major revenue of the network is generated by entertainment and sports. As one CBS producer explained:

> The news division doesn't pay for itself. We used to be nothing but the prestige thing that took a huge loss in corporate terms, always. That has since turned around now that news has become a commercially profitable thing at local stations as well as at the networks, and so the gap is much smaller . . . we never plan anything in terms of what it's going to bring back in—that's the CBS, Inc. problem.

News, however, does compete as a division for air time with entertainment and sports.

The relative positions of the networks and news departments prior to the primary period provided good indication of what they could attempt and perhaps hoped to accomplish. The most important figure in terms of the overall revenue of the networks is the entertainment ratings. During the period from September 1975 through April 1976, the entertainment ratings had CBS in first place, ABC second, and NBC third. In news, CBS was first, NBC a close second, and ABC was third. For the morning shows, NBC's "Today Show" clearly outran the other two shows; its ratings were almost higher than the other two shows combined. ABC's "Good Morning America," run by their entertainment rather than their news division, was second, and "CBS Morning News" was third.

It should be noted that at all three networks, the question was not if the network made a profit, but how much profit could be made. Demand exceeded supply in terms of places for sponsors to buy commercial time on network television. Therefore, even with low ratings, NBC was not in a position of having to reduce its rates to advertisers. It could not, however, raise them.

CBS wanted to maintain its number one position in news and if possible increase its lead. The new conditions imposed by the changes in the political rules and the criticisms were still important parts of its considerations.

But the success of the existing team and the resources which were available meant that their job was to continue doing the kind of work they knew they could do. The entertainment ratings meant there was no special pressure from CBS, Inc.

NBC, however, was close enough—just two rating points behind— to be in a position to challenge CBS for the top rating in the evening news broadcast. The network, moreover, was in a position where some successes were needed, given its low position in the area of entertainment. Adding to the atmosphere of concern at NBC was the condition of its parent corporation, RCA. NBC, Inc. was seen by some inside the network as providing an excessive amount of its own profits to RCA to make up for RCA's losses in other endeavors. Thus, decisions made by NBC to commit the level of resources to the election coverage were in accordance with its potential return to leadership in the area of the evening news.

ABC News was out of contention for number one in the ratings, although it could increase its share of the audience. Moreover, there was a strong commitment on the part of special events not to disturb a segment of their extremely profitable entertainment ranking, with some of its more successful shows on Tuesday night. As Vice President of TV News Walter Pfister explained:

> In 1972 we came on and interrupted contract programing for periods of ten minutes. We found quite a lot of resentment on the part of people having their programs interrupted. They were so angry about the interruption they couldn't remember who won. I think it is bad form to come on in the middle of a sentence or when they are doing the denouement of a story. So what we're doing now is chopping two minutes out of program content during the time that we think we're going to make the projection. We've taken two minutes out of "Happy Days" (which runs from 8:00 to 8:30) and we've taken two minutes out of "Laverne and Shirley" (which runs from 8:30 to 9:00). Depending on when the projection will be made, we can run the long version or the short version.

The ultimate decision made by each of the three networks was to go with a two to five minute period for each call, that is, the call of the results of the election; to interrupt the programing as soon as that call could be made; and then place the election special at the 11:30 hour. This avoided the conflict of interrupting the Tuesday night shows even for the less successful line-ups at NBC and CBS. These are the problems being imposed on the news divisions' time allotment as outlined by Russ Bensley, chief producer for the elections coverage at CBS.

> We're always in a squeeze for time and money. Part of the problem is that news is given only so many prime time hours a year, but those are mostly committed for documentaries and such. If we want to preempt those for a political show, then it means preempting ourselves in a way. The problem is getting time that is not normally ours; getting something away from entertainment.

At NBC, the problem of the 11:30 show was particularly crucial. The highly-rated "Tonight Show" would have to begin after the election night special, generally a half an hour later. There was no small degree of concern about moving "Tonight" and "Tomorrow" since both shows focus around strong personalities who do not hesitate to indicate their displeasure at alteration in their shows' regular appearance time.

ORGANIZATION OF NETWORK NEWS

The structure in network news organizations is related to its different products. The bulk of activity in the network news divisions is oriented toward the evening news shows. This and other regularly scheduled news shows represent major points of organization for news division personnel. For the most part their objective is to cover and present the news of the day, the "hard" news. The news departments are also responsible for presentation of documentaries and the coverage of events which will entail special broadcasts. In the latter category, the special event is usually of such significance that it will be covered live or in summary fashion by itself, and be a major topic on the regularly scheduled broadcasts as well. This division between "hard" and "soft" news is for the purpose of insuring continuing coverage of the news of the nation and the world in the hard news outlets while also making certain that the special information, correspondent assignments, and logistical arrangements are made for the special event.

Generally, producers, writers, and production related staff have their "organizational home" established by their connection with one of the regularly scheduled newscasts or with the special events units. Correspondents, for the most part, do not have the same kind of "home." They have a base of operations in their bureau assignments. That is, all correspondents are assigned to one of the locations which has all of the facilities to independently produce and transmit to the network a complete report or story. In the 1975-76 period these were New York (or Headquarters), Washington, Los Angeles, Chicago, and Atlanta for each of the three network news operations.

The formal lines of reporting to the bureau chief were, along with other formal lines of authority, cloudy. As one long-time network executive explained:

> The anchor may make a quarter of a million dollars, maybe more, I don't know. He reports to the producer and executive producer, who may make $75,000, who in turn reports to a vice-president, who may nor may not make that much. The money goes down and the supposed authority goes up. Let's face it, the reason the nightly news is going to go up or down in the ratings is because of the anchorman, and *that means millions.* So no matter what the reporting lines are, there's a lot of influence.

To gain exposure, a correspondent must be prepared to provide a story or report that will conform to the style and format of the news outlets. The particular formats or styles of the regularly scheduled newscasts are important considerations for both the correspondent and/or the coverage of the presidential election.

The formats and styles of the regularly scheduled newscasts are viewed in the network as important in determining the size of the viewing audience, while no considerations are given to the kinds of questions that seem to dominate various themes of entertainment shows, coming in various seasons such as the detective story, or the western, or the situation comedy. The style of the news show, primarily dictated by the style which best displays the assets of the anchor personnel, is considered at all three networks. Thus, for example, Walter Cronkite's approach at CBS is to involve himself heavily in the questioning of those being interviewed by other correspondents. His use of a teleprompter and other aids allows Cronkite to be on top of most of the facts and other elements going into the breaking events in the election special and other events where Cronkite is on-air for most of the time. This contrasts with John Chancellor's approach at NBC where he and David Brinkley are more passive when the correspondents are doing the interviews or giving reports. The anchormen do not attempt to integrate correspondents' reports into their own commentary.

A more important distinction, however, is the general format of the news outlet. All three networks have for their evening news show a hard news focus where reports are generally kept to two minutes or less. This includes, of course, coverage of the election, although some exceptions were made.

There is, in addition, another daily news outlet available to correspondents at NBC and CBS—the morning news show. At ABC the morning show is under the control of its entertainment division, but has a hard news segment anchored from Washington. The control over the program is not in the hands of news division personnel and therefore is not available except by very special request, to correspondents as an outlet for their story.

At CBS and NBC a clear contrast in morning show formats is apparent. "CBS Morning News" is an hour long, and generally hard news focused. Reports can be longer, but the general focus of the news show is to cover the breaking news of the day with some extended reports covering special topics. The NBC format for its "Today Show" is rather unique in this regard in that it is more like a news magazine than a straight news show. It contains a section on entertainment, sports, and a good deal of feature material. It is under the control of its news division, and with its high rating is a very important income producer and can command a good deal of attention from correspondents. NBC, therefore, has a dual personality with regard to news outlets: the evening newscast which is straight hard news, and the "Today Show" which provides an outlet for the feature-oriented or background story. Correspondents at NBC can prepare different kinds of reports, knowing that there is an outlet for them in the "Today Show" format. The difference is not only length (which can go up to fifteen minutes) but approach as well, which is not necessarily the straight hard news approach, but can and must, if its format is to be maintained, present the interesting human or background kind of story. Furthermore, the "Today Show" has a history of moving around the country in its location and, in doing so, presenting background material on that particular state or city. This is counter to the clear national mission of the CBS news outlets and the "NBC Nightly News."

ORGANIZATION FOR COVERAGE OF THE ELECTION

Primaries are special events, and this description by an NBC news executive in the Special Broadcasts Unit explores many of the aspects of how all three networks organized to cover the election.

The Special Broadcast Unit has the overall responsibility for all news coverage outside of the regular programing and documentaries, in other words, any broadcast which goes on of the nature of a presidential speech, news conference, primary coverage, election coverage, convention coverage, space coverage. To make that happen, other units are set up—some operate permanently and some are set up especially for a given coverage.

For example, a station has been constituted whose job it is to prepare us for the space shot, and we will be responsible for the actual coverage, working with the space unit. The actual getting all of the efforts onto the air in a cohesive and creative and imaginative fashion is the responsibility of the Special Broadcast Unit.

Similarly, there is the Elections Unit which operates as a permanent unit doing information-gathering as well as opinion surveying and just sort of determining the lay of the land, putting together each document, which is sort of the bible for each of the primaries and also for the general election itself.

The Special Broadcast Unit leads all of the other units which will be dealing with elections; for example, as you get close to the elections, the shows themselves, like "Nightly News" and the "Today" program will step up their coverage, and to facilitate this the Elections Unit will provide briefings, provide expertise.

Because elections are so special, obviously, they involve the news gathering function—in other words, the regular network news gathering apparatus will get very involved for the primaries because we will have to work out a scheme for how we are going to cover the primaries, leading up to them, leading up to the actual elections, as well as how we are going to cover election night itself. And all of that, since it involves more than just a special broadcast, will be coordinated on a company-wide basis.

The importance of the Elections Unit cannot be overstated. For the network executive and executive producer it is the source of information on which to base decisions about the importance of primaries to determine their coverage commitment. To the primarily generalist correspondent and field or show producer it is the source of basic material needed to understand the significance of day-to-day events during the campaign and information which will fill out a particular story. Its professional staff expertise in national politics and social science research techniques would be the envy of many political science departments. During the interviews conducted for this study, correspondents, when asked about a particular campaign event and its significance, would frequently refer the question to a' member of the Elections Unit staff. This is clear indication of the importance correspondents attribute to this resource which takes responsibility for the problems with the complexity of the new rules and provides the means to cope with many of the criticisms of past coverage.

The Elections Unit had responsibility for various tasks. Each area was headed by a professional and included the development of journalistic background materials such as names, events, issues, recent noteworthy developments for which files are kept up to date for their use during election time. Social science capabilities, such as vote projection, are also handled by the Elections Unit. This requires statistical tasks, involving both sampling procedures and the development of a model for projecting the vote, as well as the appropriate programing for the computer and control of computer facilities. Providing for analysis of the results of the elections is also the responsibility of the unit. Key precinct analyses (or voter profile analyses) and polling were two means used by the Elections Unit for such analysis. Polling will be described in detail below.

For each primary, both NBC and CBS prepared rather elaborate books, generally of a hundred pages or more, presenting the electoral rules of a particular state, its recent political and general demographic history, biographies of major figures, the styles of campaign forces and campaign activists, and the various kinds of other information that, taken together, would be extremely helpful to correspondents.

The Elections Unit had to provide information for both the correspondents in the field and anchors and commentators on the regular news shows. In addition, they had to prepare to provide the projections and analyses for election night. Because of the dual focus of the news outlets at NBC, the task of the Elections Unit there was significantly broader than at ABC or CBS.

At ABC and CBS, the basic question behind coverage of the election from before New Hampshire through November was, "what does this event or occurrence or activity tell us about who will gain the nomination of his party and then win the election and become the next President of the United States?" The focus here was national in its orientation, which meant national issues and national trends were to be stressed.

At NBC, the same hard news question represented the focus of a large part of its coverage, but both the format and frequent state and local focus of the "Today Show" added a different set of questions for which information had to be acquired. At NBC, the question could be reversed, that is, "what does this particular election event tell us about the people, their interests, and behavior in this state that would be of interest to our viewers?" Therefore, the Elections Unit at NBC had to delve more deeply in personalities and issues at the state, as opposed to national level and be prepared to provide feature oriented background material as well as the hard news information about the campaign. This pattern followed through all of its research efforts.

Planning

There were several important aspects of the plan to cover the 1976 primaries. One was the definition of winning. Another was the allocation of personnel and resources to cover each of the primaries—how much time would be given to each and where the anchor location would be. Next—the decision to focus on issues, and finally the decision at CBS and NBC to make extensive use of public opinion polls conducted by their own Elections Units.

DEFINITION OF WINNING

During the planning stages, one decision common among network executives was to shy away from the term "front runner" until a clear leader appeared. It was also independently decided that in such a large field of Democratic candidates undifferentiated by the absence of an activist campaign by someone of clear national stature (e.g., Edward Kennedy or Hubert Humphrey), the winner would be the candidate who received the most votes (or the most delegates) in the state's primary (or convention). The same criteria would be used for the Republican race. This may, on the surface, sound like a rather simple decision, but in the past, moral victories had counted for a lot. The campaigns of Eugene McCarthy in 1968 and George McGovern in 1972 had received their greatest impetus from their close defeats by Lyndon Johnson and Edmund Muskie, respectively, in the New Hampshire primary. This time there would be no victories determined by expectations; the candidate receiving the most votes, regardless of how small that plurality may be, would be the winner. The winner would secure all of the strategic pluses and minuses of this status as well as the role of interviewee on election night.

LOCATION OF ANCHOR AND OVERVIEW CORRESPONDENTS

In determining the type and location of coverage, the local orientation of

TABLE 2. Network Primary Election Night Specials

Date	State	Length in Minutes			Anchor Location		
		ABC	CBS	NBC	ABC	CBS	NBC
Feb. 24	N.H.	30	30	30	Manchester, New Hampshire		
Mar. 2	Mass., Vt.	15	30	30	N.Y.C.	N.Y.C.	Boston
Mar. 9	Fla.	30	30	30	Orlando, Florida		
Mar. 16	Ill.	15	30	30	N.Y.C.	N.Y.C.	Chicago
Mar. 23	N.C.	15	30	30	N.Y.C.	N.Y.C.	N.Y.C.
Mar. 30	—	—	—	—	—	—	—
Apr. 6	N.Y., Wisc.	30	30	30	N.Y.C.	N.Y.C.	Milwaukee, N.Y.C.
Apr. 13	—	—	—	—	—	—	—
Apr. 20	—	—	—	—	—	—	—
Apr. 27	Penn.	30	21	30	N.Y.C.	N.Y.C.	Philadelphia
May 1	Texas	—	15	—	—	N.Y.C.	—
May 4	Ind., Ga. D.C., Ala.	15	20	30	N.Y.C.	N.Y.C.	N.Y.C.
May 11	Neb., W.V.	10	16	20	N.Y.C.	N.Y.C.	N.Y.C.
May 18	Md., Mich.	30	16	30	N.Y.C.	N.Y.C.	N.Y.C.
May 25	Idaho	30	30	30	N.Y.C.	N.Y.C.	N.Y.C.
	Ore., Nev.	—	—	30	—	—	N.Y.C.
June 1	R.I.	—	—	5	—	—	N.Y.C.
	S.D.	—	—	5	—	—	N.Y.C.
June 8	N.J.	30	30	30	L.A.	L.A.	Burbank, Cal.
	Ohio	—	—	30	L.A.	L.A.	Burbank, Cal.
	Cal.	—	—	30	L.A.	L.A.	Burbank, Cal.

the "Today Show" influence at NBC was clearly important. As can be seen in Table 2, NBC originated in twice as many states as either ABC or CBS. Furthermore, NBC assigned three reporters—Tom Pettit, John Hart, and Douglas Kiker—to provide state summary pieces, a role unfilled at CBS. Finally, CBS decided it would provide an analysis of each election in the election night special by Roger Mudd. At NBC, this role was filled by Richard Scammon, an outside consultant. Later, beginning in Wisconsin, the role was filled at ABC by pollster Louis Harris. These people were in addition to the correspondents assigned to the campaigns.

A FOCUS ON ISSUES

A strong focus on the issues fulfilled the need not to fall prey to the mistakes of the past. First, in focusing on issues, the correspondent could avoid being manipulated by the candidate. Rather than accept whatever statements the candidate wished to make, the correspondent could focus interviews by seeking out the candidate's stand on a particular issue. If a candidate chose to evade answering a question on an issue, a correspondent could show this question and the response, expecting that the viewers realized that the candidate was evading the issue. The focus on issues provided correspondents with a set of benchmarks against which they could examine candidates.

Concentrating on the issues was a means of having the candidates speak to particular questions, or not allowing them to avoid questions which correspondents felt were of importance to the country. On the other side, a focus on issues would help correspondents avoid being forced into covering "media events," or simple speeches full of sound and fury and little else.

Second, the stronger attention to issues was designed to reduce attention previously given to other material which had come under criticism, specifically, stories on changes in campaign personnel and assessments of strategy and other material on the techniques of campaigning, and the structure and style of particular campaign organizations. These pieces were felt to be of interest only to the cognoscenti of American politics. Many correspondents believed that such stories were reported primarily because the subject was so important to those on the campaign trail.

Another aspect of reduced attention to other material was that attention would be redirected toward the voters. Attention would be given to what the electorate believed and wanted instead of to the interpretation of various politicians about what the public believed and wanted. The focus on issues would bring in the missing element of the electorate's place in the electoral process. The People would no longer be ignored.

Third, the increased concern with issues would directly respond to those critics who demanded that television pay more attention to the issues and less attention to who's ahead, strategy, etc. The focus on issues fulfilled the demands of those who argued that elections are primarily about issues, not the "horse race." The networks decided to fulfill a stronger educational role in the political process.

Many members of the media thought that this kind of strict focus on issues would be one means to help steer the country through the rocky times of the period, times in which a demagogic manner might be especially effective among the electorate due to the national mood of disenchantment following the end of the Vietnam War and the resignation of Richard Nixon. A greater focus on issues was seen as a proper form of behavior in a democracy.

The means by which the networks planned to focus on the issues varied. In the early planning period at NBC, one widely discussed method was to include a weekly segment on the "Nightly News" that would focus on a particular issue and summarize the candidates' positions (or lack of positions) on that issue. The issues segment would be a means of bringing together all of the candidates and getting them to present their views without being able to evade the issue or to manipulate the news process.

ABC decided that the means to proceed in the issues area would be to examine "ABC City," Columbus, Ohio. Columbus was chosen for its reflection of the various characteristics representative of the American population—their common problems, prospects, and hopes for the future. The "ABC City" segment could provide an opportunity for examining issues in terms of how the candidates were getting their issue positions across to the voters and how the voters responded to them.

At CBS, specials were considered as a means of focusing not only on the candidates and their activities during the early period, but also to bring to the fore certain issues. Walter Cronkite would conduct interviews with the candidates in a special segment in the "Evening News" during which he would specifically ask about their positions on a list of issues. In such one-to-one interviews with Cronkite, candidates would be unable to evade the issues or twist their answers into meaningless campaign rhetoric.

PUBLIC OPINION POLLS

With the shift from an elite to a mass-based nomination system, it was necessary to shift the focus of the correspondents, anchors, and others to the real decision-makers for the nomination. Public opinion polls were the natural response. Leaked sources and interviews were not fruitful for understanding the nomination process. That is, what the party, government, and campaign leaders thought about the process had been shown in 1968 and 1972 in particular and was shown to be an eminently fallible source of information. Perhaps more important was that the experience of these two elections had shown the network executives and correspondents that their own judgment was likewise flawed. They were, of course, part of the same elite. Therefore the search for answers turned to the voters themselves.

This move to extensive use of opinion polls was one of the most significant changes in the networks' approaches to covering primaries in 1976. Two networks, NBC and CBS, went so far as to develop their own in-house polling capabilities.

Public opinion polls have long been given attention by the media, particularly those by the "public pollsters"—Gallup and Harris. For many years, the results of the Gallup and Harris polls have become news events in and of themselves. As such, it is not the use of public opinion polls and their presentation in television newscasts that is of significance. Instead, it is the development of polling capabilities by the networks for their own purposes in the covering of the 1976 presidential campaign. This development is one of the major focuses of this chapter.

To better understand the development of the polling capabilities in the networks, we must examine the previous manner in which polls were used on network news and why it was decided that the development of in-house polling capabilities would be appropriate.

As noted above, public opinion polls had long been used on the network news. This was generally done after the polls were published in the *New York Times*, since the networks were not subscribers to any of the national or statewide polls. These poll results were read by the anchormen almost as one would read the weather forecast or a report of some other news event which had occurred during the day. Little analysis was done of the poll results unless the poll closely followed a particular event which the correspondents wished to discuss. A poll might be juxtaposed with an event or used as a lead-in to a discussion of the event.

Correspondents rarely made direct use of opinion polls. The reason for this is that correspondents generally prefer to present their own particular cast in their stories, and since the content of polls was not controlled by the networks, it became simply a set of figures that had appeared in the newspapers. The dilemma of a correspondent presenting opinion polls is similar to the dilemma of presenting a set of figures from a Defense Department budget request. If the correspondent cannot question "trusted sources" from various sides as to what these particular figures mean with regard to national priorities or possible changes in national defense strategy, then the correspondent would be facing an uncomfortable situation. If he cannot discuss the meaning of the figures, he finds few keys to link them to something his viewers will understand and appreciate. In such instances, the poll numbers may be worse than useless.

The difficulty of presenting a set of opinion survey results is worsened by the fact that neither the correspondent nor most of the viewers really understand the way in which the numbers were arrived at. Sampling techniques are not intuitively comprehensible, and correspondents rarely have access to the sources of the numbers in order to have them explained by experts.

The public pollsters were not the only source of opinion polls during the elections. Private campaign polls have been available during campaigns since the fifties. A member of a campaign organization may "leak" the results of a private poll to a correspondent if the results favor his or her candidate. Publication of favorable poll results may increase a candidate's support in both workers and funds. Presentation of favorable results by a candidate is not nearly as effective as presentation of those results by a national correspondent, as the prestige of the correspondent adds to the credibility of the results.

In the primary contests of previous years, these poll results were used by correspondents to set expectations for the candidates. In many reports of primary results, two kinds of winners were reported—those who received the most votes, and those who did better than expected. In this environment, campaigns have at times attempted to manipulate coverage of primaries by leaking false poll results and thereby creating artificially low expectations. If they succeed in this, they may gain favorable commentary from various correspondents.

Finally, the private campaign polls occasionally established a professional bond between correspondents and campaign strategists. Because correspondents are generalists and usually unaware of the political culture of the particular primary state being covered, they seek out information such as poll results to give them new perspectives on the population they are covering. By providing a correspondent with information which allows him to get a handle on a previously unfathomable situation, the campaign gains an ally. Since the campaign strategists may present or withhold the information at will, they are in a position to manipulate the coverage they receive.

Knowing all of the above, correspondents had become quite leery of the "private" campaign polls. Although they used them, they preferred not to do so, and they became very wary of the risk of being manipulated by the campaign organizations in this way.

In short, existing public polling resources were not oriented toward the direct needs of the correspondents or the networks. The manner in which they were conducted was not immediately available to the correspondents, and the information that was available to them was also simultaneously available to a large segment of the audience through the regular publication of the poll.

The use of polls controlled by the networks eliminated these apprehensions on the part of most correspondents, anchorpeople, and producers. The polls seemed a clear way to go as a response to the need for reducing complexity while ascertaining the issues of concern to the public. Having in-house operations seemed to eliminate many of the previous objections reporters had to the polls.

The questions and topics of the polls were to be selected by the networks, and the polls would be conducted by the networks at the times most useful to their particular correspondents. Those who actually conducted the polls would be available for questions about the meaning of the information, the manner in which it was collected, and all the nuances that reporters should have available to them if they were to make intelligent, responsible use of the polling data.

The reporters had "exclusive access" to polls for their own networks. This gave them a leg up on their competition. They knew, for example, that they were not being fed these results at the whim of a particular candidate or his campaign organization with the objective of deceiving the public or manipulating the media.

Just as important, the polls were endorsed by management and conducted by those units (elections and special events) to which the reporters normally turned for their expertise and information on a subject as complex as the presidential primaries. Those who conducted the polls also carried out the briefings on the polls and conducted preliminary seminars on the uses and misuses of polls. They gave examples as to how polls might provide background for stories to the correspondents, anchorpeople, producers, and executive producers involved in the election coverage. Knowing the personnel involved in the Election Polling Unit, the correspondents would feel free to request additional information on topics that had been covered in the polls. This gave them the potential of doing stories in line with their own interests and enabled them to put their own touches on a story by approaching it from a perspective with which they felt comfortable.

In addition to remedying the problems noted above, the opinion polls conducted by the networks had many objectives.

One objective was to understand the primary results. This, of course, was the objective of the street polls in general. This purpose was to establish which group of voters, in terms of their demographic attributes or political opinions of issues and candidate traits, was supporting or opposing particular candidates.

Another objective was to provide information which could be used as a point of departure for dealing with candidates and campaigns. This might be an assessment of strength or weakness or concerns of the public that correspondents might employ in their questioning candidates who were campaign officials.

Further, the networks wanted to catch emerging issues of concern to the general public as they developed through the campaign process, presumably as the issues would be articulated by the candidates and differing stands brought forth. They also wished to assess the emergence of concerns about particular traits of candidates, that is, their personal attributes—trustworthiness, competence, and other factors which were thought to be of importance in the post-Watergate presidential race.

The polls were also to be used to chart the emergence of trends in the area of candidate preference, the ups and downs of the various candidates through the sixteen-week period.

Finally, the polls could measure the success of the various campaign activities, that is, the degree to which the voters were being contacted on behalf of various candidates.

In addition, both NBC and CBS thought it worthwhile to establish a link with their colleagues in the print community. In 1975, when the two networks independently determined that they would be carrying out extensive polling operations, they each sought a market for their polls first with the *New York Times* and then with the *Washington Post.*

One of the major reasons for seeking poll outlets in the print media was to allow an outlet for the kind of stories the networks felt would be impossible to do over a television broadcast. Stories requiring more detailed, step-by-step analysis certainly could be presented by a newspaper or magazine far better than by television. A second advantage to the networks would be to have the prestige of the newspaper or group of newspapers attached to their poll. For instance, when CBS broadcast a poll, they referred to it as the CBS-*New York Times* Poll; when the *New York Times* printed it, they referred to it as the *New York Times*-CBS Poll. When any other news outlet used material from the poll, they cited the two journalistic establishments as being tied together. The added prestige of a major newspaper being associated with the polls was perceived as a major benefit to the networks. The caliber of the newspapers sought by the networks to join them in their polling efforts was to be clear evidence of the seriousness with which the networks were approaching the news gathering task.

The specific techniques and approaches of the networks in employing opinion polls varied. The focus here will be on those employed at NBC and CBS, with just passing attention given to ABC. ABC employed Louis Harris for on-air commentary in Wisconsin, and later in Oregon he conducted a limited polling effort at several of their key precincts where answers about issues and candidate characteristics could be determined which could not be found in the key precinct analysis format.

The differences in the approach by NBC and CBS clearly reflected their different approaches or formats in news gathering as noted above. CBS conducted a series of national polls—four in all, prior to the convention. One, in the fall of 1975, was conducted prior to the agreement reached with the *New York Times*. The purpose of this poll was to establish the issues of interest to the voters in the upcoming presidential primary season, and on this basis, Walter Cronkite would interview each of the candidates for a segment on his evening news show. This issue focus and the source of the issues of importance were seen by Cronkite and others as a major breakthrough in using a more appropriate source for determining what to question the candidates about. The candidates were informed in advance that their interviews were to be taped and edited so that only those topics which were the subject of their discussion would be shown, thereby eliminating the extraneous or gratuitous comments the candidates might wish to make.

The polls conducted with the *New York Times* were extremely elaborate in terms of their focus on the perceptions of the candidates and the various issue positions held by the candidates in relation to those held by the voters. Voters were asked to place themselves on a continuum with regard to a certain issue or the importance of a certain attribute, and then place each of the candidates on that same continuum. Polls were conducted by telephone, and a rolling panel design was employed so that there was almost a continual monitoring of the positions of the candidates and the importance of issues in their connections with the public's attitudes about the relationship of these issue positions and their votes. In addition, CBS conducted street polls in eleven primary states. These street polls were conducted on the day of the election in selected precincts drawn on a sampling basis to adequately reflect the population of this state including as well certain geographic positions and certain geographic divisions. The street polls were shorter, generally two pages long, and were completed by voters after they emerged from casting their votes. The street polls conducted by CBS were generally divided into four sections—each having an equal amount of space on the questionnaire: the vote, reason for the vote (including issues and attributes of the candidates, along with possible second choices), and then some specific questions on national issues, attributes of the candidates, and the background of the respondent. This, along with the voter profile analyses, would be used to provide the prime resource for the analysis to be conducted on the election night special.

At NBC the effort included questions about the election on its monthly national opinion poll conducted by the Elections and Polling Unit, as it came to be called. This is an omnibus poll conducted for NBC News and included a section on the presidential race, which of course, to some extent grew as the primary season increased.

NBC also conducted extensive telephone polls in the states prior to primaries. These were generally done two to three weeks in advance of the primaries, with, in some instances, double-back polling being conducted a few days prior to the primary to assess changes in voter opinion and to attempt to relate that to particular campaign activities and provide a background of the issues of importance for those particular primaries for correspondents prior to the actual election day. The results of those polls were included in the elections book for that particular state, with one of the exceptions being the "who's ahead?" question. The NBC polling operation from the beginning was concerned about the effects of early publication of its own estimates on the various campaigns, given the little-known quality of primary election behavior, and the feeling that their polls might set artificial standards and thereby affect the campaign. NBC also conducted street polls in thirteen states in a fashion very comparable to CBS street polls. In both of the preelection telephone polls, NBC had a much broader base to its questionnaire. They were likely to concern more state issues and issues of particular importance to that state, for example, questions about social security and the elderly in Florida and farm prices and products in Wisconsin. The actual schedule of polling and the type of polls carried out are shown in Table 3.

Implementation

The decisions made in the planning sessions had various outcomes for the networks, but all-in-all they appeared to have clear positive outcomes for the campaign of Jimmy Carter. First, the question of winning: sticking to a definition of winning and victory as a result of a campaign which received more votes than any other had significant effects on the campaigns

TABLE 3.   NBC and CBS Polling in the 1976 Primaries

| | | NBC | | CBS |
Date	State	Preprimary	Street Poll	Street Poll
Feb. 24	N.H.	Double-back	x	x
Mar. 2	Mass.	x	x	x
Mar. 9	Fla.	Double-back	x	x
Mar. 16	Ill.	x	x	x
Mar. 23	N.C.	–	–	–
Mar. 30	–	–	–	–
Apr. 6	N.Y.	–	–	x
	Wisc.	Democrats only	x	x
Apr. 13	–	–	–	–
Apr. 20	–	–	–	–
Apr. 27	Penn.	Democrats only	x	x
May 4	Ind.	–	x	x
May 18	Md.	Democrats only	x	x
	Mich.	–	x	–
May 25	Ore.	x	x	–
	Tenn.	–	x	–
June 8	Ohio	–	x	x
	Cal.	Double-back	x	x

of Ronald Reagan and Jimmy Carter. Reagan would give the incumbent President a race in New Hampshire that missed being successful by only a few thousand votes—an outcome much closer than that of McCarthy against the incumbent in 1968, which had been termed a victory. It would also be to the advantage of Jimmy Carter, as his victories were almost exclusively pluralities rather than majorities. But as the "winner" his segment of the vote took on a much more significant cast than their size alone seemed to dictate.

The decision of NBC to go to as many states as it chose for its anchor location during the primaries amplified an effect present in all three networks. It is a cumulative cycle effect in coverage of the primary contests.

A succession of Tuesday night primaries through this long period presented a difficult task for the network staff, correspondents, and certainly members of the Elections Unit. The challenge was to both their abilities and to their physical and emotional stamina. Preparations had begun for each state primary long in advance, so much of the basic groundwork had been completed. The bulk of primary state handbooks were ready, and only additional materials as they became available were included in subsequent editions. But after New Hampshire the weeks seemed to melt into one another, each capped by a Tuesday night.

Therefore, although the election night specials were seen by far fewer viewers than the discussions of the campaigns on the regularly scheduled evening news shows, the Tuesday night special broadcast, and preparations for it, were intellectual and emotional peaks for those most concerned with election coverage. Therefore, each Tuesday represented the focus of the elections crews' activities. The interpretation of the election as developed for that evening special carried over into the consideration of the next primary in newscasts during the week and was central in coverage of the campaign. Thus, a continuing story theme was building through the period with each successive week being influenced by the results of preceding Tuesdays, at least in terms of the all-important understanding that was growing among the correspondents and the anchors and analysis personnel.

There was, of course, an incentive to provide the thread of a continuing story in the primaries, but the effect described here is over and above that of a simple story notion. The momentum of coverage of the campaign focused around the Tuesday to Tuesday cycle, and the coverage became far more cumulative than one in which there would be a set series of stories each focusing on a particular primary or primaries, as if they were unique events.

One suspects this is even stronger at NBC where the commitment was made to travel to so many of the states with both its anchor staff and the "Today Show." At NBC the general pattern was to move most of the staff personnel on Friday evening of the week preceding the Tuesday night election with the anchor staff leaving as soon as the Friday night broadcast ended. The regularly scheduled evening news show would be broadcast on location for the Monday as well as the Tuesday of the primary week. The "Today Show" would broadcast from location Monday, Tuesday, and Wednesday; this meant that personnel would be returning to New York only for Wednesday afternoon, all day Thursday, and most of Friday. They would then prepare to move again to set up their work in the next state's arena if there were two successive location primary broadcasts. Certainly, the commitment of going to a particular state or series of states, thereby transferring all of the personnel required to prepare the broadcast to that site (which in the case of NBC might require 150 rooms alone) meant that many of the relationships established in New York were different on location, for all of the individuals were working together in new circumstances and surroundings, dealing with a common problem. This atmosphere itself contributed to the focus on Tuesday night and the overall concern with the election process itself by these personnel. Interpretations of the election developed in this atmosphere would be more likely to have lasting effects in influencing the coverage of the election activities through other outlets, such as the regularly scheduled evening news show and, for that matter, the "Today Show." In short, the cycle effect, the effect of having the interpretation of the Tuesday night broadcasts as a primary point of reference for additional interpretations of the campaign which built throughout the campaign period, occurred both at NBC and CBS, and was more pronounced at NBC.

ISSUES

Perhaps the most significant result of the intensive focus on issues was that it provided the critics with more ammunition that there was no concern with the issues. Significant allotments of time and talent had been provided for issue analysis and presentation, but there were no issues, at least as they were searched out by the networks.

First, with the exceptions noted below, the polls found no issues in the electorate; thus, the major anticipated source was eliminated. Second, the candidates seemed to studiously avoid issues. One network executive noted that Jimmy Carter had told a meeting of their top executives and correspondents that the only Presidents he knew of who emphasized the issues were Presidents Dewey, Goldwater, and McGovern.

The time allocated to issues was therefore focused on other attributes available in the polls and other analytic techniques of the network. Thus, instead of a discussion of issues or candidate attributes, the analyses frequently appeared as depicting a demographic horse race. That is, the attributes of those supporting or opposing particular candidates were all that was left in many instances in the extensive analysis efforts conducted by the networks.

The problems were described in detail by Walter Cronkite at an interview during the Republican Convention:

> Well, I was disappointed again this year in our inability to come to grasp the issues on the daily broadcasts, on the evening news. We say this every four years, and every four years we determine that it's not going to happen again— that we're not going to be swept up by the panoply of campaigning and stick to the substance. I think we made a greater effort this time. Each time we come a little closer to it, but don't quite bring it off. Now, this time I think we did an excellent job by getting the issues laid out as early as October. In October or November we ran a series on the evening news on candidates . . . . I think it was very helpful in laying the groundwork. Unfortunately, we kind of got the basement built, but never got the house put on top of it. And I wonder, maybe, what is possible with daily journalism. Because certainly we were aware of it throughout every day. . . . Maybe there wasn't any substance to cover, but I don't think that's quite true. I think we could have, perhaps, played a bigger role in the political process by forcing substance to a certain extent.

Cronkite's point concerning the problems of issues in daily journalism is worth pursuing. Several points should be considered with regard to the place of issues as they are developed on television in presidential primary campaigns in particular.

The first thing one must recognize is the low production value associated with most discussions of issues on television. This is particularly true of issues which have not been developed by the media as such, so that one or two words can convey a general position, and even more true of a program plan or other technique for dealing with the issues that might be presented by one or more presidential candidates. The medium abhors the idea of a "talking head" or the reading of a position paper, which might be quite detailed and extremely apt and effective for dealing with a particular problem area, but extremely difficult to broadcast. Alternatives available to the candidate would be considered media events, such as taking correspondents to a particular situation to discuss with those who are obviously impacted by the issue area (e.g., elderly people having difficulty making it on social security) and who would be advantaged by the candidate's particular proposal—again, something not taken to very kindly by the network correspondents. A general mode of developing an issue is to show it as an "actuality" with high capability for presenting visual material—in other words, to show the event which dramatizes the particular affair. Such visuals will not be available unless the candidate provides them himself, as in the example above.

In addition to the talking head problem and media event problem mentioned above, the question of old news comes into play. For example, if a candidate set forth a particularly significant position on an issue, it would require two or three days before the film could be gathered and the story presented. Thus television, to its horror, would have to be significantly behind the presentations of the candidate if it wished to adhere to its own values in presenting a particular story. Of course, as issues become more difficult and complex in their character—nuclear power, the flow of oil, the energy crisis—the difficulty of providing this kind of coverage means that issues in this sense are not likely to be covered according to the format requirements most correspondents, producers, and anchormen like to see.

The focus on issues was frequently discussed in relation to the overabundance of stories on the organization and strategy of the particular candidates. While it is not likely that strategy per se may be of direct significance, the type of man elected President and his particular qualifications certainly include organization as an important aspect—not only the candidate's ability to develop a smooth functioning campaign organization, but the candidate's ability to deal with other organizations as well. Given the thrust of the current focus on primaries and issues, where direct appeals are made to individuals rather than to elements of the party organization, the characteristic long looked for or at least admired in Presidents—their ability to work with Congress and other agencies outside their direct control—is a part of their qualifications, or skills, or lack of them, which we will ignore.

The third question to be raised involves the more specific relationship between issues, polls, and party organizations. There has been distress about the general atrophy, breakup and diminution of party organization in this country. The general move toward direct elections of the delegates to the two parties' nominating conventions, particularly when delegate preferences are pledged, significantly weakens the parties' structures and the voice of the party opinion leaders.

Our understanding of public opinion points toward the importance of opinion leaders in presenting and developing differing positions on major issues. The use of the polls by the networks in the 1976 primary season to locate developing issues throughout the campaign, as opposed to seeking out, for example, the "county chairmen" to find out what they saw of significance in what candidates were saying, meant that the people had few clear guidelines from political spokesmen as to the implications of particular issue positions. Therefore, the "opinion leaders step" in the development of issues was missing. The polls had blurred, if not eliminated, the distinction between the active public and the general audience of the networks in the 1976 primary elections. The members of the public who were polled, either in the primary state or in the national efforts of NBC and CBS, became the "active" elites. Differences which might have developed over some of the major issues may have been due to the absence of intervening steps provided by those who might articulate the significance of various differences, which could then become objects of specific concern to the public at large.

THE USE OF THE POLLS

Correspondents agreed that the polls did provide a very useful point of departure in dealing with candidates and campaigns. One NBC correspondent noted that his friends in campaign organizations in Washington found the NBC street polls and their analyses very useful. A correspondent at CBS noted that Carter, among other candidates, would respond when told by correspondents that a particular pattern was appearing on the polls. Specifically, the fuzziness on issues area seemed to provoke a response, even including (the correspondent felt) television ads on "Carter on the issue of."

In terms of catching the emerging issues in the nationwide race, there were none. Moreover, even in the area of trustworthiness, as one correspondent noted, it was interesting to find that while Carter's campaign was based on the theme of trust, there was no more trust placed in him by the voters than in any of the other candidates. Clearly, the polls were useful in tapping the emergence of Carter and to some extent the drop in popularity for what little popularity the other candidates were able to muster.

In this area, one of the major controversies was in the use of the polls by the networks when the inclusion of Hubert Humphrey in some of the races as a hypothetical candidate showed him to have been preferred, showed that he would have "won" that particular race. Critics of this particular approach felt that with Humphrey campaigning, his preference would not have been as high as that achieved on the polls in his absence.

In the area of relations with the press, NBC and CBS clearly improved their status. Their polls and general data collection efforts were seen as very important tools by print media correspondents and were received very well by the print media. One of the unanticipated consequences of this relationship was the drawing of the print media correspondents to the location of the network research facilities. Thus, the locus of much election night activity centered around NBC where free access would be given to the printouts produced by their Elections and Polling Unit to print media correspondents in general, and terminal connections were provided for correspondents from that consortium of subscribing newspapers. Here there was a contrary push to the idea of the reporter being free to roam with his typewriter and do his story. Availability of such information was just too strong a draw for reporters seeking to write their stories for the next edition of the newspaper. They would know, moreover, that their own editors would have seen network stories the night before which would have discussed the results of the primary in terms of these very same street polls. The reporters had to rely on them to some extent in preparing their own election story wrap-up for each of the states.

The Futile Search for Issues and Candidate Attributes, The Cycle Effect, and the Success of Jimmy Carter

Alas, 1976 was neither 1968 nor 1972. Among Democrats, and to a lesser extent among Republicans, great issues did not divide the public nor direct their vote for or against a particular candidate. Neither did particular attributes of the candidates—their character or other facets of their personalities—provide a key to the electorate's decision-making in 1976. In the Republican primary contest, Republicans who had initially perceived few differences began to see Ronald Reagan as the more conservative of the two candidates, and according to their own positions, began relating to him on this basis. Republicans who opposed the Panama Canal Treaty were also likely to support Reagan. In personal terms, Reagan was also increasingly seen by Republican voters as the more competent of the two candidates; although this did not affect the loyalty of many to Gerald Ford. These differences appeared on the national CBS polls rather than on their state polls. The nation's Republican electorate apparantly was learning something about Ronald Reagan and how he and Gerald Ford differed through their campaigns via the coverage of those campaigns by the network media.

On the Democratic side, issues and attributes of candidates seemed to play little if any role in the voters' choice. The polls did, however, provide on a state-by-state basis a clear picture of the different grounds of support for the candidates in terms of their previous political behavior, ideological self-identification, and other attributes of those who voted. This became the focus of the election night special segments devoted to analysis of the voters' choice in these primaries.

Several important factors contributed to the appearance of Jimmy Carter as the choice of an ever-broadening base of support within the Democratic Party. The different demographic and ideological bases of the Democratic Party in the primary states and the selective focus of Udall (and other liberal candidates) and Jackson (and other conservative candidates) led to relative ambiguity in Carter's vote-getting ability. Having committed to enter each primary, Carter was heir to the votes not being courted by the candidates entered in the particular state (e.g., the conservative vote in New Hampshire and the liberal vote in Florida).

The commitment of the networks to analyze these primary elections, including the commitment of resources, especially the polls, and the use of high-prestige correspondents, such as Roger Mudd at CBS, or outside consultants, such as Richard Scammon at NBC and Louis Harris at ABC, for the presentation of the results on the air was intended to allow for a broad range of topics to be presented. The street polls, along with the analyses of certain precincts, provided for four major types of information to be included in the analyses of why the voters chose as they did. These included the issues, the candidates' attributes, the voters' own personal background characteristics, and voters' political attitudes.

The fact that differences were found only in the latter two categories meant that the analysis was focused on these particular items. Issues did not appear, as noted above, nor were attributes of the candidates themselves of any great significance to the voters, either in direct link-ups in terms of their reasons for supporting a candidate, nor in terms of patterns of association between those holding a particular issue view and their vote, nor those having seen certain characteristics associated with a particular candidate.

Thus, the networks presented a continuing show of Carter's strength with different voting blocks in different states on successive Tuesday nights. The picture that emerged was of a man who could bring back the Democratic party coalition of FDR days. However, the only consistent support Carter actually received was among blacks and southerners.

With hindsight, this can be seen as foretelling the later softness of his support as shown in his sharp drop in the polls between the Democratic convention and the November election. It must be remembered that Carter received a minority of all Democratic votes cast in the primaries. The early showings of tremendous support for Carter following Democratic and Republican conventions can be interpreted as primarily a show of the same kind of residual support; that is, Carter was supported more by those who did not want a Republican or Gerald Ford in the Presidency than those who had a strong commitment to Jimmy Carter. Therefore, the picture of Carter which emerged during the primaries which seemed to show him as capable of appealing to all segments of the party was true only in a limited sense. He had the only capacity not to fragment the party. Members from all segments of the party would not reject him. This is quite different, however, than having the capacity to unite all of those segments behind him.

The network polling strategy, especially the street polls on primary election day, did, therefore, help Carter's effort. The broadcasts provided hard data that Carter was accomplishing what he had said he could do, that is, appeal to all segments of the party.

Added to this factor was the effect of the schedule itself. The correspondents and staffs of the networks, like Carter, had to perform every week. A candidate who entered every primary presented a continuing story. The correspondents and staffs of the networks also had to appear to present an analysis of that continuing story during those same primary weeks. Thus, the story of Jimmy Carter's race was the single continuous thread throughout the period. It was and could be developed each week by the same network personnel who had to give shape to their own coverage of the primary season during the same period.

Just as important was Carter's success, particularly according to the definitions of "victories" and "winning" used by the networks. These "victories" gave him an advantageous position, given the building cyclical nature of coverage at the networks. Clearly, the electoral news during this period built to a peak every Tuesday night. Correspondents, anchors, and to a lesser degree the staff of the Elections Unit were required to prepare for the coming week as if they were moving between the troughs of a wave pattern. Their discussions of the future were necessarily tied to their findings of the preceding week. Thus, the candidates who entered a selected set of primaries were at a significant disadvantage in relation to a candidate who appeared in all primaries by losing the context that was provided by the preceding week. This lack of context was particularly significant when contrasted with the candidacy of Jimmy Carter, who appeared in the primary each week, was successful, and could therefore provide a basis for continuity in the story of the 1976 Democratic presidential race, as that race unfolded from New Hampshire to California.

Concluding Remarks

The challenges presented by the 1976 presidential election coverage offered the networks opportunities and difficulties. The use of the polls and the focus on issues represented efforts to try to come to grips with the complexities of the political system, the large number of candidacies, and the criticisms of past media coverage. Clearly the polls are here to stay, but other aspects of campaign coverage, particularly issues, must rest in the hands of the politicians. As those in the networks themselves admit, however, they frequently find themselves in the position of having made superb preparations for the last war. With fewer changes in the political system itself, the networks may be better able to cope with what is coming in the future.

James David Barber

5

Characters in the Campaign:

The Literary Problem

Ours is the post-Hitler generation: we know that "advanced" civilization is no safe protection against tyranny, that modern technological rationality stands ready to enlist in dreadful causes. Ours is the post-Vietnam and (one continues to hope) the post-Nixon generation: we know that the marriage of high technique and low purpose is no peculiarly German phenomenon. We have got past the naiver versions of the myth of progress, past the habit of relegating intense political evil to the olden times. We know that attention must be paid to *now* and *here* lest yet another Pied Piper lure away our children. Eternal vigilance, alas, really does turn out to be the price of liberty.

Yet for all our generation's weary sophistication we still get mesmerized by political magic. Meg Greenfield in "What Is Merit?" (*Newsweek,* March 13, 1978) says that:

> The great holy grail of American political reform is an idealized, unattainable—and frankly weird—state in which there is no discretion, no judgment, no flesh and blood, no better and worse—in short, no human politics. We have a couple of broad, if doomed, techniques by which we are continually seeking to achieve this elusive and beatific condition. One is to put the thing on automatic, to opt for wheel-of-fortune choices, as distinct from deliberate political choices for which someone has to take responsibility. I have in mind, for instance, the lottery reform of the draft, or the seniority principle of selection of Congressional chairmen, procedures that may end up working great injustices, but which we nevertheless believe have the enormous advantage of *not being anybody's fault.*

The quest for that holy grail, the search for some systemic Automatic Pilot to relieve us of reliance on flawed discretion, got going in 1787 when a generation of squire-politicians, fumbling quickly through their intellectual baggage, found Montesquieu and Locke and Newton and the idea of the well-balanced machine. Some opposite instinct reacted to insist on a Bill of Rights—however plausible that the machine might work, several motions must be explicitly denied it. From then to now, as Orwell's year approaches, we Americans have been revering our Constitution as we bend it to serve new purposes, banging at its gears and flywheels, attaching auxiliary wires and pipes and safety valves. The chant of the mechanics echoes down through the years, like Dean Rusk's toot-toot litany on Vietnam, whistling through the graveyards of 600,000 dead in a *civil* war, another 600,000 in one battle in the mud of the Somme, and a few children in a ditch at My Lai, not to mention the milder ways we have continued to wound one another here at home.

In recent years the search for no-fault politics has focused on elections—the key democratic choices—and particularly on the choice of the President—the fatefulest choice of all. The result (and there were other causes) is a system in which the voices of the traditional recommenders—political party leaders, public officials, and other elites—fade out. The concept of nomination, some leaders naming other leaders as worthy of election (the original *idea* of the electoral college), has given way to "name-familiarity" as the touchstone of notability. The parties are shattered. No one seems to care who Father Hesburgh prefers. Announcement of Tip O'Neill's allegiance fails to electrify. Neither Max Palevsky nor Derek Bok can deliver much of their worldy and spiritual treasures; not even Bruce Springsteen can make the lightning strike. Just who was it, for example, who nominated Jimmy Carter?

There are those who think that Jimmy Carter was nominated by Mr. R. W. Apple, Jr. of the *New York Times* in a front page story on an Iowa poll, headlined, one envious candidate staffer thought he remembered, in type as large as that announcing the fall of Saigon. The line of thought that attributes the fault or glory of serving up Jimmy Carter to Apple—or the press or "the media"—leads into a vast quagmire of speculation about power that has been drowning intellectual talent since Aristotle sketched out the forms of causality. It is a topic which fits smoothly into the mechanistic approach because it suggests rearranging power relationships as the cure for whatever seems problematical: reshape the FCC, break up the networks, license reporters, subsidize competing newspapers, et cetera ad infinitum. Much political science writing on power winds up shaking a finger at various hypothesized dummies who supposedly do not realize how complex it all is. What gets lost in such enervating debates is the common sense observation that what the press in this country does or does not do is a very important factor in the process by which we pick a President. Reporters do not invent the world they see, nor do they take note of every stimulus-bit that invades their sensory equipment. What the press says is not universally noticed or believed, but nearly all the public's political information and wisdom comes through the press. Re: power, full stop.

What is the alternative to the mechanistic, Tinkertoy approach? One might try to find out how, within the more or less structured constraints, journalists grapple with politicians. One might suppose that both sets of grapplers have minds (and thus memories and anticipations) and that they come at their encounters with different desires. One might make the normative assumption that decisions on both sides have consequences—for instance that it makes a difference who the particular President is and how he is evaluated. In other words, one might focus on the personal and cultural blood of the situation, on what makes the machine of human politics stop and go. My thesis is that the mode and manner of the journalistic enterprise have significant effects on reporting about potential presidential characters, and that significant improvements may be possible if journalists want to make them, leaving the machinery roughly as it is.

I will concentrate on three problem areas.

The first is the problem of news reporting as a literary endeavor. As writers, journalists are artists whose vocation calls them to the muse of truth. As news reporters, they are responsible for carrying back to their readers a representation of reality. How do old and new news genres depict political characters? Does "objectivity" mean reducing politicians to objects? Does "subjectivity" (as in the honest admission that the reporter is *there*, reflecting) mean unleashing the fictive imagination? What of the new mixtures, such as "faction" and "docudrama"? In the rough and tumble of the quotidian contest, how can the reporter tell the truth he knows while reporting the facts he sees?

The second is the problem of psychologizing. Journalists don't like to think of themselves as psychologists; but they are, as any random sample of their writing demonstrates. They practice under a broad license. Moving out from facts, they draw inferences. What are the methods of this science on the hustings? Before that, what are the hypotheses? Have we got to the point where a journalist can tell—and tell us—when we have got another Nixon on our hands?

The third is the problem of popular education. Call it merchandizing the news. We are a voluntary citizenry with much besides politics on our minds, and the least of us has a vote. How can the candidates as (slangwise) "characters" and "personalities" be brought across? Can the great unwashed be lured to the political baptistry? Should they be? Formal invitations will not suffice; so is the alternative more hype, con, pitch, and come-on? And who are "they" anyway?

Examples are taken from 1975-76, but in a way that I hope will draw on the past and throw light ahead. That season was, I think, a propitious one for understanding character reporting. No large, clear issue happened to coincide with our rigidly quadrennial election schedule. No obvious winner dominated the scene; the incumbent had not been through a national election and new rules had ruined the old calculations. The standard ideological left-right cadence was lost in a bewildering cacophony of scattered themes. And strong attention was focused on character because experience with Johnson and Nixon had brought home a hard lesson: we the people, for all our savvy and data, could still err mightily, could freely choose the tragic course. For these reasons, 1975-76 is probably as nearly pure a case for character as history is likely to hand us.

I hope I may be forgiven for saying obvious things, as strangers are wont to do.

What Reporters Are After

The reporter sets out not to find facts, but to find a story (preferably a story that happened today or that can first be told today or that says a new thing about tomorrow). Indeed, to remain a reporter he must find a story. The luxury of silence is denied him. Perhaps if he does not write today, he is thinking. If he does not write tomorrow, perhaps he is composing. But if he carries on that way, he is not a reporter anymore. Like Scheherazade, he will die (professionally speaking) when his story can no longer be continued. His story-seeking is not merely for his private amusement or instruction. The story becomes real and professionally sustaining only if it is put forth for others to share. When he was dispatched on his mission, his editor may well have told him why the trip might result in a tellable tale, and when he returns he may well have to argue that he found it and that it is worth telling—especially compared to competing stories. He has to work quickly lest all his effort be garroted by a deadline. Tomorrow he has to do it again. And he may never produce just the same story twice or repeat it just as told by another. Thus the first fact of journalistic life is not that the reporter is skeptical or naive or biased, but that *he will tend to notice those aspects of the situation that lend themselves to storymaking.* He looks in order to show. He listens in order to tell. At peak form, his whole perceptual apparatus is attuned to pick up, in the cackling confusion which surrounds him, the elements of a new communicable composition. He grows a "nose for news."

The first whiff of a story is a lead and a lead is like a joke. It gets its punch from the juxtaposition of incongruities, much as a comedian's one-liner is a crisp combination of elements ordinarily apart. Dog bites man will not do. Thus *a story begins when one notices contrasts coinciding.* The reporter's raw material is differences—between what was and what is, expectations and events, reputations and realities, normal and exotic—and his artful eye is set to see the moment when the flow of history knocks two differences together. The simplest spark of a story is figure-against-ground—the appearance, for example, of yet another candidate through the political fog. Better yet is a previously-unremarked contradiction between, say, liberal Bayh and liberal Udall, and best of all is when those two have at one another.

Watching candidates, the political reporter is struck by their *distinctive* qualities—their contrasting and identifying idiosyncracies and (better) eccentricities. Fresh as we are from 1976, there is no need to supply the names for these fellows we met, one at a time, decked in their assigned personae:

" . . . a tall and witty former professional basketball player . . . . "

" . . . gentlemanly President of Duke University . . . . "

" . . . Earthy, barrel-chested new radical with a folksy populist pitch and a quick mind . . . . "

" . . . low-key former cable-television executive with the look of a persecuted nebbish . . . . "

" . . . shrewd and ambitious politician with strong labor support and a deceptive veneer of country-boyish looks and backslapping cordiality . . . . "

" . . . husband of Eunice Kennedy Shriver, brother-in-law of Ted Kennedy . . . . "

" . . . stocky, boyish-looking foreign policy specialist . . . . "

" . . . the freshest of new faces, preaching the politics of skepticism and diminished expectations . . . . "

" . . . veteran of thirty-five years in Congress and recognized expert . . . . "

" . . . rich and antiseptically handsome . . . . "

" . . . soft-talking, evangelist-sounding peanut farmer . . . . "

" . . . crippled, confined to a wheelchair, hard of hearing . . . . "

(from Jules Witcover's *Marathon*)

Then the contrasts could be seen to coincide. Each noticeable candidate acquired a question to be asked about him—a surface contradiction upon which many a lead could be based. A clear series of examples is in the titles of the impressive *New York Times Magazine* series in 1975 and 1976:

"Puritan for President" (Jackson, November 23, 1975)

"Peanut Farmer for President" (Carter, December 14, 1975)

"Wallace's Last Hurrah?" (January 11, 1976)

"Liberal from Goldwater Country" (Udall, February 1, 1976)

"Peach-pit Conservative or Closet Moderate?" (Reagan, February 22, 1976)

"What Makes Hubert Not Run?" (April 4, 1976)

"The Rockefeller Campaign. Campaign?" (June 27, 1976)

New questions and thus new stories proliferated from these.

The story form is exceedingly old, perhaps the very oldest form of human discourse, compared to which even prayer and argument may be late-life novelties in the biography of mankind. The reporter's requirement of novelty bars him from that strange appeal the repetition of already known stories has for people but connects his writing with the nearly-hypnotic effect one notices when a child settles down to "once upon a time," an adult sighs and eases as the lights go down in the theater. This appeal is mysterious, but an obvious part of the lure of, in Sir Philip Sidney's words, "a tale which holdeth children from play, and old men from the chimney corner" is the promise of action. But it is action of a special kind—interior action—that entices. Descriptions of scenes, personae, and motions are beside the point unless they intimate (explicitly or not) what is going on in the minds and hearts of the characters.

This point deserves pausing over, I think, because many journalists would question it. Action is to be distinguished from passion, event from meaning, happenings from "soul stuff." Yet I would contend that for journalists, too, the story—even if it depicts only physical actions (e.g., a fire)—takes off only if it displays or implies inner action. Journalism as literature shares a reversal contrary to the common sense that motive precedes and thus explains action; rather actions are used to educe motives, and actions which fail to meet this criterion are "irrelevant." In a story, what seems concrete is really symbolic. Somehow, the lead must lead inside.

That is evident in the oldest stories, long before Proust and Joyce, as in Aesop's tales—crackling with action, but only action which lights up character. Similarly, reports of Odysseus' travels, the chronicles of the Crusades, and Ernie Pyle's war reporting. Even peoples we would suppose to be utterly dominated by the physical facts of life and .death make inner stories of outward events, as in the tales Eskimo hunters tell.

If it is true that reportage and literature both pulse with inner meaning, it is also true that neither can get along with *merely* motivational peregrinations. One can imagine long and even interesting passages of interior dialogue—say, Birch Bayh in the style of Penrod, Fred Harris as Molly Bloom, Milton Shapp as Herzog. But even such would be full of metaphorical *action.* Wendy Robineau surveyed a thirty-five-hour sample of videotaped network news campaign stories broadcast between December 1975 and May 1976 and reports in an unpublished research paper that nearly all newscasters (with the notable exception of the female ones) in nearly all their stories drew on action metaphors from sports ("kick-off," "race," "sparring," "cross the goal line," "winning streak," "trading punches," "decisive knockout," etc.) or war ("political battle," "friendly territory," "survivors," "media blitz," "left flank," "campaign wounds," etc.). Journalism insists also on at least some element of real-world action to peg down the story in actual life. It shares with literature an initial concentration on the act as primary datum. In the process of creation, plot comes first.

In journalism, then, *the story consists of actions selected to reveal character*. Almost all the actions journalists observe politicians doing are verbal actions, physicalized into "stands," "postures," "positions" perhaps, but consisting in fact of verbal pronouncements. That the system now requires the candidates (they think) to travel endlessly helps with physical story material, but the main facts are words—quotations—and thus the main literary link is to the drama. Jules Witcover, in an interview, said a good campaign on issues goes "he said—I said—he said," a running dialogue in which the stuff of action is the verbal duello.

A story is a drama in another sense: it develops. At a given moment in its progress, it points forward, its "rising action" piques expectation. This is true for any single story-within-the-drama, which cannot be just one damned thing after another, bumping down the inverted pyramid; ideally the plot thickens piece by piece. Thus *the reporter is prepared to notice patterns of causal linkage*—threads potentially available for dramatic sequencing. The simplest form is action-reaction, but there are also unfolding, unmasking, confirming, and a thousand other patterns. Not that the reporter necessarily explicates these patterns (or any others), but he will avoid, if he can, tossing around in the random salad his senses serve him—a candidate's ploy, the shape of a teacup, tomorrow's strategy, the reek of Ramada Inn rugs, his headache.

Like Suzanne K. Langer's definition of dramatic action, a good news story is "a semblance of action so constructed that a whole, indivisible piece of virtual history is implicit in it, as a yet unrealized form, long before the presentation is completed." As Erving Goffman points out in *Frame Analysis*, even "when the lead neatly encapsulates the story line, giving the show away, as it were, the story can still be written in the gradual disclosure form, as though the reader could be counted on to dissociate his capacity for suspenseful involvement from disclosive information he had been given a moment ago." The reporter watches for action pressing forward, for a causally *connected* narrative linking past to future.

Writing The Future

In political reporting, the drama continues beyond any one news gig. Indeed, one reason the campaign is so heavily reported is that it is a natural, structured, long-lasting dramatic sequence, with changing scenes, pauses and spurts of action, heroes and villains, winners and losers, and a measure of suspense. The reporter may aspire to move from story to saga; news magazine writing stretches the perspective to a week, the monthlies and quarterlies beyond, and "book journalism" has emerged as a new genre. Straining against the perpetual demand for novelty, the reporter hopes for the luck of a "running story" he can board and ride for awhile. An analogous lure for the literatus may go vignette-anecdote-short story-novel-trilogy. Thus, *a reporter is on the lookout for stories that will lead to other stories.*

The clearest example from campaign reporting is the "scenario," a term picked up, I think, from movie-making, and developing as a journalistic form out of the "violin" at the first of the news magazine (to sing like a gypsy violin and thus entice the reader onward) and then the cover story and "situationer." But everyone in the news business commits scenarios—any business must, to plan, and every human does anyway—and many get published. Explicitly, the scenario story is a summarization and prediction, an ordering and projecting. The ground is chaos, the figure is order. But an evident secondary function is to define a new ground against which new figures can appear. *Time*'s Stan Cloud sees that "by doing such a story you create a situation that creates further stories off of it"; *Newsweek*'s Ed Kosner smiles as he says "whatever we think now is going to be wrong." Mel Elfin notes that "deviations from a straight line make life exciting and adventurous." Similarly "investigative reporting" turns over little rocks to find big dragons, and the assignment of reporter to candidate commits the reporter to discover dramatic development in the quest of middle-aged man.

One could argue that news is not essentially about what happened, but about what is about to happen. If its zest is partly attributable to its artful portrayal, through action, of inner life, part of what it links to there is a fascination with the future. George Steiner in *After Babel: Aspects of Language and Translation* notes that the metaphysician and historian Ernst Bloch thinks man's essence is his "forward dreaming," a bending into the future without which "our posture would be static and we would choke on disappointed dreams. . . . Natural selection, as it were, favored the subjunctive."

Ace reporters are of mixed mind about the virtues of "forward dreaming" in journalism, though they have no doubt it happens continually. Thus in a feisty and relaxed interview, Martin Nolan and Anthony Lewis (in their tennis togs on the way to the Duke courts, March, 1976) resolved a mild disagreement about scenarios in their common disdain for one mode thereof:

NOLAN: I will try to kill scenarios with one stone. The metaphor in political writing has shifted in the last few decades from that of the race track to that of the theater. Nobody really writes about front runners and dark horses and grooming candidates for sweepstakes—if they do they ought to be thrown out on their ass. Rather we go with something more sophisticated. We have candidates projecting their image and how the charisma works, et cetera. But scenarios are what we used to call hedging bets and ought to be treated as such. It is just a wonderful way to say, "Well, on the one hand, and on the other hand," but to do it by using these fairly novelistic dramatic techniques. And it's utter bullshit to sit down—anyone that really sits down and says, "Here's what's going to happen"—and then Ted Kennedy gets a phone call in Hyannis and Hubert does this and that—they're crazy to do it.

LEWIS: Well, if it involved that sort of thing I would agree, but I don't see how you can avoid looking ahead to an extent . . . For example, we were discussing the impact of Jerry Brown. You can have, I think, a useful speculation in a political column about whether, when you finally get to California, Carter and Jackson will be so clearly the serious candidates and that Jerry Brown will merely look like a stiff and the voters will not transfer to him as a presidential candidate, so-called, the awe they show for him in the opinion polls in California. That's a thing that one can use for speculation. . . .

But Lewis and Nolan agreed that magazine scenarios were "too wearying to read," "frivolous and futuristic," "so hyped and frantic and frenzied." Yet it would be fair to say that these newspapermen, in their own styles and modes. have also been known to peep over the wall to the future, looking for a story that might spawn publishable progeny.

Romance and Irony

Literature has its styles, and writers of an age tend to share them. The available repertoire is wide, the typical selection therefrom much narrower. Political reporters write pastoral pieces (New Hampshire), mythic tone-poems (the South), ritual exercises (election night), and any number of other generic effusions. But these days (post-everything, pre- we are not sure what) *two genres, the romantic and the ironic, predominate* in political journalism and perhaps even feed on one another.

The empathetic journalist can hear, in this outline of medieval romance, themes more than rarely encountered in stories on the quest for the Presidency:

> The protagonist, first of all, moves forward through successive stages involving "miracles and dangers" towards a crucial test. Magical numbers are important, and so is ritual. The landscape is "enchanted," full of "secret murmurings and whispers." The setting in which "perilous encounters" and testing take place is "fixed and isolated," distinct from the settings of the normal world. the hero and those he confronts are adept at "antithetical reasonings." There are only two social strata: one is privileged and aloof, while the other, more numerous, is colorful but "more usually comic and grotesque." Social arrangements are designed to culminate in "pompous ceremonies." Training is all-important: when not engaged in confrontations with the enemy, whether men, giants, ogres, or dragons, the hero devotes himself to "constant and tireless practice and proving." Finally, those engaged in these hazardous, stylized pursuits become "a circle of solidarity," "a community of the elect." (Erich Auerbach, quoted by Paul Fussell in *The Great War and Modern Memory)*

Obviously this type of quest romance—in fiction or in politics—need not be naive nor even sentimental. Bunyon's *Pilgrim's Progress* is no tea party; Christian is jolted again and again. But the drama's force derives from encounters, of uncertain outcome, between our hero and external obstacles to his progress, in which his *virtue* is tested. The question is whether or not he will prove strong and good and true enough to win. And romance is hopeful in the sense that the process of testing culminates in a just decision, that justice inheres in and is produced by the process itself, as in medieval trial by combat or John Stuart Mill's wrestling match between truth and falsehood.

Irony makes no such assumptions. Odds are, the process and the outcome are farcical—just, if at all, only by accident. The forceful scenes are not fighting encounters but discoveries of erroneous calculation, of Don Quixote mired down in misplaced intentions. The devil refuses to wear his uniform. The question is not one of virtue but of insight: whether the protagonist, brave and true as he may be, will realize in time that he is playing the fool. Romance arouses indignation as our hero is temporarily bested by the beasties. Irony sees him win and then fall off his horse, and smiles knowingly.

Northrop Frye has thought his way down analogous transitions in modern literature and Paul Fussell gives a succinct summary:

> "Fictions," says Frye, "may be classified . . . by the hero's power of action, which may be greater than ours, less, or roughly the same". . . . [T]he modes in which the hero's power of action is greater than ours are myth, romance, and the "high mimetic" of epic and tragedy; the mode in which the hero's power is like ours is the "low mimetic," say, of the eighteenth- and nineteenth-century novel; and the mode in which the hero's power of action is less than ours is the "ironic," where "we have the sense of looking down on a scene of bondage, frustration, or absurdity . . . "In literature a complete historical "cycle" . . . [goes] . . . myth and romance in the early stages; high and low mimetic in the middle stages; ironic in the last stage. Thus the course of literature from Hebrew scriptures to Roman comedy, or of modern European literature from medieval through Renaissance [myth, romance, and high mimetic] to bourgeois [low-mimetic] to modern [ironic]. And the interesting thing is the way the ironic mode [in the modern cycle, Joyce, Kafka, and Beckett are exemplars] again "moves steadily towards myth, and the dim outlines of sacrificial rituals and dying gods begin to reappear in it."

One can make too much of cycles. In political journalism, though, there may be a similar rough drift toward the ironic and beyond. In television, from Walter Cronkite (the romance of spaceshots) to John Chancellor ("low-mimetic" Dickensian realism) to David Brinkley (Old Irony Asides) to Tom Snyder ("sacrificial ritual and dying gods"). In newspaper work, the drift may go from James Reston (America) to Tom Wicker (Dickens again) to George Will and Garry Wills (the willful ironists) to Hunter Thompson (the Kierkegaard of the causeways). From a larger perspective, the news magazines are generally romantic, as witness their bicentennial celebrations; the newspapers ironic; and television flickers gently in between. In specifically political campaign reporting, I think one could inoffensively consider Jules Witcover tending romantic—as witness his indignation at candidates who wouldn't talk issues and his subsequent book, *Marathon,* chronicling "a marathon obstacle course that consumes time, money, and humans like some insatiable furnace," a race in which "nearly all stick it out as long as money, physical endurance, and emotional stability last, and the dream of success is not overwhelmed by the reality of failure." And Richard Reeves might agree to serve as ironic exemplar since his book *Convention* starts with an anecdote in which Clare Smith, youngest delegate, arrives in New York and goes in a couple of hours from feeling "sort of flattered" to "Oh, screw you!" The book ends with Robert Strauss being served the wrong sandwich.

Romance and irony are symbiotic opposites. In order for irony to work, there must be hopes abroad. Thus F. Scott Fitzgerald feeds on the ghost of Rudyard Kipling. In order for romance to work, the threat of defeat must be real. Thus *Gone With the Wind* is nourished by *The Red Badge of Courage*.

The ironists and the romantics need one another, lest either lose their distinctiveness. It is an open question whether anybody needs Tom Snyder and Hunter Thompson; perhaps they will do for journalism what Kurt Vonnegut and Donald Barthelme are doing for literature. But if Frye is right, yet another mythic era may loom ahead. The acids of irony may bubble away, as the audience tires of the tales of error. Maybe Jimmy Carter's success signaled that.

What Gets Left Out

At this point it is no longer possible (if it ever was) to continue characterizing political journalism as a whole, or even that part of it concentrated on the candidate's character. Already the romantics and ironists are distinguished. What may be useful is to pause to reflect that each of the regularities I have hypothesized—as emphases—implies the tendency to neglect its opposite. Thus journalists tend, I think, to pass over aspects of the situation which do not lend themselves to narration, which lack story potential. They tend to ignore commonalities among the candidates, in favor of the distinctive. They tend to slight contrasting elements which remain, in the flow of observable history, apart from one another; which is why, for example, Catherine Mackin's famous 1972 juxtaposing of what-Nixon-said-McGovern-was-saying with what-McGovern-was-saying got yanked off the air as shockingly unprofessional. Reporters are generally loath to speculate directly about the inner life of the humans (candidates, voters, etc.) they observe, preferring revelatory actions (statements, polls, etc.). But in selecting actions to report, they tend to disprefer those which do not in some significant way represent or affect the actor's inner life. The reportorial focus on the story as a minidrama directs the reporter away from causally-isolated items; if a noticed action appears to be causally-isolated (take Ford's slip, in the 1976 debates, that the Soviets did not dominate Eastern Europe), the reporter will tend to seek out plausible linkage (as, say, to Ford's intentions or memories or rigidity or intelligence) —to "make something of it," something developable. Similarly, in the larger dramatic framework, the reporter is likely to be unstruck by dead end, one-shot, used-up stories, unresurrectable in the future he strains to foresee; perhaps Hubert Humphrey's passion for extended argument should be an example from last season, or, more significantly, Nixon's compulsiveness from the season before that. And journalists covering politicians tend to craft along the main highroads of contemporary literary culture, turning aside from old timey byways and dangerous new trails.

The Sentient Reporter as His Own Man

Departing from the general to the individual, we encounter in modern political journalism the reporter on the way out of the closet of objectivity. He is not alone; for centuries the literati have been tensing over the issue of the relation of the artist to his art—art as extant or expressive, the artist's self as enhancer of or detractor from the aesthetic experience. Aristotle sounds like an avuncular editor wising up a cub when he advises in the *Poetics:*

> As far as may be . . . the poet should even act his story with the very gestures of his personages. Given the same natural qualifications, he who feels the emotions to be described will be the most convincing: distress and anger, for instance, are portrayed most truthfully by one who is feeling them at the moment. Hence it is that poetry demands a man with a special gift for it, or else one with a touch of madness in him; the former can easily assume the required mood, and the latter may be actually beside himself with emotion.

Probably good reporters do the same thing: as a technique for discerning more clearly the candidate's subjectivity, one gets vicariously into his shoes, feels as he must feel, notes the other in himself. But does he *publish* these notes? Increasingly, I think, reporters feel ambivalent about this. Walter Mears, the former wire service ace, says proudly, "I don't give my impression of him; I collect material on what he *did,* how he performed." A lead Mears would disdain is Norman Mailer's opener, "Plains was different from what one expected." The *Washington Post's* Howard Simons worries about "that creeping little feeling in the back of your head, when a reporter comes back with an interpretative piece—are we sucking our thumb?" But television's Jack Perkins says, "You make your own judgment first, because over four or five days you can find film to support any kind of piece you'd like to do." Certainly one can find, in the journalistic fraternity, pledges of allegiance to every conceivable flag of "objectivity."

One need not pause long over the image of the reporter as a mere mirror, reflecting a world he randomly discovers. Not even Mears would buy that. What Charles Beard, in *The Discussion of Human Affairs* wrote of "the broad and general field of history, sociology, and interpretation" is true of journalism:

> [E]ven the person who claims to proceed on no assumptions is in reality employing some hypothesis in the selection of facts real and alleged from areas of apparent order and areas of apparent chaos. If no hypothesis is consciously adopted, then subconscious interests and predilections will affect the selection, for such interests and predilections exist in every human mind. If anything is known, that is known.

But even the most icy-eyed newshawk, his mind a tabula scrubbed rasa for each new assignment, totally devoid of sentient selectivity, blankly inquiring "what happened?"—even if such exists—his analogue among the readers does not exist: the story will be turned into evidence for or against a supposition.

Nor are the important questions exhausted in the continuing debates about "bias" and "balance" and "fairness." There is no objectively definable Golden Mean. One man's middle-of-the-road runs through another's left field. Today gets canted askew when one tries to balance it against yesterday. Of course one should try to be fair. But the reporter in his persona as writer—as a literary man—has a deeper problem: where, if anywhere, is there a place for *him* in the story, for his own "special gifts" or "touch of madness"?

In practical terms, objectivity seems to mean not letting your emotions get mixed up with your reporting and sticking to the facts.

In the first meaning, the reporter stands apart, noticing and even fostering his apartness. The *Post*'s William Greider, his sensitivities undulled by years of close professional work, told me he thought a hard look at the reporter in action would reveal the romantic-ironic tension in the reporter's emotional involvement: "I just bet if you go out on the campaign and see people covering stories and how they react, you will see that the cynicism in the humor and the hard-boiled stuff is very shallow and that basically, when you get past that, they take it very seriously." But even more seriously, the reporter can come to love his independence, "the purity of the calling," his sense of himself as "the outsider, working for an organization, yes, but really out there alone, slogging along doing something clean that the organization doesn't have anything to do with. And you know, this is very powerful." Greider thinks he "could think of two dozen reporters of similar class and background and education" who had similar feelings when they went into journalism:

> We all read Riesman and William H. White and we looked around us at our

college classmates and we thought, "My God, that's right—that is the way the world is and I don't want any part of it." . . . You looked for a sate harbor where one could keep his ideals, where you didn't have to wear a hat to work and carry a briefcase, and they might even tolerate some eccentric habits . . . . And in terms of the real world where real things happen and people get killed and buildings get built and trains run on time, you don't really have much responsibility . . . I mean, sure, in a very narrow limited sense, if I go out on a story, I have a responsibility to do a good job and come back with all the information and write it clearly and so forth. . . . But I am not *doing* anything. I am an observer. And in my sort of blindered perception, I'm not hurting anybody . . . . I know that that can be horribly wrong but that's the way reporters look at it . . . . I remember this vividly because it hit me as so true: Holden Caulfield is in the elocution class at his prep school and they gave little elocutions on things. And if you wandered off the subject the rest of the class would start yelling, "Diversion! Diversion!" and heckle you until you got back on the subject. And this boy got up and started talking about his family's pig farm or something and pretty soon he had wandered off into his uncle's cancer. And Holden thought the uncle's cancer was really interesting, but the class just shouted the kid down and trampled all over him. I mean, that is a little of the juice reporter's feel: we are kind of off into the diversions of life. The rest of the people have to keep their minds on the subject, but we can flit around everywhere. There is this chaotic freedom of being a reporter . . . . You can move from the CIA to politics to something else—all of these subjects kind of parade in front of you . . . . But still, the basic enterprise is a one-man thing . . . . And most reporters believe that the truth shall make you free and we are not going to leave any of it out if we can help it.

Russell Baker sees the reporter as Willie Loman,

> on the road, laden down with a typewriter in one hand and a suitcase in the other and a trench coat, trudging his way through the mob, living a rather dreary life with the reality of it romanticized with good booze, sitting up nights and telling old tales. Basically, he's a guy who is riding out there with a shoeshine and a smile, and he's easily shot down. (from Lou Cannon's *Reporting: An Inside View*)

Holden Caulfield or Willie Loman, these visions share an image of the reporter as a loner, a man free—or abandoned—to see and say the truth. Those who pay him haven't bought him. He flits or slogs *his* way, loyal to his muse, not his masters. That is a large item in his covenant of objectivity. He is unbeholden to those above and he stands to one side of the history he observes. Greider's theme implies, I think, that the reporter would lose his essential definition were he himself to step into the action.

Other Objectifiers

CBS News' Richard Salant says that, "Our reporters do not cover stories from their point of view. They are presenting them from nobody's point of view." Other newsfolk adopt, if not nobody's point of view, at least the interest of those off-the-scene "nobodies," the readers. The journalist's profession warns him not to lust after mere popularity and not to lapse into the didactic and exhortatory modes. But in a subtler way, the reporter can use his sense of "the reader" as a check on his own subjectivity. David Broder, in a 1975 interview, explained:

> At the early stages, most readers don't give a damn and those readers who do rarely find it convenient to be where the candidates are. So you are eyes and ears for particular readers. And you do have a responsibility there. I think in any situation in which you are asking questions, you ought to ask yourself whether the question you are pursuing is simply a matter of personal interest or whether you have some reason to believe it's the area that needs to be brought to an audience. I am going through that exercise right now, because I'm on a "Meet the Press" panel with Ford this Sunday. Now there are 300 things I would like to ask Ford about personally. Assume you've got perhaps ten questions—what ten are really most important to push him on? There you really do have to think for the public, in your role as a proxy or surrogate for people who are not going to have that chance to ask those questions themselves.

Broder and his colleague Haynes Johnson (who agrees with the above perspective) spent many an hour in 1975 searching out and listening to *voters,* as such; no doubt some were also readers, but that was not the focus of the research. Reporters in general, like professors, are remarkably incurious about how their audiences are receiving them. Editors used to tell *New York Times* reporters to write for a twelve-year-old girl, a category with which not many reporters were known to hang around. Broder facing "Meet the Press" is thinking, I think, not how Suzy Jones would question President Ford, but what he should ask in her interest. His own "personal interest"—his subjectivity—is subjected to that discipline.

Like creative artists in other fields, journalists may guard objectivity by avoiding introspection, lest the caterpillar tangle to a halt.

Broder's boss, Howard Simons (who would not so describe himself), says, "You just automatically *do it,* because if you ever stopped, you would never get started again." Simons' boss, Benjamin Bradlee, brasses on by the question how the press chooses candidates to cover—"We decide by fiat who a serious candidate is." Behind a physical and mystical barricade at the other end of the floor, Philip Geyelin—"I report to the publisher, and we're totally distinct from the news side"—maintains his editorial writers in the purity of their anonymity—"it's kind of a monkish life." Such separations, though never complete, protect the writer from drowning in external and internal chaos, free him to get on with his work. Little time is taken in thinking through how his separatenesses shape that work.

Sticking to the Facts

It is in the work itself, many reporters would say, that objectivity or the lack thereof inheres. The work is a *Ding an sich,* whatever the worker's intestinal condition. The work "stands on its own feet"; even an obviously autobiographically-based novel like *Memoirs of a Fox-Hunting Man* can be wrenched away from the life of Siegfried Sassoon, objectified, and evaluated for what *it* is. Which brings us to the second facet of objectivity: the journalist's injunction to stick to facts. Admitting they are his facts (see above), how does he handle their recounting?

A few brief passages highlight the beginnings of the reporter's passage—in his work—from Invisible Man to Man in the Scene.

Theodore White has been our age's most influential artist of pointillistic journalism: microscopic fact-dots blended by the mind's eye to compose a meaningful conglomerate. (White's other major contribution, incorporating demographic analysis into popular political writing, is less often remarked.) White got into the candidate's hotel room and took it all down. His books are chock-a-block with facts. "It would be good," White writes in *The Making of the President 1964,*

> if the private lives of public figures could be sealed off from their political records, and their leadership discussed as an abstract art in the use of men by other men. The politics of an open democracy, however, dictates otherwise. Men and women both vote, and they choose a leader by what they catch of his personality in the distortion of quick headlines. Yet the private lives of public figures are as three-dimensional, as complicated, as unyielding to interpretation by snap judgment as the lives of ordinary people.

This is the philosophic prologue to White's exploration of Nelson Rockefeller's divorce and remarriage, the facts of which, he thinks, merit attention "as much to show how greatly public report distorts, as for their shattering impact on the politics of the Republican party in the seeking of a candidate for 1964." And now the scene:

> It is the estate at Pocantico Hills that gives the clearest impression of the isolation and separation so characteristic of all the Rockefellers—as well as the near-paralyzing effect the Rockefeller fortune has on those who approach too casually its field of force. Only forty minutes from Manhattan, off a winding road in Westchester County, surrounded by a low fieldstone wall, the estate stretches away to the Hudson, so hidden from the public eye that the hurrying motorist will miss the gate unless forewarned. Behind the wall stretches some of the greenest and loveliest land anywhere in America—low, rolling hills, perfectly planted yet not manicured, that come to a crest in a Renaissance mansion built by the original John D. Rockefeller shortly after he transplanted his family here from Ohio in 1884. It is a beautiful mansion, yellowing now with mellow age, with grottoes for children, a loggia, a terrace, a swimming pool. From the terrace on the far side one looks out over the Hudson River as it winds majestically down from the

north, with all its freight of the American past, before it is squeezed into the angry present by the Palisades. Both sides of the valley are equally green with grass and forest, and as one gazes down in enchantment on the broad-flowing river, it is difficult to imagine sorrow or anger or any ordinary human concern penetrating this paradise.

Here White is not merely rambling around the outdoor inside of a country place, like a Junior League guide on a house tour. His mind commands his eye and the facts he sees evoke the sense he seeks to convey: isolation and the "near-paralyzing" oceanic feeling a city boy can get in too wide-open spaces. More subtly, the finished lineaments of God's and man's architecture — "equally green with grass and forest," "grottoes for children" — and the flow of history from "freighted" past to "angry present" get us ready to feel along with Nelson Rockefeller when, it turns out later in the narrative, he feels imprisoned there.

Ward Just thinks "Teddy White did for political journalism what *Madame Bovary* did for the novel" — but Just also thinks the trend has gone too far. "To Teddy White" has become a verb form roughly translatable as "to write the scenery." Part of White's objectivity is the primacy of ineluctable fact in his reporting. The adjectival material may verge poetical, but the material stands out, reinforcing the reader's sense that he would sense it as White does. Another part of his objectivity is White's literary economy. His imagination is disciplined, prevented from ranging beyond the boundaries set by his thematic purpose. A third part of his objectivity is the unobtrusiveness of his person. Obviously he is there — the "hurrying motorist," the "one gazing, the surveyor of his own feelings finding it "difficult to imagine sorrow or anger" — but not very obviously, not as an object of *primary* interest in the account.

Compare the following. From the December 1, 1975 *New Yorker,* here is Elizabeth Drew on the campaign trail with Mo Udall:

Monday, October 20th: Buffalo. Mercifully, Udall's plane did not arrive in Boston until eight, after which it had to be serviced, so we were not awakened until seven-forty-five. The pilots had not wanted to fly the plane to Boston during the night. Some of Udall's staff members were up most of the night talking to people in New York and Washington, rearranging plans several times. One staff member says that a hairdressers' convention beginning today in Buffalo made it impossible to arrange for a commercial flight there. On his way out of the hotel this morning, Udall was interviewed for a Worcester television station. After driving to Boston, we boarded the candidate's chartered plane, and are now arriving in Buffalo at twelve-fifty, over four hours late. Normally, Udall's plane — called Tiger, after the candidate's nickname for his wife — makes it easier for him to get around. The plane, an F-27 twin-engine turboprop, seats sixteen and is comfortably appointed. It costs fifteen thousand dollars a month to lease. Udall can afford the plane now, because when he travels he is accompanied by anywhere from six to ten Secret Service agents, whose way is paid by the government. The Secret Service agents are also helpful in making it easier to get to and from airports, on and off planes, and through traffic, and in various other ways.

From the February 20, 1976 *New Times,* here is Marshall Frady watching Sargent Shriver:

> [Shriver] is by far the most zestfully urbane of the whole company, carbonated with champagne urbanity, an ebullient insouciance for all his unlikelihood. A certain tautness in his movements, a starchiness in his neck and arms, in his crisp speech, with heavy eyebrows like stripes drawn by charcoal, and a heavy cap of hair like a toupee over his rosy chicken hawk's face, he had at Jackson with a gleeful, flurrying combativeness unmistakably Kennedyesque, that same spry and spiffy incisiveness of licks in exactly the same kind of creaky, crinkly voice like cellophane crackling, like a speeded-up tape recorder.

From the September 26, 1976 *New York Times Magazine,* here is Norman Mailer reporting his interview with Jimmy Carter:

> Having failed with the solemnity of this exposition, but his voice nonetheless going on, beginning to wonder what his question might be—did he really have one, did he really enter this dialogue with the clean journalistic belief that ultimate questions were to be answered by Presidential candidates?—he now began to shift about for some political phrasing he could offer Carter as a way out of these extensive hypotheses. The sexual revolution, Mailer said hopefully, the sexual revolution might be a case in point. And he now gave the lecture he had prepared the night before—that the family, the very nuclear family whose security Carter would look to restore, was seen as the enemy by a large fraction of Americans. "For instance," said Mailer, clutching at inspiration, "there are a lot of people in New York who don't trust you. The joke making the rounds among some of my friends is 'How can you put confidence in a man who's been faithful to the same woman for 30 years?"
>
> Carter's smile showed real amusement . . . .

Each quotation illustrates a departure from White, at once sharing and shedding different aspects of his literary objectivity. Drew is reporting what happened, facts the accuracy of which could be directly, immediately verified by any other reporter, whatever his mind-set. Hers is the authority of the industrious person on the scene, like the war correspondent who has smelled the cordite, touched the chilly mud, hefted the sack of grenades. She herself barely appears, as one of "we." But the point of her observations is obscure, her principles of economical selection less than self-evident, so the reader is significantly more dependent on her personal authority than he is on White's. In another passage, Drew takes nearly two *New Yorker* columns listing the cities the candidates visited in October 1975. As far as I know, she tells no lies. But what is the truth of the piece?

Frady's claim to credibility is parallel to Drew's—his data also consist of candidate observations—but his heavy foot is on the adjectival accelerator, racing out beyond the independently-testable facts. He risks the accusation of idiosyncracy in order to gain the authority of sensibility. Unlike Drew, who presents none, he presents too many interpretative themes, like a stage drama composed of nothing but asides. Shriver himself is shattered in a kaleidoscopic visual cacophony. For that to work, we-the-readers must, to a significant degree, enter the world of Frady's imagination, suspend disbelief, take his words for it, and try, as the art appreciation teacher would say, to "get inside the artist."

The Mailer passage is a sample; there is much more to the same effect. One must read well down into the paragraph before who's who is clear. The object—Jimmy Carter—is virtually absent, exists only as a foil for the Mailer drama. The language is straightforward enough—even the joke is flat—and the thematic topic perfectly evident: Mailer wrestling with Mailer. It is an interesting match. Mailer is like a city (he contains multitudes), so that Mailer quoting Mailer quoting a joke Mailer heard barely ripples the narrative flow. But it has nothing in particular to do with What's-his-name, the politician. Insofar as it is factual, the facts are about Mailer.

I do not mean to pedestalize White as a guru of objectivity. He was wackily wrong about Nixon, that genius at ambushing journalists. White's drama is operatic in part because it is retrospective; knowledge of the outcome always reinforces the tendency to see fate at work in the gambles of the past. But he did, it seems to me, stimulate in political literature a fresh sense of seriousness and sensibility and artistic discipline—a standard against which the work of the Drews and Fradys and Mailers can be measured—as he sought to see through the facts to the truth.

Across the Line to Fiction

For all his admiration of Theodore White, Ward Just thinks Teddy Whiting "has gone too damn far." Journalists "are promising more than they can deliver, not really living up to what they can do best, playing to their weakness rather than their strength. And it is going to get worse before it gets better." Just's admiration for working newsmen is also intense; his is the criticism of a caring colleague, who spent his life in the craft and nearly gave it his life when he was severely wounded by a grenade in Vietnam. Now he writes novels in Vermont because, he feels, he could not tell his truth as a journalist. When we talked in January 1976 he was working on understanding that decision.

A lot of journalists are now fascinated by Hunter Thompson—which is a bad fascination because there is only one Hunter Thompson. He stands absolutely alone. I think Thompson is goddamn wonderful. There isn't anybody like him. He is a national treasure. Teddy White—there can be a lot of Teddy Whites. Dave

Broder can write a Teddy White book. Haynes Johnson can write one. I could. It is journalism of a very high order—I don't mean to denigrate it in any way. But it is duplicatable. Hunter isn't duplicatable. I think reporters are thrashing around for these new forms, but that's because the whole business has gotten so goddamn nervous and excitable. Hunter Thompson breaks the mold—I mean, Hunter is a sort of broken mold figure. Now presumably somebody will take Hunter a step beyond. I don't know. But the traditional form of political journalism I suspect will stay pretty much the way it is now, unless the worst of all possible things happens and some editor of *Time* or *Newsweek* or the *Washington Post* or the *New York Times* decides that what the public really has to know is all the intimate, personal details about a candidate. When that happens, I think we are really in trouble.

For too long now—what with Watergate, the war, the Pentagon papers, impeachment—reporters have been "living on adrenalin." Just continues.

And since in the United States it seems to be unacceptable to revert back to anything—you always have to step forward in this country—there is a desperate search for this new form, for a way to tell the story all at once. And it means that everybody is jumpy. There isn't any sense of reflection or relaxation or going out and simply writing a story, whether it is dramatic or isn't dramatic. There is a sense now that some metaphor must be imposed on every public event, a kind of national metaphor illustrative of something deep in the American psyche or a vision of the future or mirror of the past—you know, whatever. Each public event must be invested with mythic significance.

In the search for novel metaphors, Just thinks Richard Reeves "has had a terrific effect" as has Martin Nolan—"a Nolan phrase will enter the air and will stay around for awhile." *Post* editor Harry Rosenfeld's question: "New cliches are being made—shouldn't we be making them?" A prime example is Morley Safer's story.

He was the guy who got them flicking the cigarette lighter and burning down the village—which had an enormous effect on everybody. It was one of those leaps of the imagination. All of a sudden one story changed the context in which the war was reported. All of a sudden, all those things that guys had seen and hadn't reported—it wasn't that they were trying to down play it or anything like that, it was that they didn't see the context in which to put it. Morley Safer gave them a context. And after that the stories just came like drum fire.

Just's own path in Vietnam took him away from his professional home:

I ceased to believe that facts could lead me to the truth. And when that happens, when you really lose a certain essential respect for fact, you are useless as a journalist. Useless. You are not worth a good goddamn. And when I came back from the war, I did this sort of Nixon thing and then started to write editorials. But I am not by nature either a preacher or a teacher. I mean, I was okay at it, but I knew I didn't want to do that for the rest of my life. I had always wanted to write fiction and I knew damn well that if I didn't do it then—I was thirty-five years old then—I would never do it.

I asked Just to explain how facts no longer lead to truth.

If you assemble for yourself fact A, fact B, fact C, fact D, and fact E, all you essentially have are those five facts. Because of my particular view of the unknowability of human motive, I don't think you can go beyond that to anything larger that's very damned helpful in trying to convey the essence of the situation, the terrain of the human heart—not to get too elaborate about it. But that's really what I mean. I find no way in journalism to do that, because there isn't a way nor should there be. That isn't the journalist's terrain: it is the terrain of the novelist. Once you become fascinated by motives and the connections of people one to the other, journalism doesn't take you very far. Say you become fascinated with Haldeman and Nixon, just as a relationship. You can poke around the edges. You can find out how many times Haldeman sees Nixon in a day. You can go back into Haldeman's background and back into Nixon's background and you can make a couple of pretty good educated guesses. But by Jesus you never really know what that *was*. If you were lucky you would see them talking together twice, but that would be all askew because you are there watching it. Okay, so the tapes come out and you know a little bit more, and if you can listen to the tapes to hear the tone of voice, you are a little bit farther. Even with all that evidence, you can't do it as well as a fellow can do it in a novel. I am not talking about a *roman à clef,* such as "I am going to take Nixon and I am going to take Haldeman and I am going to imagine what they might have been like and I am going to write my novel about this." That's silly. I am talking about creating two people—make them a university president and his aide or a police chief and his sergeant—two types of men and what draws the one to the other. If that's the sort of thing you are interested in, journalism won't take you very far down that road. There isn't much of a form to work it into print. It is very difficult. I mean, the form is very hard, but well, it won't work anyway.

Then what *would* work? Just is not sanguine, given the recent journalistic history he has shared in:

As Nixon would say, let's look at the record. What do we have for the last twelve years? We've got Nixon, Lyndon Johnson who got us into the worst war in history, and John F. Kennedy, who, now in retrospect—there is going to be no hide left on that poor bastard in about five or six years . . . . With Kennedy we voted to move the country ahead and we got the goddamned Bay of Pigs and a whole passle of other difficulties. With Johnson it was "no wider war"; we got the widest war in history. With Nixon it was "bring us together" and we have never been more divided. In each the reverse has turned out to be true, so you do have to wonder at the ability of journalists to fulfill the contract.

But still, what is the alternative? Should everybody quit journalism and go write novels?

Oh hell no. But in my heart of hearts I am not sure that in the real world we live in—not Plato's *Republic*—journalism can be done much better than it is being done. On Watergate, everybody goes back now and says, "Oh, we should have done it a year before, two years before." Oh, bullshit. To me it was just an extraordinary demonstration of old-fashioned, hardworking tenacity. Look at the people who are in journalism now. They are really a collection of the most able, by and large intelligent, by and large decent people. No, my question is a little darker than yours: if those guys can't do it, given the form—hell, I was about to say maybe the form is wrong. I think the form is okay. I can see no alternative to the form. I mean, I am up a blind alley. We shouldn't expect anybody to peer into the future. If a fellow simply reports on what he sees and hears and what his best judgment tells him appears to be the situation—Christ, that's all you can ask of him. And if it turns out wrong, you shrug your shoulders, because events aren't always satisfactory and the future doesn't always fall into place, as it ought to, like a row of dominoes.

Just's insights clarify strikingly several dimensions of objectivity in political journalism. He sees how reporters, seeking stories, are pressed to impose novel orders on the flux of reality—to find, in progressive American fashion, new metaphors, new cliches, new leads, new juxtapositions of incongruity, and that that professional demand makes necessary the intrusion of the reporter himself, his own creative artistic imagination. He recognizes the power of new metaphors to redirect radically the vision of the journalistic fraternity, not just that of the creating individual: Safer's soldier's lighter burns down the current perceptual structure as it ignites a grassfire of new sensitivities. That process moves well within the standard journalistic *form*, anchored in external objects and actions.

Hunter Thompson slips that anchor, but not all the way. The danger is induplicatability: unleashing Thompsonian gesticulation from the discipline of potential replication. The further danger is a fundamental corruption, a muddy mixing of forms, each of which has its own purity. It is not that Thompson is a poet, but that he pretends to be a journalist. Formwise, he is a moderate masked as a radical.

Case in Point: Roots

Just has concluded that facts—however many facts—cannot add up to truth. He used to think journalism "could deliver *anything,*" he says. Now he thinks the gap between fact-based journalism and the most significant kind of truth—truth about motive—is unbridgeable. It is not a matter of the journalist trying hard and doing better. Essence, not accident, separates the disciplines. Not only does the inner truth perpetually elude the journalist; factuality ruins fiction, renders it "silly."

An example Just might nod yes to happened in the translation of *Roots* from book to television film, as described in *The Inside Story of TV's "Roots."* The book was already a mixture of novelism and journalism; the novelism enabled Alex Haley to tell what his characters were feeling. But the screenwriter, William Blinn, had to represent feelings by actions: "I had to find ways for Kunta Kinte and other characters to visualize or verbalize things that were inside their heads." Thus the Wrestler was brought forward as "someone for Kinta to *talk* to," to make Kunta's thoughts dramatically extant. Blinn then confronted a second formal problem, telejournalism versus telefiction:

> The first drafts for the telecast were very different from the finished product. In the original concept, Alex Haley was to have played a considerable role. The film would have begun in the present, with Alex Haley tracking down leads about his ancestors. Then there would have been a flashback to the day Kunta Kinte left his village to go look for a tree to make a drum for his father. Then we would have flashed forward to Haley again, and back and forth, until the whole story was told. In one early version, the first scene was to have been the assassination of Malcolm X.

It took four or five months for Blinn and the producer, Stan Margulies, to see that "the plan was dull" and decide to drop Haley. "Suddenly the story became stronger and clearer." Margulies explains:

> The minute we dropped Alex . . . the thing took off. Bill and I have talked about how two experienced people like us got into that terrible spot. The answer is that we were simply seduced by Haley. I felt at first that we could best tell the story through a sophisticated citizen of the United States of America in 1977. We'd understand him in a minute because he is obviously one of us, and if we liked him—and most people love Alex Haley—we could then get into his story.

Margulies faced Haley, the narrating journalist, with Kunta, the fictional character, and told Haley, "You can't stand up to Kunta Kinte. Kinte is bigger than you are. Any time we take away from Kunta Kinte is lost time." Haley grasped the point immediately. His attitude was "I know the story and I know what it takes to write a book about it, but I don't know anything about movie-making . . . . Is it really much better without me in it?" Margulies said, "Alex there is no contest," and the decision was made.

The forms work when kept apart, fail when folded together.

Case in Point: Broder's Hope

From the other side of the barricade between fact and truth—or is it truth and fiction?—David Broder has fought for a way, within journalism, to get at the inner life. Back in 1966 when he left the *New York Times*, Broder wrote his editor an explanation of his departure. Good political coverage, he thought, should include

> the portrait of men under pressure, their gaffes, their gropings and their occasional moments of greatness as they strive for power in the Republic. This is the dimension of politics that you described to me at one of our early meetings as "gossip and maneuver." I believe that one has the right to expect in a paper like the *New York Times* that the major actors in the political drama will emerge as live

human beings. But that is not the case today . . . . (quoted in Bernard Roshco's *Newsmaking*)

Unlike Just, Broder thought that *could* be the case: "Any good paper can get live human beings on its pages if it just lets its reporters know it wants them there, and then gives the reporters space and freedom to sketch them." Instead, the message came through loud and clear: "Stick to the spot news, buster, and those nice safe formula leads . . . ."

Nine years later, Broder was still chafing against the lead rope. He tried hard to get the *Washington Post* off the campaign racetrack—all those set pieces about "front runners" and "home stretches"—with at least some delaying success. "The real work of political journalism," he wrote with only a blip of humorousness, "is not to provide advance insights into coming events; that is clearly beyond us. Our true skill lies in inventing imaginative rationalizations after the fact for any implausible thing that occurs." Broder knew what it felt like to guess wrong about the future: his *Post* series on the constituencies of *ten* presidential candidates in 1975 did not take him to Georgia. But more important than what's ahead was what's within: reporters should ask:

Where do the candidates come from? What motivates them to want to be President? What kinds of records do they have? Were the governors and former governors good leaders of their states? How do they get along with others they work with? How do they treat their underlings? Are they aggressive or weak? When they have to make a decision do they pull in a big group of people or go with whatever seems the consensus or do they go off by themselves and meditate on what they should do? Do they have a sense of humor? Are they really open for questioning, or do they go into a debate or press conference to defend their own views? (*Washington Post*, November 2, 1975)

Broder thinks there is room in reporting for these characters. Still, he is glad there are Ward Justs around. For example, he told me,

There is a limit to how much of Fred Harris you can get into the neat corners of a typical *Washington Post* news story about a campaign and a candidate. There are wonderful and terribly important dimensions of him of which you really have to say, "I am dealing with a character out of a novel here" and write him in those terms.

Hadn't there been some pretty poetical Fred Harris stories in the *Post*—the campfire, Ladonna, the Winnebago van? Yes, but that is "the tip of the iceberg," said Broder, and asked me to turn off the tape recorder so he could delve deeper. The important thing, Broder thought (and I think Just would agree), is that "the reader ought to be able to tell, fairly early on in an article, whether it is fiction or nonfiction he is reading."

Mixing the Forms

And that is the point. What rattles objectivity out of the brain are the mixed forms. On the one hand, fiction, however clearly labeled, has enormous power to fix the imagination. Who can hold tight to objectivity with respect to, say, Richard III, Huey Long, and Martin Luther, undistracted by their depictions by Shakespeare, Warren, and Osborne? Who can hold steadily in mind that *Roots* expresses a particular vision of eighteenth century African village life, or that the screenplay for the television series *King* shuffles a few historical sequences in order to convey a more striking truth? We get public Nixon, then the doctored tapes, then the transcripts read theatrically by first newsmen and then actors, then Ehrlichman's lightly-disguised "President Monckton," then the television dramatization *Washington Behind Closed Doors* starring Jason Robards, then Robert Coover's *The Public Burning*—"real historical people and events, mixed with made-up people and events, mixed with made-up events happening to real people," says Arthur Levine in the March 1978 *Washington Monthly.* The ragged confusion of the Cuban missile crisis is crisply tailored for television. It is rumored that one of the networks contemplates a Carter drama spliced together from film of real and fancied performances. Scenarios zip out past subjunctivity to plausibility ("Robert Strauss screamed, 'Stop this goddamned thing, we're losing control.' Albert: 'But a roll call is in progress.' ") to wowsville ("Carter dueled Wallace first, both men playing plectrum banjos, taking off on *Foggy Mountain Breakdown.* It was thrilling! We were at the apex of the entire American political process! . . . Hombre!"). And at the factual base, Anonymous Source slips into They Say and on into Apparently. The footprints of Capote's *In Cold Blood* and Doctorow's *Ragtime* are all over this no man's land.

On the other hand, when real history blazes forward scattering sparks of fact, standard journalism seems to shine. The "whirl of experience" can blow a reporter's mind, reduce him to a twitching telegraph, juice up all the old *Front Page* excitement.War is in the long run dangerous for journalism, not only because some professionals get killed or hurt, but also because thousands of amateurs can check what they read against what they see. But when it is happening, war is very short run. In covering Vietnam, Charles Mohr said, "You see these things, these terrible things, but in an odd way they're good stories." Julian Pettifer of the BBC said, "There is simply no point in arguing whether the war is right or wrong. You're always left with the fact that it is there and it's your job to cover it." The professional passions are fully engaged in getting it right, now. Even there, even then, the fictive imagination intrudes. Phillip Knightley in *The First Casualty* gives two examples:

Michael Herr, making a dash, with David Greenway of *Time*, from one position at Hue to another, caught himself saying to a Marine a line from a hundred Hollywood war films: "We're going to cut out now. Will you cover us?" One should not be surprised, therefore, to find that GIs sometimes behaved, in the presence of television cameras, as if they were making *Dispatch from Da Nang*. Herr describes soldiers running about during a fight because they knew there was a television crew nearby. "They were actually making war movies in their heads, doing little guts and glory Leatherneck tap dances under fire, getting their pimples shot off for the networks."

Later, David Halberstam saw what had gone wrong and why:

The problem was trying to cover something every day as news when in fact the real key was that it was all derivative of the French Indo-China war, which is history. So you really should have had a third paragraph in each story which would have said, "All this is shit and none of it means anything because we are in the same footsteps as the French and we are prisoners of their experience." But given the rules of newspaper reporting you can't really do that. Events have to be judged by themselves, as if the past did not really exist. This is not usually such a problem for a reporter, but to an incredible degree in Vietnam I think we were haunted by and indeed imprisoned by the past.

Michael Herr concluded that "conventional journalism could no more reveal this war than conventional firepower could win it." Gavin Young closes the circle: "The Vietnamese War awaits its novelist."

Political campaigns in their climactic phases are not all that different from battle campaigns: events harden, speed up, hurl causatively into one another. Not even Broder could stem the tide of horse race stories; indeed he wrote a few. To see how the press for facts can turn aside the quest for truth, consider Edmund Muskie, leading Democratic contender for the Presidency, as the 1972 season opened.

Case in Point: Muskie Mad

Campaigning in 1968, Muskie had impressed reporters with his cool handling of an antiwar heckler, conveniently decked out in long hair and dirty jeans. Muskie invited him to the microphone and gave him ten uninterrupted minutes to discover the difference between passion and eloquence. Then Muskie quietly told the story of his father's coming to America and, before he died, seeing his son elected Governor. "Now that may not justify the American system to you," he said, "but it sure did to him." Even the students applauded. The incident appeared on all three network news shows.

Then in November 1970, Muskie came on television right after a speech by Nixon at his worst, raging defensively at a partisan rally. John Mitchell called it Nixon running for sheriff. The scene shifted to Muskie sitting quietly in a Maine kitchen. He spoke of the need to be fair to your opponents. From then at least until he was thought to have wept in public in New Hampshire (Muskie denies it) in 1972, the image he had with the great American public was "Lincolnesque."

A goodly number of reporters knew otherwise. In a postelection book, *Us and Them*, James M. Perry said he knew that

> Muskie is not quick and, God knows, he is not cool. He is a very special breed—a plodder with a roaring temper. It takes him weeks, sometimes years, to make up his mind about things like equal rights and the war in Vietnam, and then it takes him seconds to unleash lightning and thunder on those who wonder why it took him so long.

The *Boston Globe*'s Richard Stewart knew and wrote—back in June 1970—that "when Muskie is frustrated and bored, his irritability threshold is down around his ankles. The public appearance of calm and control belies the monumental temper he can display in private." In February 1972, Muskie, the odds-on front runner and poll leader, took to blowing up at questions from students as he toured New Hampshire high schools. One night, playing poker with reporters, Muskie failed to draw to an inside straight and, swearing, threw down his cards.

In *The Making of the President 1972*, Theodore White recounted, again after the election, that beneath Muskie's

> image of the grave moderate were, however, two essential qualities not yet recognized by the public but more than casually troublesome to Muskie's staff. He had a tendency to emotional outburst; and an even graver disability—a lawyer-like, ponderous way of dealing with all issues and even the most trivial decisions.

Hunter Thompson in *Fear and Loathing on the Campaign Trail* put it more pungently:

> It was not until his campaign collapsed and his ex-staffers felt free to talk that I learned that working for Big Ed was something like being locked in a rolling boxcar with a vicious 200-pound water rat. Some of his top staff people considered him dangerously unstable. He had several identities, they said, and there was no way to be sure on any given day whether they would have to deal with Abe Lincoln, Hamlet, Captain Queeg, or Bozo the Simpleminded.

The *Post*'s Lou Cannon made up his mind at the poker throw-in that Senator Muskie "seemed a little temperamental to be President of the United States." Cannon's candid reflections in *Reporting: An Inside View* highlight the problem: "What does a political reporter do with this kind of insight? Frankly, I don't know. Muskie was known to have a temper, but I had yet to read a story saying that he was showing it all over New Hampshire in response to questions asked him by high school students. I didn't write the story, either." He did check out the facts in one student's complaint, found them correct, and ended his column with this passage:

" 'Sen. Muskie doesn't suffer fools' gladly,' says [press secretary] Dick Stewart. The best guess of the New Hampshire primary is that the 'fools' category includes anyone with the temerity to question the plans or policies of Edmund S. Muskie. "

Cannon wishes he had a second chance:

> If I had it to do over again, and could get away with it, I might lead with the poker game. In my crowd, a poker player's blowup when he fails to draw the statistically-unlikely inside straight on five cards is considered more significant than the bawling out of a high school student. Whatever the lead should have been, I wish I had brought the independent perspective of that campaign trip (where I knew few of the reporters) and that column to more of my political reporting. Usually we find it difficult to write that most important of all stories: "The emperor has no clothes." If we took that approach we would have written several stories about key political figures at various head tables falling fast asleep, literally, during speeches by Gerald Ford. We might have written also, as Tom Wicker once suggested, that "Hubert Humphrey opened his 1972 campaign today by misrepresenting his 1968 campaign." And we certainly would have written differently than we did about Nixon in the same campaign.

Here Cannon is saying what the philosopher Michael Polanyi in *The Tacit Dimension* put this way: "We know more than we can tell." That is in the large sense true of all knowing-telling relations—it would be true if Cannon had all the space, time, and freedom his heart could desire. The answer is not simply more facts, getting it all down and out. Polanyi notes that "an unbridled lucidity can destroy our understanding of complex matters." Nor is the answer in some new mechanical form: "the process of formalizing all knowledge to the exclusion of any tacit knowing is self-defeating," makes it impossible to decide what to call a thing before one knows it, what questions to bring to bear. It was Cannon's hunch, germinated by the fall of a card, jelling into an "independent perspective," growing into definition as a journalistic problem that let him see Muskie in a new light. There he follows in the path, not only of all the great creative artists, but of all great creative scientists. Polanyi explains:

> It is a commonplace that all research must start from a problem. Research can be successful only if the problem is good; it can be original only if the problem is original. But how can one see a problem, any problem, let alone a good and original problem? For to see a problem is to see something that is hidden. It is to have an intimation of the coherence of hitherto not comprehended particulars.

But Cannon, like Halberstam, having glimpsed a new problem, a different kind of story, bumped smack into journalism's literary tradition—not only in the instructions of their editors (one supposes) but also in their own professionally-reinforced habits of mind. The reporter listens in order to tell. Especially when standard journalism is working well, in the sense of throwing up plenty of storiable event-clashes, he may feel that, "like a beaver whose teeth grow constantly, he must chew incessantly, not to eat, not to build dams, but simply to keep his jaws from being locked shut." (Wallace Stegner, "The Writer and the Concept of Adulthood," in *Adulthood*, Erik H. Erickson, ed., p. 233).

Would Muskie's slow deciding and fast exploding, transposed to the White House, have radically endangered his country? Picture President Muskie drawing to an inside straight in the Cuban missile crisis. The question was barely raised in 1972. Indeed, the opposite ("Lincolnesque") image prevailed. Ward Just's worry about the track record seems justified as does the plaintive appeal Stan Cloud imagines a reader addressing to him: "You are able to see what this guy is really like. *Tell* us for God's sake."

Case in Point: The Wallace Problem

George Wallace would make a terrible President. If on nothing else, the nation's press agreed on that. The editors of *Time*, for example, "judge George Wallace not fit to be President," says one of their Washington reporters. And the *Washington Post* came out squarely against him editorially, in the only exception since 1952 of their nonendorsement rule, says Phil Geyelin. Yet coverage of Wallace in 1975-76 illustrates, I think, how reportorial tradition can get in the way of objectivity, of the reporter trying to tell that reader what he knows. Most especially, what he remembers.

Even now it is hard to remember how seriously threatening Wallace was reckoned in 1975. *Time*'s William Shannon wrote in July:

> The persistence of Mr. Wallace's political strength despite his lack of seriousness, the emptiness of his "program," and the fraudulence of his posing as a Democrat—is a sinister phenomenon. His appeal derives its motive power from racial hatreds and fears and from the popular fantasy that there can be simple answers to complex problems such as crime, poverty, and economic injustice.

Wallace was guilty of "nasty innuendoes" and "false bravado." Herblock took out after him with his powerful pen. Tom Wicker's January 18, 1976 *New York Times* column titled "Back in the Gutter," led this way:

> George Wallace has lapsed for the first time in years into his true gutter style. At a news conference in Montgomery the other day, he cast off the respectable robes in which too many politicians and too much of the national press have tried to drape him and came out snarling and kicking like the alley fighter he is.

Television commentaries, while taking note of apparent changes in Wallace's "message," did recall his old cry for "Segregation Forever!" Journalism's *editorial* voice was clear enough.

What made Wallace suddenly newsworthy was that this time he might really have a chance—if not to be President, at least to wreck what remained of the Democratic party. In March 1975, Gallup gave him 22 percent of the

Democrats, compared to Humphrey's 16, Jackson's 13. He was rolling in money and it kept rolling in, thanks to a highly-professionalized direct mail operation. The new finance and delegate selection rules played into his hands. While it can be argued in retrospect—and was argued by Jules Witcover and a few others at the time—that it was awfully early to take the poll results so seriously (and to neglect the fact of massive *anti*-Wallace sentiment), the press had cause to fear Wallace. Clearly a major element in early stories on Jimmy Carter and Terry Sanford was their potential as Wallace-killers.

Wallace sought the Democratic party nomination, but leading Democrats were loath to take him on. Senator Eagleton had commented on his sincerity; Senator Kennedy had blessed him with a Fourth of July visit in 1973, noting mildly that he and Wallace "have different opinions on some important issues" but share other values, such as Wallace's devotion to "the right of every American to speak and be heard." Wary of offending Wallace's followers, the active candidates avoided direct reference to his racist history. Birch Bayh was on record that he could "see circumstances where there might be a balancing effect: I would support him for Vice President," though Bayh was now edging away from that. Even the Republicans cozied with Wallace: Nelson Rockefeller said casually, "George and I didn't always agree, but we always respected each other, and were the two who stood up for what we believed." President Ford noted that on domestic issues he and Wallace "have many similarities." With fine impartiality, the official Democratic party gave him a hand: "We're helping all of the candidates," said the party's national chairman. "We're giving all of them lists and information and advice on delegate selection and everything else. But the truth is we're giving Wallace more help than any of them" (quoted in Arthur T. Hadley's *The Invisible Primary*). The scenario going around the top journalistic circles in the spring of 1975 was that Wallace might well come into the national convention with 30 or even 40 percent of the delegates; that and other chaos-generators might well capsize the creaking party hulk. In an April 1975 interview Broder worried:

> The presidential selection process is in such bad shape now, in terms of mechanisms, procedures and values, that it is likely to be perceived by the end of 1976 that we really do have a national crisis in the way in which we choose our presidential leadership. . . . There is going to be a great hue and cry to say we've got to rationalize this process. At which point if Congress takes it on, there is a substantial danger their answer will be to nationalize the process—some form of national primary, an open primary . . . . And at that point, any hope of party cohesion or identifiable party positions is essentially down the drain.

If the Democracy was incapable of innoculating the public against the Wallace Yellow Peril, who could? With his usual precision, Jules Witcover in *Marathon* describes how journalism went about it:

In early 1975, at a dinner meeting with a group of Washington-based reporters . . . Udall's plight as a liberal *and* a pragmatic politician became painfully obvious. Settling his long and wiry frame into an armchair, he nursed a scotch and water and fielded repeated questions about Wallace. Was Wallace a demagogue? Well . . . . If he thought so, why not say so? Well . . . . Would he have Wallace on his ticket? If not, why not say so? Udall tried patiently to explain, then and through dinner, that he saw no need to go out of his way to antagonize any segment of the electorate. He would run his campaign and let Wallace run his. The voters would decide. Muskie had seriously erred, Udall said, in calling Wallace "a demagogue of the worst kind" after Wallace trounced him and the rest of the field in the 1972 Florida primary. That statement was an unnecessary dig at Wallace's constituency and he was not going to make that mistake. But still the questions came. Was Wallace a racist? If so, why not say so? In the end, the harried candidate reluctantly acknowledged that he couldn't run on the same ticket with Wallace, but he wasn't going to throw rocks at him either.

The interrogation by a group of political reporters who had been out around the country and had some feel for what was going on made a strong impression on Udall. He began to worry more about "the Wallace problem," his aides later acknowledged, or more exactly about how the press and liberal circles viewed his handling of it. At breakfast with another group of reporters several weeks later, Udall was still playing it cozy, but not confidently.

Eventually, Udall attacked Wallace openly, said he would have no part of him.

To get into the news columns of the newspaper, Wallace had to make news—or it had to be made for him. In the summer of 1975, the trouble was that Wallace would not *do* anything. "I'm just sitting here not saying a thing, and not straining," he said, "And it seems I'm the one all the others are talking about." In September he led all other Democrats in a New Hampshire NBC poll. In October it came out that in the previous two years, Wallace had raised over $4,000,000, more than all the other candidates combined, including Ford.

The subsequent coverage of George Wallace, far too extensive for detailed review here, came to focus on events, including revelations by enterprising reporters. Factual material about Wallace's health was reported—that unlike FDR he was paralyzed from the waist down, that he suffered from deafness, that it took him some three hours of preparation to begin his daily work, and that on the other hand he could easily lift a fifty-pound barbell. Television and news photography rarely left out his wheelchair, and when his leg was broken, one saw the doctors in the hospital hallway. He would not let reporters go with him to Europe, but his gaffes and gaucheries were headlined along with such nonevents as his failure to see the Pope or German leaders; his inability to think of anything to say in Berlin but "I am a Berliner"; his reflection, on returning, that he had seen nothing much he couldn't have seen on television. He was quoted in the September 11, 1975 *Washington Post* as saying he hoped to "see some electrocutions in this state," as he signed a bill restoring the death penalty.

The February 1, 1976 *New York Times* noted: "Wallace Isolated by Tight Security." Wallace's record as Governor was raked and piled—from welfare to liquor permits, from the number of hospitals constructed to Alabama's cellar standing in most any comparison among the states. His media campaign was skeptically dissected; CBS let the camera's eye rest on him as, filming a commercial, he fumbled with a telephone and his hearing aid and his thick glasses.

These stories were to the point. But reporters struggling to get across the truth—the Brechtian absurdity of "George Wallace for President"—were up against hard obstacles. They knew—everyone knew, didn't they?—that this was the George Wallace who, well into his grown-up political life, boiled with the rage of a frustrated hit man:

> Nigguhs start a riot down here, first one of 'em to pick up a brick gets a bullet in the brain, that's all. Let 'em see you shoot a few of 'em, and you got it stopped. Any truck driver, steelworker would know how to deal with that. You elect one of these steelworkers guvnuh, you talk about a revolution—damn, there'd be shootin' and tearin' down and burnin' and killin' and bloodlettin' sho *nuff*. Hell, all we'd have to do right now is march on the federal courthouse in Montgomery, lock up a few of those judges, and by sunset there'd be a revolution from one corner of this nation to the other. (quoted by Marshall Frady, *New York Review of Books*, October 30, 1975)

He talked that way; his men had done that way, as any number of veterans, black and white, of the struggle for justice—never mind mercy—in Alabama could testify. Could one count on those voices echoing between the lines of stories about, say, Wallace's chances in the Florida primary? Some blacks in Alabama had had to learn to live with George Wallace, even to work with him politically. But as Roger M. Williams of the Southern Regional Council was given space in the *Washington Post* on November 16, 1975 to recall,

> Wallace rode to political success on the backs of black people. Playing masterfully on white prejudice and fear, he defied the federal government and the courts, and he helped create the climate in which civil rights workers were murdered, a Birmingham church was bombed and a twisted allegiance to "states rights" was elevated to the highest rank of public virtues.

Out in the American countryside, one had to strain to hear Old Wallace behind New Wallace. From the start of October 1975 to the end of April 1976, the *Houston Post*, for example, had forty-four news stories featuring Wallace; one two-incher on November 11 quoted his memory that the South "never did have any segregation except in the schools." Another (by Eleanor Randolph) mentioned a bit of his racist history. Otherwise, it was health, polls, money, travel, issues, and the rest.

If the echoes were soft at home, they were weak indeed abroad. The *London Daily Mail* found him smashing: Wallace "is emerging that most beloved of U. S. figures, the folk hero." And the *London Times* found it "impossible not to admire the shrewdness, good humor, courage and sheer willpower of a man paralyzed by the bullet of a would-be assassin in 1972, but determined to fight on."

Poetic Marshall Frady in the *New York Review of Books* saw literary connections in the continuing Wallace story: "George Wallace's life by now has taken on symmetries of irony that would be almost too pat even for hack melodrama. It's as if he has passed out of reality altogether, and become a character in an Allen Drury novel." Frady spotted

> a constant gap in vision between pleasant assumption and the gutteral actualities . . . [a] polite disparity magnified to a continental popular dimension that [Wallace's] campaigns have always operated on. They have, in a sense, proceeded on that most ominous of all disruptions and divisions in American society, beyond even race—the increasing disconnection between language and meaning in the conduct of the nation's life.

I think it could be argued, as Ward Just would, that it was precisely journalism's restricted vision that let Wallace climb onward. Journalists who tried to let him show through the news hole were continually distracted by optical illusions. Wallace could shut out the press, as he did on his Europe trip, or just shut up in their presence. But reporters given access could find, almost every time, good copy. He had only to be courteous to suggest he had changed. He could be outrageously funny. You could count on him to attack. His language was full of dialectical action. You couldn't be sure what he was going to come up with from one day to the next. He was dangerous—a real scenario-buster. He was a walking bundle of contradictions. Whenever the great saga started to sag, Wallace was there to jack it up—from Birmingham to Boston to Bonn—or to enliven his shallow tragedy with new hamartia. He came from America's storyland, down South; James T. Wooten's excellent profile in the January 11, 1976 *New York Times Magazine* starts out like Aesop or Uncle Remus:

> One fine afternoon last spring, at just about the time of day when the scarlet-and-white colors of the Old Confederacy were being reverently lowered over the chalky dome of the Alabama Capitol, a middle-aged black man timidly poked his head around the corner of a door to the Governor's office and asked permission to enter.

The escalating crash of momenta in the spring of 1976 did not leave much room for accounts of Wallace's past, or anybody else's. Every time he appeared—in a list, a vote, a scene—the legitimacy he had been lusting for so long got another lick of gilt because of what was *not* said. The early historical profiles, largely published back when, as Broder put it, "most readers don't give a damn," were often curiously balanced—Wallace *had* built some hospitals—and murkily contextual, as in the wispy debates about whether or not he was a "Populist." What was needed, I think, was not more history as much as some way for the reporter, writing news, to evoke a certain memory.

The *New York Times* on October 26, 1975 reported that George Wallace, touring Scotland, told a reporter, "It's not your background so much as what you stand for in public affairs that counts at election time."

What Might Have Been and Might Yet Be

If it is an objective fact that journalists, as literary men and women, inevitably convey a *particular* vision of reality, how might it be possible, within their system, to write news stories communicating the truths most needed by the choosing voter? Suggestions from outside the craft have been notoriously Utopian, notoriously blind to the real world constraints of space and time that no mechanical reformist magic is likely to charm away. But inside those constraints, there are, I think, significant freedoms. Confinements of the mind can be escaped. Experiments in new traditions are triable. Literary assumptions need not be carved in stone. The common culture, strengthened by sharing, is not beyond the reach of imaginative invention.

Much "media criticism" is at once too pessimistic and too optimistic. The indignant mode prevails—righteous wrath directed at journalism's moral turpitude, often accompanied by a demand for return to mythic good old ways. That happens in every age of transition, which every age is. It supposes that nothing but moral revival will work—and that that *will* work. On the contrary accusation arouses defense; the past is forever gone, and worn out visions give way only to fresh ones.

Recognizing the possibilities might begin with an expansion of the dramatic horizon. Agreed that news reporting must hook into today, what questions should guide selections from among the nearly infinite array of phenomena? Clearly events cannot define themselves as newsworthy. The questions bound the answers. More often than is necessary, I think, concentration on immediate consequences of today's actions restricts the scope of operations. Scenarios projecting into the middle-range future are not entirely useless to the voter, because he does not want to waste his precious attention on hopeless cases. But in practice, scenario writing, while it pretends to concern itself with the future, is in fact unrealistically reifying the present, weighting down a current configuration of chancy changes with more responsibility than it will be able to bear. Once published, the scenario itself becomes an event and very shortly drops like a wet diaper into the can of the past. It seems no one ever reviews scenarios to see not just whether they guessed right or wrong, but why.

The larger trouble with scenarios is that they do not reach far enough ahead. The campaign's basic dramatic force is there because the race is for the

Presidency. Yet campaign drama and Presidency drama are curiously disjunct. It is not that the Presidency is neglected: "Ford," for example, appeared in front page headlines of the *New York Times* late city edition 239 times in 1975 and there were 88 front page pictures of him in the same period. What is mostly missing is a perspective on the candidates as potential Presidents. To get at that a reporter must shift his stance toward the subjunctive, tune his imagination out of New Hampshire's Wayfarer Inn and into the White House, sniff out the presidential qualities in the campaign smoke. Certain practices—such as assigning the same reporters to cover the Presidency and the campaign, providing more opportunities for professional intercourse between reporters with these different tasks, holding editorial sessions on which qualities it is essential to notice—recommend themselves. Far from detracting from the drama, such sensitizations could lend the story a new liveliness, against the grayer background of yet another primary.

For Just and Broder are right—Just, that the track record in choosing Presidents does not inspire confidence; Broder, that the official and empowered nominators do not perform effectively. Journalism cannot fix all that, but the opportunity for an expanded contribution is there.

Journalism's "forward dreaming," then, might be encouraged to dream on past the upcoming primary to the Presidency itself.

Once stories on that theme were encouraged, it would follow that the candidate's past, and with it the journalist's memory would gain relevance. That need not be a loophole for idiosyncratic reportage. In Wallace's case, for example, the truth about him was very largely agreed on; it was not some individual reporter's flight of fancy. Here again, the dramatic horizon can be broadened and can enrich coverage of the day-to-day. One focuses on the person as embodying his historical development, playing out a character born and bred in another place, connecting an old identity with a new persona—the stuff of intriguing drama from Joseph in Egypt on down. That can be done explicitly in biographical stories. Jimmy Carter must have recognized the appeal a "life" can have when he wrote and published his own campaign biography. But it can also be done inexplicitly: the reporter adjusts his vision of today's whirl of experience to glimpse therein those facts typifying and contradicting the historical who behind the what. Or the reporter asks him to explain what he thought he was doing, back then, when he was moving and shaking a different banana tree. How much more interesting—and useful to voters—such stories are, compared with, say, his "stand" on alternative baby-prevention techniques!

But it is perhaps in an expanded literary space, rather than time (backward, forward), that the promise of political journalism could best go exploring. Journalists who understand that they are sharers in their age's literary conversation, with all its false starts and stutters, might seek through that connection a deeper discipline that reliance on the facts alone can impose. Particularly in news reporting, the discipline of fact is indispensable. The drift to docudrama and faction is threatening because, as these forms pretend to speak the journalistic language, they impose a false sense of order—invented, not discovered—on events. An artificial neatness results and can have extraordinary esthetic power, adding to the enticements of historical curiosity the overwhelming propensity of the human mind to believe a really good story. If the discipline of fact did nothing else, its contribution in demonstrating that life is not neat would justify it.

But one can stick to the facts without getting stuck in them. The literary imagination has its disciplines, too—economy, for example. News stories which jam together in a few paragraphs "everything" that happened in the campaign today break that rule. Antifloridity is another—the Christmas tree should show through the adjectival tinsel. Concentrating on the artistic product, not the artist, is a third. There is nothing wrong with Mailer writing about Mailer, but if the object is to unravel Jimmy Carter, Mailer should focus his mind on that. There is nothing wrong with writing "I asked" or "I said" when that is a true part of the story—but only then.

Novelists have often done poorly as reporters. Hemingway's dispatches were notoriously dull and inaccurate. Yet reporters might, if they would and could, draw on their own insight and creativity much as a novelist does. At a minimum, they might insist on getting across those facts which, from time to time, impel them to a major conviction. At a maximum, they might consider whether the only live alternative to the predominant ironic and romantic modes is a descent into the genre of sacrificial ritual and dying gods. For their thoughts will mother deeds.

James David Barber

6

Characters in the Campaign:

The Scientific Question

Journalists are clearly writers; they are also scientists insofar as they draw inferences from evidence. The lines separating these high callings are not nearly as hard and fast as amateurs tend to think. The "scientific method," it's true, is partly the patient, highly systematic, rule-bound accumulating of evidence. Even there, one can see analogies to the literary artist as he gathers impressions and experiences—for years perhaps—so that one of these days he will have something to write. But there is poetry in science. Like the poet, the scientist gathers selectively, and his gathering is guided by a theme, hypothesis, a theory, the shape of which may be only dimly apprehended at first. Like the reporter, he starts with a potential lead which he must be prepared to chuck overboard as soon as it fails him. And the progress of science, examined historically, can be seen to jolt forward in leaps of creative imagination, large and small, very similar in form to the inspiration the poet knows when a verbal illumination dawns on him. The journalist as scientist is in the same boat: if his science is to transcend the routine, he too needs Aristotle's touch of madness.

If journalists had to pick a scientific home, few would opt for psychology. In the July-August 1976 *Democratic Review* David Broder found the prospect of "journalists as amateur psychologists" a "terrifying" one. R. W. Apple led off the *New York Times Magazine* character series with a valiant and incisive attempt to track down the real Henry Jackson in the streets of Everett, Washington ("They thought me mad"), concluding, as early as Thanksgiving, 1975, that the task of lighting "fires among the suburbanites and intellectuals and young people and minorities" seemed "well beyond Scoop Jackson's capacity." Early in this piece Apple points to one specifically psychological approach to President-predicting that was apparently helpful in his Everett peregrinations. But another time, at the 1975 *More* convention, he spoke for many of his colleagues when he said the whole business "makes us nervous, because most of us feel incompetent to try to do much psychological interpretation." Jules Witcover, speaking at the same convention, thought there was validity to the criticism that "we don't do enough looking at the candidate and finding out what makes him tick," but "at the same time, we are reporters: our job out there is to say what the candidate says, to analyze what he says, and in general to hold his feet to the fire of the campaign—to throw up issues to him that are being raised or should be raised." He is loath to "draw psychoanalytical conclusions." The examples could be multiplied: a consensus was jelling among sensitive and serious journalists (a) that character counts in a presidential race and (b) that reporters had better go slow with their Freudian free associations.

I contend that like it or not journalists are psychologists. They are right to go slow. They exercise their craft in a society gone dippy over "personality"— from the teenage fear of not having any to the all-pervasive search for the book or the chemical or the guru or the group which will guarantee a life of uninterrupted personal exuberance through self-cultivation and "success" through the conscious exercise of bad manners. Their common sense sees through the vapidity of the instant psych-out. But in fact, his line of work impels the journalist to make psychological judgments, such as what a candidate means, what he is likely to do, where in his past his present behavior comes from. Those judgments may be made with one blind eye or vaguely or by derivation from absurd psychological principles. But the judgments themselves are unavoidable, as every extant news item of any human interest indicates.

That is as it should and must be in presidential campaign reporting. The central question is what these human beings would do if they were elected—a prediction about human behavior. If one thinks he can get that by listening to the candidates' issues stands, then that in itself is a psychological proposition. If he thinks it doesn't make a tinker's dam who gets elected President, then that too is a psychological proposition. Both are, in form, hypotheses subject to verification, suppositions to be tested. And both are ineluctably of the psyche.

In good old psychoanalytic fashion one ought to be able to "analyze the resistances" reporters throw up against their culture's psychological landslide. In interviews, journalists tell about all kinds of practical (i.e., craft-tradition enforced) difficulties in delving into the candidate's background. It is old material. We said it already—for example, about the candidates who had been around Washington a long time. It's too long a take, too cumbersome and complicated; one experienced hand thought it could take a whole *week* to write up a candidate's record in office. Furthermore, it seems somehow unfair. *Time*'s Bonnie Angelo told me, "The American way is that a man can rise above his background," and some reporters in 1968 were clearly convinced that Nixon's background "shouldn't be held against him."

Going back in time is one thing—lots of journalists think of themselves as sort-of-historians, and it is amusing to notice how quickly the journalistic product—disdained by many academic historians while it is being produced—becomes "primary data." But going inside the soul is riskier yet. Journalists who would not mind an identification with C. Vann Woodward or Frank Friedel shy away from Ann Landers and Dr. Joyce Brothers. Some reject even a personnel psychology approach: "strictly speaking," journalists should not make judgments of presidential job qualifications, "should just report what the guy's doing." Some rely on a division of labor: "Communicating presidential qualities is *their* job, not ours." Or, like lawyers, shift the burden of proof: "I really don't know what the skills are, frankly. It is a lot easier to put your finger on lack of skills." Or into modesty: "You don't want to play God," says Apple, and "It is preposterous to think you can do psychoanalysis in daily news coverage." And there are those who, looking back at the track record, draw a negative lesson from the apparent failures—all those insights that discovered a "new Nixon," "forged by fire," a "changed man," for example. Still others view the record as more mixed, but stress the difficulties: the press can perhaps psych-out a more-or-less normal fellow with some weaknesses, such as McCarthy, Robert Kennedy, Hubert Humphrey, but "a real scoundrel, such as Yorty, Rafferty, or Nixon, is very difficult to portray."

But probably the main reason journalists resist psychologizing is that they have seen it so badly done. It can be a mask for character assassination or scandal-mongering. "Personality" pieces can lap over into gossipy goo, as in all those stories about the "New York City radical chic liberal with-it beautiful people" in politics. Reporters who went marching into Georgia for a day or two sometimes came back with a less than complete portrait of the Carter tribe. On another front, psychologizing opens a path to sycophancy: the candidate media managers are ready to supply any number of illustrations that their man has the "charm and talent and brains" that make for good Georgetown dinner parties. Or the "ongoing, over-riding attempt to 'people-ize' the news" can result in snappy little two-line reductionisms or facty "profiles," meant, like silhouettes, to evoke much more than they convey—the man wears a vest, has a three-legged dog, was born in Iowa, served as Japanese Trade Ambassador in Lisbon, etc., etc., etc.

But journalistic opinion on this problem is no monolith, as will soon be illustrated. Plenty of practitioners read the record as prescribing more, not less, attention to character. *Newsweek*'s Ed Kosner speaks for many when he says, "Find out what kind of person I am and my decisions on Portugal will come out O.K." For if character interpretation is difficult and risky and often ill done, so is interpretation of issues and chances and travels, and, unlike those topics, character interpretation is directly relevant to the campaign's largest purpose: choice among persons. Obviously the point is to do it well. That calls for better science, not a retreat from the task.

The Skeptical Stance

Journalists share with scientists at least two key attitudes, skepticism and wonder, without which their parallel progresses would falter. "There can be no higher law in journalism," quoth Walter Lippmann in *Liberty and the News,* "than to tell the truth and shame the devil." In 1975-1976, these two commands seemed to have merged into one law. We were going through one of those recurrent periods in which the talk around many a cocktail campfire was how the old myths were shattered, the old chiefs gone, a few battered warriors like Gerald Ford and Carl Albert stumbling around in a leadership gap. Every leading figure turned out to have at least one clay foot. The public was variously painted as alienated, angry, disillusioned or depressed—in any case, nonenthusiastic, and two young bucks (Robert Redward and Carl Dustin Hoffstein) had become rich beyond their fondest dreams of avarice by holding steadily to their faith in skepticism. Mencken's preachment, that the only way for a reporter to look at a politician was down, rang true. It fell to Garry Wills, in the September 1975 *Harper's,* to write the inevitable piece to the effect that politicians were not so bad after all.

There is no logical necessity for journalists to be doubting Thomases and in many another time they have believed all too readily whatever the powerful were passing out. But skepticism is clearly an item in the ethos. Persons who succeed at a profession are likely to be those who can adopt the appropriate stance without calculation: cool surgeons, adaptable actors, curious researchers. One can speculate about how such connections get made. At least until recently "going into journalism" was a fairly gutsy thing for a young middle-class fellow to do; perhaps there is a residue of rebellion in the journalistic ego. At least until recently "news" was largely bad news—was defined as such—and he who spends his life with mayhem and misery may learn to steel himself against hopeful impulses. (Today, one could argue, the psychological ground is error and failure, the notable figure ["news"] anything that works well.) Whatever its roots, skepticism flowers in the news garden.

Richard Salant puts it succinctly when he says, "They are trying to sell us a bill of goods, so our job is to get behind the bullshit." Apple calls the "they're-all-crooks" attitude "post-Watergate macho"—but admits he got a zing—"utterly delicious"—when he caught out a leader. Hamilton Jordan says the appellation "honest public official" has become a contradiction in terms and Lou Cannon says that "politicians have made candor a cant word, have destroyed it as a value." William Greider says lightly, "I'm an optimist—the only hope for America is reducing the legitimacy of its leaders." Dan Crossland has it clear: "I don't like this government, and I didn't like the last one, and I won't like the next one."

Wise Peter Kaye, who has worked both sides of the lot, puts the professionality of it this way: reporters and candidates are in "an adversary relationship, not an unfriendly one." But wise Hugh Sidey thinks the contemporary press "deeply suspicious of men in public life. To approve is seen as a kind of weakness." And wise Dan Schorr sees the same thing in television: it is "almost required that you bring a note of skepticism into your script—'Oh boy! You really shoved it to him there!' If you don't, you're a patsy."

The going contemporary wisdom—that politicians are to be doubted—affects journalism profoundly. Similarly in science, the going way tends strongly to carry the living scientist along with it, always has. Witness physics from Copernicus to Einstein, genetics from Mendel to the double helix. For like journalists, scientists are culturally embodied. Thinks Edwin G. Boring:

> We shall not be far wrong, if we regard the scientist as a nervous system, influenced by what it reads and hears as well as by what it observes in nature and in the conduct of other men—the smile of approbation, the sneer of contempt—and affected also by its own past experience, for the scientist is forever instructing himself as he proceeds toward discovery and is also forever being instructed by other men, both living and dead. (from Phillipp G. Frank's *The Validation of Scientific Theories*)

Thus the skeptical stance, seemingly of the essence, may be a passing phase, so that not long from now we may need to worry again that journalism is too charitable to politicians.

Journalistic skepticism can find many a friend in the psychological tradition. Much of psychology grew out of pathology and curative therapy (as distinguished from eupeptic therapy, à la, e.g., Esalen). Little wonder then that so much of psychology focuses on the ways people experience trouble, sorrow, need, sickness, and adversity, and that so much more seems to be approximately known about the ills than the wells.

Relatively recently the insightful stage-typing of Erik Erikson, the close scientific work of Daniel J. Levinson and colleagues, and the popularization of the idea by Gail Sheehy have importantly extended psychology to the understanding of progress, through mature choice, in individual development, and Robert Coles, in his *Children in Crises* series, continues to illustrate how the strengths of personality can be marshalled, even in childhood. But the assumption that "patients" and "subjects" are not as nice as they make themselves out to be and that they do not really know what they are talking about prevails. In political science, too, a fear of appearing academically tender-hearted seems to reinforce an emphasis on the politician's ambitiousness or obsessiveness or pretense. In short, journalism alone neither invents or sustains skepticism. It is part of our intellectual way of life.

There is a noticeable difference, though: the scientist's skepticism focuses strongly on theories and on the adequacy of evidence. Journalists share a corner of that when they challenge the *candidate's* theories and the factuality of his data base. Worth discussing more is how journalism's day-to-dayness makes it hard to find leisure for questioning—by the active journalists themselves—of their own theories and methods. For it is a fact that "what the facts are cannot be discovered without reflection," that "sensory experience sets the *problem* for knowledge," and that "just because such experience is immediate and final it must be informed by reflective analysis before knowledge can be said to take place" (Cohen and Nagel, *An Introduction to Logic and Scientific Method*).

The Mysterious Politician

Much of creative science depends on unlearning. True, long immersion in the data bath and patient study of previous explanations are requisites. But to jump from elaboration to invention the scientist has to be able to clear his head of the buzz of contemporary wisdom so he can hear what he is about to say. That can be very difficult. The students who came to Socrates had their heads full of opinions, the validity of which seemed self-evident to them; therefore much of their teacher's work was disillusionment preparatory to a fresh look. In a sense, he had to help his students find the child inside them, first puncturing balloons (skepticism) and then breathing the airs of inspiration (wonder). Einstein, Newton before him, Galileo way back—all had that capacity for regression in the service of the scientific ego. It is not very normal. Most people do not do it very often.

Professional journalists here again link to science. Their skepticism does not extend to questioning their sense that the candidate is *mysterious*, their wonder about who he really is. Thus "the only real story" about Carter is "who the hell is he?"; this "Southern mystery—who is this guy?" A minor Reagan obscurity sends reporters to barber shops to check his hair scraps for dye. One had to "cut through to the real Fred Harris" and the problem about Edward Kennedy was "getting through his armor." John Chancellor is "mystified by Brown" and Eric Sevareid agrees: "I don't make him out." Part of what was "frustrating" about Jackson was how hard it was to find in him "a puzzle to untangle." And perhaps the ultimate in mystery-making: "Jerry Ford remains quite an enigma." A large part of the journalist's job is digging behind the sweetness and light to get to the real person," who exists "behind the surface," by using "the old onion routine—peeling, peeling, peeling."

A diligent researcher could array plenty of historical material to show that nearly every newfound presidential candidate has had his mystery noticed, including Harry Truman, Alf Landon, and Calvin Coolidge. Campaign managers complain that their man is not taken at face value, but they do not really want that to happen, because mystery is a prime element in charisma. Probably many voters also want to perceive mystery so they can wonder what their king is doing tonight. Surely it helps the journalistic enterprise—dependent on new stories to write—to see the as yet unpierced shadows in the politician's aura.

But it is more than a simple utility. Year after year of campaign reporting teaches a reporter to let his wonder loose to forage for new characterological hypotheses. It is part of his stance, a mental practice he cultivates. He gambles that his explorations will turn something up. What sustains that quest is close to faith: that in truth there is something there to interpret. In that sense, too, he is a practicing psychologist.

The Seriousness Question

A scientist embarking on an empirical inquiry has to bound its scope, at least tentatively, lest his energies ooze away in a million marginal rivulets. The same for journalists. In the early phases of campaign reporting, money and manpower limits make it necessary to define, at least tentatively, who the candidates are. The candidate's own wanting of it is an insufficient desideratum—scores stand for office who stand no chance of getting it, and others (Kennedy, Humphrey) must be thought about despite their apparent reluctance. The editor can wait for some external signal, such as qualification for matching federal funds or a poll or even a vote in an early caucus or primary, but none of the mechanical criteria quite work. Popularity, for example, might seem the logical definer, in which case the reporters would look to the pollsters. But we know that the pollsters, in making up their early lists, rely heavily on what they read in the papers and see on television. Obviously pollees cannot prefer candidates they have never heard of, and these days—except for the tiny minorities who go out to lean over airport fences and get touched—voters learn about candidates from reporters.

Dan Schorr told us as much: "To whom does TV pay attention? To those who merit it. Who's that? If you have been on television then you are recognizable and if you are recognizable then you have been on television."

Into this calculation gap steps consensus (one hears the same names over and over again) and assertion (deciding "by fiat," which might be called decision by announcement) and well-exercised instinct ("seat of the pants," "top of the head," or "gut" reactions). The candidate names actually allotted space or time in reporting are very few. Insofar as the matter gets argued about, it turns on who is "serious."

Listening to leading journalists talk about who's serious, a pattern-seeking professor can hear a pattern. In fact, I think, journalistic seriousness-assessors use a scheme in which "personality" considerations appear in the dark before the heavy coverage season dawns.

A serious (and thus to-be-covered) candidate is one who has in his bucket a combined sufficiency of motive, opportunity, and resources. Here motive means ambition—how desirous is he? Opportunity means chances—early in the game this is roughly what we used to call "availability." Resource means not only money and time, but also "organization," advisors, skills, etc. A candidate without fairly high scores on all three factors is unlikely to come through, but the more interesting point is that, to a fair degree, the factors can substitute for one another. A rich Lloyd Bentsen gets in because his resources (including his status as Senator) substitute for his apparently mild and fragile motivation and the broad political odds against yet another Texas millionaire in 1976. A poor Fred Harris is serious, not because anyone that "radical" is likely to win, but because he is just damned well determined and because he has succeeded in generating an energetic cadre. An Edward Kennedy is on the list because some think he could have the nomination for the asking (opportunity), however much or little he might want it now (motive), given his considerable resources. Similar calculations for Terry Sanford, Morris Udall, Jerry Brown, and the rest would illustrate how their different weights balanced them into serious consideration. The scheme is rough—nearly impossible to quantify, for example—but appears to be about what reporters are doing when they decide that, as far as seriousness is concerned, Milton Shapp is, Julian Bond is not.

Focusing on motive, a newly-widening split is visible between running for and being President as the object of ambition. In 1974, Senator Mondale, surveying the rapids ahead, decided to paddle ashore: much as he wanted to be President, he did not want to be a candidate for President. Wallace, on the other hand, was as bored with running Alabama as he would be running the White House: it was running *for* the Presidency that gingered his lust. With the exception of accidental-President/candidates Johnson and Ford, all the nominees starting with Kennedy and Nixon have been ardent runners for, some of them spending nearly as much time campaigning as they would ruling as President. Thus part of the calculus of ambition has to be, in this day and age, ambition for what? The word means "going around," as in ambling or ambience, but even in the Latin it referred to "soliciting votes." Increasingly, one must ask whether it takes the same (or, in an imperfect world, roughly the same) stern stuff to run as to serve. A "serious" candidate could make a comic President. One of our system's operative qualities is the effective elimination of the Mondales, whose motivational ambience forks wrong at the turning.

Rough reasoning about motive-opportunity-resource combinations churns out a list. Most of the names are, alas, familiar to the journalist, thoroughly fondled talismans on the political chessboard. But with one exception, typically, candidate identities are obscure to the public. The exception is the incumbent. The incumbent leads by a long chalk in "name familiarity," which means that people "recognize" the name as belonging to a certain newsmaker. Unless he says what General Sherman said (maybe even then) or he has run out his Constitutional string of years, the incumbent is assumed to be serious. There were doubts raised about Ford due to his peculiar ascension and his early Sherman-verging intimations—but not very serious doubts. As President he had only to show his face and open his mouth to get covered; even his hesitations were reportable, as one front page headline in the April 3, 1975 *New York Times*, the nation's Newspaper of Record, illustrates: "Ford Reported Undecided on the Tax Cut Bill Until End." One suspects that only in the remotest of the severer monasteries and alienated youth communes was there any countable collection of successful Ford-avoiders, while a Lloyd Bentsen had to struggle against confusion with the former Secretary of Agriculture. The incumbent got into the family of our attention because he could act, while his rivals-to-be could only opine and deplore and predict. Meanwhile, in the early campaign months, the challengers, seriatim, peek through the front page news hole for a moment, and are gone.

The point here is not that such frequent coverage gives the incumbent electoral advantage. It does, in the "name familiarity" stage; later, that depends on what is said about him. But assessing his presidential character poses peculiar journalistic challenges. During his incumbency, the underlying question of interest is, given who he is, what will he do? Everyone "knows" who he is. When he departs markedly from his supposed character (as when Ford pardoned Nixon), that is big news. But regular news flows on without perpetually (and irrationally) reraising the question of whether or not he should be President. He already is, for better or worse. And having kicked around with him for years, we feel already acquainted with him and more interested in his positions than in his personality.

As the context shifts toward the election, the basic question shifts to the incumbent-as-candidate. Invariably his actual and potential Presidencies get mixed as it becomes necessary, once again, to assess him against rivals. Like Coriolanus, he must be brought down into the marketplace to show his wounds. It is hard to make a mystery of someone who has spent so much time in our living rooms, hard to convince a skeptical editor that, for example, a reporter should be dispatched to Grand Rapids one more time to poke among the roots of Gerald Rudolph Ford, Jr. It is hard to jimmy the incumbent, whose presidential *plausibility* has been treated as if established, over into comparison with challengers for whom that is a very live question. It is hard to connect the popular image of his presidential character (his basic, personal orientation toward his political life)—stamped into the public mind long ago in a different context—with the new and invariably different criteria. As news, the incumbent is a has-been, and when you hypothetically slip his power out from under him, there may not be much more to say about his inner life.

Yet the incumbent's character—as commonly perceived—has a profound influence on the way his potential challengers are explored. He tends to define the election's major characterological question. When Ford came in, Nixon's behavior had made the overwhelmingly-salient question "Is he honest?" Three hundred-odd FBI agents combed the nation for flecks on Ford's honesty. When Ford went out, his image as honest was intact, but his behavior had raised a different question: "Is he smart?" Eventually he was beaten by the image of a philosophic technocrat. We jolt through history by action and reaction—Wilsonian uplift, Hardingian ease; Harding corrupt, Coolidge clean; Coolidge sleepy, Hoover vigorous; Hoover stonehearted, Roosevelt compassionate. After the war, Truman the "influence peddler" gives way to square soldier Ike, who eventually looks lazy and is replaced by active Jack, and so on..

Inexplicit Theories

It is often said nowadays that the media set the national agenda. They decide what issues and persons are worth attending to this season, this week, today. Journalists joke about "the candidate of the month." Attention is one of our polity's scarcest resources; so agenda-setting is powerful decision-making. Recognizing that is a step of abstraction above the directional questions—bias, preference, substantive interpretation. Social scientists know that most persuasive attempts fail at just this point. Thus, deciding who's serious—bounding the universe of inquiry—may be journalism's most influential decision.

But at still another abstractive remove, journalism as science sets agendas of agendas: out of experience, criteria of relevance are invented and traditionalized. That is rarely done explicitly; the assumptions are rarely dragged out into the light of conscious deliberation. In science, too, consensus, assertion, and instinct often substitute for reason; actually-operative theories are often only dimly perceived; causes and effects are loosely linked; and agenda-setting principles are assumed rather than examined. Yet science does, at its best, fight these temptations. The question about questions strains the brain, but it turns out to be worth asking.

Political journalists stake out the campaign's field of contention, staying open to the possibility of boundary-breaking, as when a "new face" appears on the scene or an old one fades out of it. Calculation then turns to structuring. Given the campaign's overarching purpose, a definitive choice among alternative persons, it makes sense to concentrate on the comparative mode. As other chapters in this book make clear, the dominant comparison concerns chances of electoral success, particularly in the short run, and thus a very strong focus on early success-predictive events, such as the New Hampshire primary. The question shifts from who's in the game to who's ahead, a continuing application of the criterion of attention-economizing. But increasingly, as the chances sort themselves, journalists look harder at the candidates emerging at the top of the structure, not only as probable winners but as possible Presidents.

The psychology of that predictive enterprise is rarely sorted out clearly. Character-as-President gets mixed with character-as-candidate, character in a moral sense with explicitly political character, general mental health with the brand of that a President specially needs. Interpretation rarely reaches beyond the next primary to pose—out in the open—such questions as:

1. What are the particular skills needed in the modern Presidency, and how do the candidates' working habits compare with these needs?
2. What major political beliefs ought to grip a modern President, and how do the candidates' basic world views mesh with these beliefs?
3. What does the modern Presidency call for in the way of character, given its peculiar demands, and how do the contending candidates stack up on these criteria?

Situational questions (as distinguished from these personal ones) get asked more often but are rarely linked directly with presidential performance:

1. What configuration of power will the new President have to work in, and how does that anticipation help to discriminate among the candidates?
2. What forecast can be made of the politically-relevant public mood—the climate of expectations—the Presidency will confront, and how would the candidates life and challenge that mood?

Some such set of questions guides the editor as he makes assignments, the columnist as he pokes around for an interpretative scoop, the "news analysis" writer as he edges past the facts. But the danger is that in leaving them unstated he will leave them unexamined. Precisely as the scientific researcher cannot really get underway until he wrestles a thesis out of his topic and pins it down in propositions, so the journalist flounders when he cannot quite grasp what he is writing about.

The Campaign Stress Test

On the face of it, campaigning for President is not much like being President. Presidents do not run around to shopping centers shaking hands. Presidents do not make the same speech ten times a day. Presidents need not spend half their energies raising contributions. Presidents are not forever calculating how to get on the television evening news. Presidents are not followed around, day after day, by some of the nation's best reporters. Presidents wrack their brains, not their bodies.

Nor, on the face of it, is New Hampshire much like America. Among many deviations, it is prettier, smaller, ruraler, whiter than your hypothetical average state. Its ethnic minority is French-Canadian. Its television comes from Boston, and its only important newspaper is run by an eccentric egotist who parks his .38 automatic next to his office telephone. New Hampshire is old, in a new nation, off in a geographical and cultural corner of the country.

Nevertheless, there are arguable reasons for putting potential Presidents through these paces and for the extraordinarily heavy coverage of the New Hampshire primary. A common argument on the first is that it educates the candidate by forcing him to rub around with citizens and get acquainted with their common discomforts—perhaps like forcing the president of General Motors to work six months on the assembly line and eat in the cafeteria. Even with all the artificiality of crowd-generation, the nonconversations at plant gates, and the well-planned, media-saturated strolls down Maple Street, campaigning may do something to counteract the natural tendency of the big shot to view himself as a human exception. Provided the experience does not make the candidate hate The People, it may deepen his democratic memories.

The argument for New Hampshire is that it may be good for the public in that, with few historical exceptions, the front runner there has won the nomination, so the result can help guide public attention. Atypical it may be, but that primary is the first real public vote, as distinguished from unreal polls.

Neither purpose has anything much to do with assessing presidential qualities. *That* argument boils down to hypothesis by analogy: campaign life is seen as like White House life in the tests it poses for the person's skills, beliefs, and character. Walter Mears calls the campaign "pretty good on the job training." Witcover calls it "a preview." Cronkite thinks it "tests them in fire." But just what is being compared? In science, Cohen and Nagel tell us, "We generally begin with an unanalyzed feeling of vague resemblance, which is discovered to involve an explicit analogy in structure or function *only by a careful inquiry.*" In the journalistic accounts, specification comes hard.

For example, organizational skill in campaigning might predict that skill in the Presidency. But the historical record strains that faith. Clearly Wilson cooperated with the bosses to get elected, then turned on them. FDR's campaign organization under Howe and Farley was apparently a good deal more efficient and lean and targeted than his (purposefully) chaotic White House system. Kennedy tried to carry over his hellbent campaign techniques into his relations with Congress—with disastrous results. And then there was Nixon's campaign-effective, White House-defective CRP.

For example, "issue" positions in campaigns may presage issue actions in the Presidency—but then there are all those past elections in which We The People were profoundly mistaken on that score. Little time has passed, but already it is hard to recall how terribly important in 1975-76 abortion and busing and tax reform were taken to be.

For example, the candidate's capacity to perform under stress may be analogous to the President's capacity to perform under stress. The logic here is clear enough. The White House is a stressful place. The campaign is a stressful race. And the latter tests for the former. The generalized assumption is that the stresses are analogous or at least equivalent. I think careful inquiry would reveal few direct, explicatable similarities—but whatever the outcome of that research, it cannot be addressed reasonably until the supposed stresses are specified. A skeptic might ask whether the Boston Marathon, say, or a series of forty-eight hour-long "Meet the Press" sessions would not do as well.

An inside view of one campaign can highlight these scientific difficulties. William Wise of the Bayh campaign saw how frustrated the press got when candidates were unwilling to respond to queries on issues arising during the campaign. Suddenly the Mayaguez incident happened and "Bang! Every stop [the candidate] was asked for a reaction. He's on the road. He hasn't read a newspaper. He may not even have heard a radio broadcast. Therein lies a danger for any candidate." In such a contingency, a Bayh staffer, tape recorder in hand, would call into headquarters to get a quick rundown and recommendation which he would record. Bayh would wind up his meeting, the staffer would pass him the tape, and "the minute he walks out of that meeting—before he gets hit by any reporters—he walks into the nearest john, he hits the button on the recorder, five minutes he listens to it," and emerges, mysteriously knowledgeable about current events. Where in that episode are the presidential equivalents?

The campaign stress test is a relatively new challenge. George Washington would not have admitted that he campaigned at all. Andrew Johnson tried it and ruined himself on the "Swing around the Circle." McKinley did not stray far from his front porch. As late as Harry Truman's time, the candidate taking to a train was considered a sacrificial novelty. In 1976 Ford may have been slightly swozzled when he declared he would go into all the primaries. What was very recently a stroll among the people has been turned into a frantic race, thanks to the zeal of the mechanistic democratizers. An indicator of seriousness has been transformed into a test for fanaticism. Udall's advisor John Martillo says, "We don't *need* that kind of maniac in the White House." At least as plausible as the argument that the experiences are analogous is the thought that they diverge to the point of contradiction. The larger problem is that the matter is allowed to rest in plausibility.

The campaign stress test reaches its apex in the gaffe. Reporters, like classical Freudian psychoanalysts, tune their ears to hear slips of the tongue that suddenly clarify something "real" about the candidate. Gaffes show up the candidate as a fool or knave or both; they go way back—to Truman "considering" the use of atomic weapons in Korea, Eisenhower telling a press conference that the budget he just gave Congress could be cut, Kennedy's campaign "missile gap," Romney confessing his brain had been washed. In 1975-76 they ranged from Ford's mild malapropisms ("Growth National Product," "the ethnic of honest work," "our nation is resolent," etc.) and physical stumbles to the darker implications of Carter's "ethnic purity" phrase to Wallace's intimation that the U.S.A. might have been on the wrong side in World War II to Reagan's plan to cut the federal budget by $90 billion. In the Ford-Carter debates near the end of the campaign, the President, no doubt holding in mind an old Republican hope, brought a large smile to the faces of his interrogators when he put the wrong verbal twist on the idea that we should never give up on Eastern Europe—and repeated it. Typically the candidate first seeks to dismiss the incident as trivial, becomes defensive when explanations are repeatedly demanded, struggles to change the subject, is pressed to apologize and recant, and the story at last fades away.

With the advantage of retrospection, judgment is easy: substantively, none of these gaffes amounted to a hill of beans. Ford was not about to take action to free Poland, Carter has not moved to set up pure Polish enclaves in Milwaukee. The larger—scientific—question concerns the logic of induction. The analogue in science would be the single, key fact or experiment which demonstrates a truth, like Pasteur's success with the sheep. In psychoanalysis, a single flash of insight may suddenly light up the minds of patient and doctor. Carter's "ethnic purity" gaffe, then, might be taken to reveal, of a sudden, that beneath all his talk of love and inside all his history of black playmates and hard stands against the racist tides of Plains, lurked a hateful ghost. But neither in science nor in psychoanalysis does the "key" observation, all by its lonesome, solve the puzzle. Its power spreads out in two directions: it enables the scientist or physician to explain in a new and convincing manner past observations the sense of which had been obscure, and it suggests that future observations will be consistent with the key one. The verifiers are representativeness and replicability. The significant question about Carter's phrase, then, was not what it in itself revealed, but what it implied; the proof of the pudding would require evidence ranging far beyond the immediate event.

The campaign stress test rarely reaches that far. Given the enormous volume of verbal productions candidates spew forth and the semiexhausted state in which they compose them, it is a wonder they do not gaffe every day. Partly because journalism's methodology defines today's quote as the key data type, single slips of the tongue and mind get blown out of proportion. Walter Cronkite says reporters have to travel with candidates because "something might happen—amusing, revealing, a character revelation." But John Lindsay views the gaffe scene less sanguinely: "Some nice rational guy has a hotassed conversation with the candidate—and rushes off with words the candidate didn't realize, didn't mean, and screeches them into a phone." To its credit, the *Washington Post* decided it had been hasty in overemphasizing Wallace's World War II realliance gaffe, and said so.

But from a scientific perspective, the problem is not moral but perceptual. Like all of us, journalists need to be urged to try hard and do better; a scientist would say, "Yes, but while you're at it, try readjusting your sights."

Concepts of Character

Many an interpretative journalist did, in 1975-76, delve into the candidates' pasts for clues to their present personalities and—though mostly by implication only—tc their potential Presidencies. It was a biographical year. Significant style questions were explored. Did Ford's history show him too dumb to be President? (Did Franklin Roosevelt's?) Was Jackson's diseloquence disqualifying? (Was Eisenhower's?) Had Carter shown himself poor at political negotiation? (Had Kennedy?) Important worldview propositions were looked into—journalists peered past campaign issue-stands to search out the basic political beliefs that had shaped the candidates' actual doings. Records were scanned and added to position the candidates along the old left-right continuum, though that ground had grown a good deal swampier than it had been. What Carter's serious Christian commitment might mean for his politics was assessed. Like questions regarding the political situation the new President would face, up close and at a distance, these questions of skill and belief were critically important, lest we wind up with a man for the wrong season, an accident-prone chief executive, or a politician who detests politics. Each such dimension would be worth intense inquiry, beginning with the bounding of the universe.

The emphasis, though, was on character. Trying to unwind what was genuine and real and operative in the tangle of manipulative artifice, journalists (remembering) approached the candidates from a variety of angles familiar to psychologists. These approaches illustrate how different concepts of character research guide the researcher to different types of data—how questions shape answers.

Patterns of Adaptation

Approaching Henry Jackson's character, journalists met a hard problem: his lack of developable mystery. Not only did it seem that the inner layers of the Jackson onion were much like the outer ones, but also he had been probed and squeezed for years by the Washington press. In an interview with me, Stan Cloud found the Senator's transparency "frustrating to a reporter, because you keep finding that Jackson the public man is the same as Jackson the private man—there is almost no distinction there." Cloud explains:

> A cynical reporter finds that difficult to accept. You assume that the public image is something that he projects and when he is at home and doing something else, then there is the real guy. I have seen too many politicians where I know there is a difference. But time and time and time again, his friends and his enemies would say, "No, no, Jackson for better or for worse is what he is, what he appears to be. "And the more I dealt with that, the more it became a puzzle to me. I found it hard to believe, that Jackson was so completely under control.

Perhaps as bad, from the viewpoint of a reporter responsible for bringing his readers newsness of life, was that Jackson was old copy, fishwrapping, a project done already and embalmed in the dead morgue of the past. Strange to the public, Jackson was as familiar to Washington newsmen as, say, Jerry Ford was in 1974. When I talked with *Newsweek's* Mel Elfin in January 1976, he kindly gave me a rundown on how the candidates were trying to affect their coverage, with sprightly comments on Ford, Reagan, Carter, Udall, Harris, Shapp, Shriver, Sanford, Wallace, and Humphrey. When he seemed to have finished I noted, "You didn't mention Jackson," and Elfin said, "Isn't that funny! Isn't that funny—it was inadvertent. I forgot about him."

But nearly a year earlier, *Time's* anonymous prosists had begun to glimpse Jackson's character through a glass darkly. If he was "still notably opaque for a man in public life," *Time* said on February 17, 1975, a few clues were visible:

> The private personality behind the long face, doleful eyes and resonant voice is known only to his family and a few close friends, though one crony insists: "There is no such thing as an off-the-record Scoop. What you see is what he is. He's that way at home, he's that way with his friends." Almost completely dominated by politics, Jackson has shown himself to be aggressively ambitious, rigidly self-disciplined and often unwilling to tolerate criticism or forgive a slight. He has

been known to berate hostile questioners, but normally he is unemotional in public, though on rare occasions he explodes in private. One close associate has seen him in a rage on only three or four occasions, but each time Jackson became sick to his stomach.

By late November 1975, R.W. Apple, Jr. had discerned in Jackson's history a pattern and found that "the same pattern has held in Washington: *work, work, work, a Spartan existence, life is serious"* (*New York Times Magazine,* November 23). Did Jackson's Puritanic dedication, which had brought him the respect due a vigorous expert, also indicate a dangerous rigidity, a prospect of Nixonian perseveration, an "active-negative" character as my jargon called it? A month later Jules Witcover, in the December 21st *Washington Post,* wrote of "Sen Jackson: Conscientious Loner," including the pros and cons of the thesis that Jackson was compulsive and authoritarian. It would be unfair to "conclude that Jackson is an aloof and inaccessible man," Witcover said, "but he is a man driven by his own diligence, who seemingly runs scared, and consequently—in the manner of such men—is often impatient or misunderstanding of those who either don't run scared, or don't care to stay up with him." What a Jackson friend called Jackson's "single-minded motivation" had brought him a long way, but, Witcover psychologized, "his straight-arrowness seems to have inspired in him, more than one Jackson-watcher had observed, a macho complex, a need to demonstrate his masculinity in ways other than hard drinking and talking, and otherwise carousing." In February, *Newsweek*'s Peter Goldman, Hal Bruno and William J. Cook collaboratively discovered Jackson "a hopeless workaholic—a dawn-to-midnight ironpants," with "breath-taking command of detail," who, however, "tramples jokes, flares at criticism, has no small talk and, in the words of one admirer back home in Washington State, 'has never uttered a memorable sentence' . . . Jacksonians insist that he is a warm, vital and thoroughly qualified man whose hidden charisma will be discovered as soon as he wins his first primary."

Thus the main character question with respect to Henry Jackson (as distinguished from the style question—his rhetorical wretchedness—or the worldview question—his ideological position)—was defined early and lasted late. No sizable flow of commentary was directed at Jackson as, say, a Harding-like patsy for his pals, a musingly detached Coolidge, a Rooseveltian manipulator. In this way, a preliminary data scan helps one focus attention, by imaginatively blanking out the less plausible and concentrating on the more plausible possibilities. The data are largely observations and opinions—if available, by and from someone other than the reporter. The descriptive hypothesis is that a concept, rigid effortfulness, characterizes a significant range of Jackson's behavior. Various explanatory hypotheses are suggested: that the pattern of rigid effortfulness traces to a need to control anger, "demonstrate his masculinity," counteract fear, or satisfy a perfectionistic conscience. The political relevance of this line of thought comes from an appreciation that certain highly important presidential failures have developed out of this particular pattern. While none of the journalistic accounts array much evidence, they do not rely on a single gaffe and they bring to bear several different observational standpoints.

People given to overcontrolling themselves are familiar to psychotherapists and the pattern of "obsessive-compulsive" behavior is perhaps the one clearest bundle of problematic characteristics. The pattern has its payoffs—it contributes mightily to "success" in our culture—so that "the same qualities that make these people seem so rigid in one context endow them, in another, with excellent technical facility and an impressive capacity for concentration on a technical problem." (David Shapiro, *Neurotic Styles*, p. 30)

The scientific problem in this example is relatively simple: does the pattern of rigid effortfulness fit Jackson's behavior? Leaving aside the motivational question, pattern-discerning and testing call for evidence, including evidence of exceptions. In other words, the motivational guesses are not essential to the descriptive hypothesis. Neither is it necessary, for this restricted purpose, to get etiological about it in a developmental sense. Psychiatric experience suggests where in the life-historical roots one might want to look for that:

> Compulsion can be described as a command from within. The idea of "being commanded" certainly is rooted in the child's experience with grownups who used to "command" him, especially, in our culture, in experiences with the father. In compulsions this father commands from within; and an "inner father representative" is called superego. (Otto Fenichel, *The Psychoanalytical Theory of Neurosis*)

But for assessing *political* character, we may with reason be far more interested in the adult upshot than in the childhood putdown, particularly if the pattern is pretty clear. The therapist is trying to cure a patient; the public is trying to choose a President. Getting the pattern straight is step one.

Unconscious Motivation and Its Development

It is unlikely that Henry Jackson would deny that he tries to work hard, and very likely that he would deny having a "macho complex." Sometimes reaching behind pattern to explanation is a good idea; particularly so when the pattern is not all that clear.

The 1976 season's sharpest case example featured Jerry-son-of-Pat Brown. If Jackson was not mysterious enough, Brown was too much so. Brown reduced Eric Sevareid to puzzlement—"I can't make him out. I think something's wrong with his mind,"—and led a "mystified" John Chancellor to think Brown had "a serious mother and father problem." Richard Reeves found Brown "the most interesting politician in the United States" and, in the August 24, 1976 *New York Times Magazine,* took note of "the tortured father-son relationship"; but Reeves hewed close to the descriptive—quotes and facts casting grave doubt on Jerry's filial piety.

It remained for Garry Wills to go the distance: Brown the younger mistook his own motives and Wills would explain them. Journalist Wills is also a learned professor, capable of erudite observations on his subject's "cenobitic appetites" and mild wonderment that Brown "seems to think that Alaric lived in the Alexandrian age." In "Anti-Papa Politics," *New York Review of Books,* June 10, 1976, Wills salts facts with interpretations which, it seems to me, owe much to psychoanalysis. Thus Brown's complaints are not to be taken at face value: "He found ways to boast of the [campaign] effort's very rigors, tireless in his claim that he does not tire. He kept telling reporters how long it had been since he ate, how long since he slept." When Brown "does refer to his father, he misleads, no doubt unintentionally." Topics Brown neglects to mention may be important: he "talks easily" of much of his history, "but he never talks, if he can avoid it, of the eighteen formative years in his father's house." His conversational gaps are attributable to denial: "The one debt Brown is most anxious to deny is that he is really just a politician following in his father's footsteps." And behind what Brown says lurk powerful emotional meanings: exploring Father Brown's decision in the Caryl Chessman case, Wills asked Jerry "point-blank what he would do in such a position" and "Jerry answered: 'I would make the decision and not agonize over it.' The sentence is a ringing condemnation of his father."

Wills' piece is not presented as a hatchet job on Brown. On the contrary, he explains,

> None of what I say reflects on Jerry Brown as a politician. Indeed, I am arguing that he should be judged precisely as a politician, not as an intellectual. The only reason he encourages the displacement of these priorities is to prevent people from thinking he is a politician in the same sense that his father was. As a politician he has major claims to make.

But for the reader who doubts person and politician can be so easily dismembered, the prospect of a President given to displacing priorities to divert attention from his father—especially when, if Wills is right, the relationship is loaded with intense anxiety and condemnation—is discomforting.

The point here is that behavior which seems mysterious on the face of it can be clarified, not only by looking inward for motive, but also by looking backward in the life history to see where the pattern came from. Again because the purpose is not therapy but prediction, the major task is to get the pattern straight; once that is done, digging into the past is less important for political analysis. As Fred Greenstein in *Personality and Politics* puts it, "It is the aspect of psychological interpretation that most readily can be agreed upon"—the pattern—"which proves to be most urgent." Political leaders from Martin Luther to Gandhi, Hitler, Wilson, Stalin, Kennedy, Johnson, Nixon, Ford, and Carter (among others) have shown in their patterns of adaptation interesting and clarifying representations of their fathers. In Brown's case, understanding is advanced when we know, even roughly, that the son is reacting against his father's main identity—even if we cannot know very precisely the deep, unique private origins of that reaction in, say, the drama of Brown's infantile sexuality.

Analysis of the Transference

One of the reasons psychoanalysts must themselves be psychoanalyzed is that, to be effective therapists, they have to understand—up front in their consciousness—who they are. This patient-doctor relationship is a very intense one, at least from the patient side, soul-baring surgery, letting every little thing hang out. Time and again, patients try to turn their doctors into their fathers or lovers or devils—they "transfer" past relationships into the present one with that fellow at the end of the couch. If the doctor brings to that encounter powerful unresolved conflicts of his own, the theory goes, he may use the patient as the patient is trying to use him, smuggling all sorts of distorting feelings into his quiet questions and comments. In his previously cited work, Otto Fenichel explains:

> It is not easy to face the innumerable and various affects with which patients bombard the analyst without reacting with counter-affects, whether conscious or unconscious. The unconscious tendencies by reacting to transference with countertransference must therefore be eliminated through a training analysis.

Thus the doctor must, so to speak, shrink from involving his personal feelings with the patient at the same time as his professional attention is fully mobilized. And not only that: he must pay close heed to how the patient is feeling about him, as critically important material for interpretation.

One can get an idea of how this problem shapes up—and a hint of the analogous problems journalists confront—from Lillian Carter, candidate for First Mother, when she told that distinguished soul-plumber Robert Coles what it felt like to be psychiatrically objectified:

> I was interviewed by a psychiatrist in Chicago, over and over again. He kept asking me why, why, why I wanted to leave a comfortable life at my age to go live in a distant place like India. Was there anything "wrong" in my life? Was I "running away" from something? After a while I became tired of his questions. I began to wonder about *him,* and what *he* was like, and what *his* motives were. I didn't say anything for a long time. I knew they required those psychiatric

interviews of everyone, and I didn't want to be rude. I tried to get the *doctor* talking; I wanted to have a *conversation* with him, not his endless questions and that noncommittal look on his face. I wondered what answer would satisfy him, anyway! There he was, the expert. There I was, the old lady from South Georgia. He kept on asking me where Plains is. I became tired of the same questions: how long had I lived here and there, and why did I want to go abroad, and what was on my old mind and what would happen to me overseas? I thought of asking him as respectfully as I could about *his* life. I wanted to ask why there aren't more psychiatrists from places like New York and Los Angeles "running away" from their private practices to the ghettoes a few miles away, never mind India. I kept my mouth shut, though. I kept my impertinent questions to myself. I got by. I got to India. (*The New Republic*, June 26, 1976)

Candidates off for their India (all but one of them fated, like Columbus, for a different destination) had similar complaints as they were zapped by reporters from behind the redoubt of anonymity. The journalists could hide, the candidate was exposed. No one was checking up on them; his casualest comments got thrown back in his face. What looked like a conversation—two human beings taking turns at talk—was really a one-way test, an interrogation masked as a chat. He knew his desperate gamble depended on how he got reported. In the dark of night, that could madden him.

But journalists tend to feel the converse dependency. What the candidate puts out is "the same old offensive bullshit," one says, but "I have to report it." "We are prisoners of the news," complains another, and a third sees the candidates "holding the hot hand. They've got the information. We want the information. You come to them as a supplicant."

The professional defense on both sides is cool detachment. Americans are supposed to be friendly and relaxed, open and easy, to like (not quite love) whomever they happen to be talking with. Candidates rein in those feelings because they have seen how spontaneity can ruin them. "Don't let down your guard" and "don't blow up at the press" are two cardinal lessons. Press people maintain their skeptical distance (see above). Thus Robert Novak sees the danger in candidate-covering: "A reporter falls in love with him or hates him—it's hard to be neutral after so many days together." When an interviewer asked Novak, "Do you socialize a lot with the people in the campaign?" he replied, "Socialize? Would you define that?"

At the same time, reporters learn by watching the candidate watching them and by taking note of their own personal reactions to the candidate. Normally the tradition is that "you use other people's perceptions to express your own," for instance by how "effective" his "political act" is with the public, how well or poorly he "comes across" with audiences. There it is not only admiration that must be guarded against: Greider confesses to a certain heart-jerk sympathy when he sees a candidate "getting the hell kicked out of him." But there are also scenes of close-in introspection. For instance, candidates who once would have come to Washington or New

York mainly for private confabulations with the politicians now head straight for the Sperling breakfast group with Washington reporters, elegant lunch with the editors of *Time*, little dinners at the tops of various glass buildings. The idea is that "off the record" the candidate will let his hair down, ease into candor and genuineness. Occasionally a substantive news story will grow out of such sessions, but the dominant journalistic purpose is to get a sense of the man, his style, how he handles himself in that situation of apparently pressureless pressure.

In groups and scenes and tête-à-têtes, reporters trying to discover "what kind of guy he is" watch their own reactions: how well did he "impress us?"; does he "know how to use the press?" A natural tendency is to like the candidate who likes the press. For example, Birch Bayh's assistant Ann Lewis (whose candidate, however, did not get the best imaginable coverage) has an attractive attitude: "What we do, 95 percent of the people don't care about. The only people who do are people in the same business, and reporters . . . . So we really enjoy being with reporters, telling stories and jokes. I feel like we're members of the same road show." By contrast, Stan Cloud thought Carter the campaigner was "massively unimpressed with reporting, the triviality of it, reporters who drink and smoke too much." The point here is not that such attitudes impel to bias (they may) but, on the contrary, that reporters cultivate a conscious, scientific interest in the phenomenon, learn to take it into the account.

Reporters also tend to like candidates who are like them. "Mo" Udall was a prime example—that "blithe spirt," that "chatty, funny, down-to-earth" fellow, that "fun guy to be with." Udall was rather like John F. Kennedy, who was "dear to us because he would let his hair down and just say anything." Jackson, on the other hand, struck some reporters as "mean, vindictive, petulant"—egregiously unblithe. The candidate's ponderous "seriousness" gets in between him and the reporter's attractively adolescent mode—that fey and funny, nicknaming, Army-cussing, limerick-limning, unbuttoned, gauche-verging, wit-winding, camaraderie (that regression in the service of the ego) which affects even your most serious and grown-up journalist when he gets on the bus to go on the road. A candidate who can be less than all business gains the advantage of familiarity at the same time as he risks contempt. Udall's characterization of himself as "Second-place Mo," for example, fit that mode—and contributed to a sense that he was not to be destiny's child.

The analogy between psychoanalytic transference and campaign news relations would be easy to overdraw. On the campaign trail, there are many doctors, not one. The candidate is seeking victory, not cure. The journalist is after a story, not a diagnosis. And the whole scene is fraught with activity, not like the quiet of the couch. Still, there is a connection as the journalist, reaching for insight, probes inside self and other.

The Perils of Pathologizing

For some time now, political scientists have been worrying that Americans revere their Presidents too much and have a wildly exaggerated vision of presidential power. The President's surface popularity waxes and wanes, but deeper down are strong tides of emotional allegiance, as shown historically when a President—any President—dies in office and the public weeps. Many people who had reluctantly concluded that Nixon was not a good President were, in the early stages of his defeat, unready to have him leave office; later, many who thought he ought to leave were unready to see him "impeached"—that strange and frightening new idea. Aware of our worshipful tendency, a fair collection of political scientists thinks we ought to deimperialize the Presidency through realistic disillusionment.

Add to that trend journalism's skepticism and psychology's concern with illness, and you are likely to develop an agenda of attention accentuating the negative. Too easily, realism and negativism can slop together, seem one thing. In journalism, for example, the very definition of a lead as a contradiction highlights contradictions of character. A lie is a story, a truth may or may not be. The problem runs deeper yet in psychology, where so much of the language is pathologese, a shorthand for shortfalls in coping with life. Only quite recently have such psychoanalytic thinkers as Erik Erikson and Robert Coles begun to spell out what health looks like. Older definitions are curiously vague, compared to the precision of the illness jargon, and concentrated on the *absence* of blocks of health. Health seems peculiarly bloodless, while the blood of illness splotches vividly through our vocabulary.

Presidential power is dangerous; so is presidential weakness. Negative virtues—peace, for example—are important; but peace needs making. Not only should the criteria be reexamined, the research and presentation strategies should be too. For instance, the division of labor some journalists would prefer—the candidate touts his virtues and the journalist grasps his defects—works only now and then.

The problem is hardest when scientific experts are asked to contribute, always briefly, to candidate coverage. Lacking space to explain and particularly to array much of the pro and con evidence which would give the reader a crack at inferring contexts and balances, the force of the author's argument comes to rest in his authority as an expert. If the expertise is psychological, the negative jargon leaps out of the page. An example, plucked unfairly out of the context of a fascinating and balanced account of three stages in Carter's development, appeared in *New York*, August 30, 1976. It was written by a professional psychohistorian, Bruce Mazlish, and a professional media critic, Edwin Diamond, and illustrates the point.

Some translations from the confessional to the psychological mode can help at this point:

Carter told Moyers he recognized his own "shortcomings and sinfulness. . . ." *In psychological terms, he was depressed.*

Carter felt filled with pride. "I was always thinking about myself . . . ."*The psychoanalytic term for this is "narcissism."*

Carter says that he used people. *The analyst hears, "I can't love . . . ."*

Carter says he had "the need to improve . . . ." *The textbooks talk of the "crisis of generativity."*

Depending on the context (and the authors supply one), these Carter confessions could be taken differently—in psychological terms. A candidate who talks easily about even his former faults and failings is rare; he might be demonstrating freedom to learn through experience. One who enters a period of intense self-concern may be taking a giant step forward in breaking through prideful resistance. One who sees that he has used people may be learning to love them. And recognition of "the need to improve" could represent an emerging achievement orientation as well as a crisis of generativity. As Heinz Hartmann insists (and I am pretty sure Mazlish and Diamond would agree) "a healthy person must have the capacity to suffer and be depressed." That is hard to hold in mind, post-Eagleton, and the standard pathology-language makes it harder. The point is not that in character work on candidates only common English should be spoken—those words, too, like "pride," are encrusted with moralism—but that diagnostic and journalistic negativities can powerfully reinforce one another, particularly when, as I have done artificially here, the technical labels are ripped off the packages of evidence.

Psychologies change. New journalists might join new psychologists in balanced attention to personal strengths and in pondering what Erikson meant when he wrote in *Childhood and Society* that "the patient of today suffers most under the problem of what he should believe in and who he should—or, indeed, might—be or become; while the patient of early psychoanalysts suffered most under inhibitions which prevented him from being what or who he thought he knew he was."

The Scientific Journalist on the Campaign Trail

An inordinate proportion of the journalist's gusto gets eaten up in bookie work, figuring the odds on the next primary; but insofar as he tries to see character, he is a scientist and a psychologist. That work counts, if history is any guide at all. After the fact is too late to discover that an Aaron Burr has been elected in place of a Thomas Jefferson. It will count even when—especially when—we have an election in which big issues dominate, for it is on such big issues as war and peace and the integrity of the

Constitution that presidential character has called the tune. If it should turn out that 1975-76's character emphasis was a passing phase in the fashion parade, we will once again be in danger. Interpretative journalism has at least this responsibility: to set a rational agenda of inquiry, whatever moody breezes blow across the land.

Science is one of our civilization's names for reason. It marks itself out by its intense self-consciousness—focusing reason on reasoning itself. Even that can and does exaggerate itself into irrelevance, as in so many social science studies that ape physics and produce peanuts. But for the journalist who cares whether or not his interpretations hold beyond tomorrow morning, and most good ones do, his intellectual brotherhood with the scientist can strengthen his mind. He will ask himself, as he trots along, what he is thinking about, where his hypothesis is taking him, when he will recognize the appropriate data, how to use the facts to test his thoughts, and why, in the first place, he is called to this work. Like Galileo, he will foster and protect in himself that odd combination of skepticism and wonder that every day's encounter with "common sense" seems to shred.

As a practicing psychologist, proudly amateur, the journalist shares more than he might realize with his less fluent colleagues in the clinics and universities and research institutes. The "assessment of men" is an old topic in psychology; during World War II, for example, psychologists contributed importantly to figuring out who was fit for the OSS, and no doubt at this moment CIA psychologists are tracing what motives move various Pekinese and Muskovites. The campaign stress test is one way—an improvable way, I think—of checking up on character in Presidents-to-be, a way well within journalism's taste for behavior as the key to motive. The scientific guts of that enterprise concerns equivalence, and that inquiry is not going to go very far until attention gets paid to what the stresses of presidenting amount to. No sudden single verbal burst of incandescent illumination will show far along that way.

The journalist whose fascination focuses on campaigns can and should let his mind seek patterns. "Rigidity" is not the only one, but it is probably the easiest one to spot and the most dangerous one to elect. Back before that is a live question; the journalist has to decide, with or without knowing it, what "seriousness" consists of. And after that, when systematic work still leaves the pattern murky, journalists can find systematic ways to reach inside the candidate for understandings the man himself may not see clearly and outside the candidate to include how he and they react to one another.

What the campaign stress test misses is life history—and that is what journalism excelled at in 1975-76. Would Caesar cross the Rubicon? The answer, may be, was coded into his Julian genes or buried in some trauma of his infancy. But even he could remember when his uncle Marius made him "Priest of Jove" before he was a man; when, scarcely a man, he had married the wealthy Cornelia and, a mere year later, was stripped of his priesthood because he refused Sulla's command to divorce her. His alliance with Pompey and the popular party; his bribed election as Pontifex Maximus; his service as quaestor in Farther Spain; his diplomacy between Crassus and Pompey; his winning ways with the legions in Gaul (he knew his men by name); the death of his dear daughter Julia, wife to Pompey; Marc Antony's brave and perilous support—in short, his life, as he had experienced it and the situation at the Rubicon that January day and what "Caesar" had come to mean—knowing and weighing that, and saying what he thought, a wily enough Roman journalist might have scratched into history a character never to be forgotten.

James David Barber

7

Characters in the Campaign:

The Educational Challenge

One can picture Thomas Jefferson seated at his desk in Monticello, his collar loose and the glassed doors open to catch a bit of the evening breeze at the end of a hot August day. The candlelight flickers gently on the old wood, on his lined, attentive face, on the sunbrowned hand that moves his pen across the page. He pauses, looks out into the gathering darkness. His mind's eye sees the pen and hand moving across another page, nineteen years ago, inking into the second paragraph of the Declaration, " . . . governments are instituted among men, deriving their just powers from the consent of the governed . . . ." Jefferson sighs and returns to the letter he is writing. We hear his mind composing as he writes:

> . . . I do most anxiously wish to see the highest degrees of education given to the highest degrees of genius, and to all degrees of it, so much as may enable them to read and understand what is going on in the world, and to keep their part of it going on right: for nothing can keep it right but their own vigilant and distrustful superintendence. I do not believe with the Rochefoucaulds and Montaignes, that fourteen out of fifteen men are rogues: I believe a great abatement from that proportion may be made in favor of general honesty. But I have always found that rogues would be uppermost, and I do not know that the proportion is too strong for the higher orders, and for those who, rising above the swinish multitude, always contrive to nestle themselves into the places of power and profit. These rogues set out with stealing the people's good opinion, and then steal from them the right of withdrawing it, by contriving laws and associations against the power of the people themselves. Our part of the country is in considerable fermentation, on what they suspect to be a recent roguery of this kind. They say that while all hands were below deck mending sails, splicing ropes, and every one at his own business, and the captain in his cabin attending to his log book and chart, a rogue of a pilot has run them into an enemy's port . . . .

173

For my part, I consider myself now but as a passenger, leaving the world and its government to those who are likely to live longer in it. That you may be among the longest of these, is my sincere prayer . . .

What would Jefferson, transplanted to our time, think of the American multitude and of the prospects for our civic education? Could his sanguine intelligence comprehend the masses of the propertyless, the blacks, the immigrants, the women, and the young people who have come crowding into the electorate? In the United States today, there are more than a thousand "functional illiterates" for every soul alive in Boston the day Jefferson worried over the degrees of genius and the proportion of rogues. The minimasses of his day—that "swinish multitude"—were largely unfranchised; our contemporary hordes can vote if they want to.

That is the central fact confronting civic education today. No reasonable writing from the Federalist Papers on down has supposed that the great public can be educated into expertise or persuaded to devote most of its time and attention to public affairs. Indeed there are reasonable reasons for hoping it never will; Hitler had his people pretty well involved. Rather the problem is one of learning readiness. When the time comes for the people to judge, will they bring to the judging such knowledge and values and interest to choose, if not the best, at least leaders good enough to keep the ship afloat? If we cannot make Everyman a Solon, can we at least equip him for the "vigilant and distrustful superintendence" Jefferson thought essential?

Who Are Those People?

It is a tribute to American teacherdom that they have tried as hard as they have to find out who their students are—though it is a bit disconcerting that all those researchers have yet to tell us definitively how to teach reading to grade school kids. But compared to journalists and college professors, "educators" are hellbent to understand the audience. In Ron Powers' *The Newscasters*, Richard Salant sounds very much like a professor irritated at being asked to pass out course evaluation forms: "I really don't know and I'm not interested . . . . I take a very flat elitist position. Our job is to give people not what they want, but what we decide they ought to have. That depends on our accumulated news judgment of what they need." Newspapers sometimes do surveys asking people what they like and would like more of (people know how they are supposed to answer that), and the circulation department has a rough idea of market demographics, but when print journalists are asked to imagine what their own readers are like, they go blank. The ready rationale is professionalism: the surgeon does not inquire of the patient where to cut; the lawyer does not ask his client when to move for a mistrial; the minister does not poll his congregation on what sort of gospel they would like today. Even a little knowledge of the audience could be a dangerous thing if it warped the journalist's professional judgment away from truth-telling to popularity pandering. Better to craft the best possible product and let who wants it take it.

The great exception is television market research, and television news is the great medium for reaching the politically unwashed. Polls in 1975-76 indicated that three out of four Americans say they get most of their news from television and half say they get *all* their news there. Sizable majorities also say they "trust" television news more than other sources. People untouched by higher (i.e., later) education are far more likely to say they rely on television than are the cognoscenti. Compared with the circulation of any newspaper or magazine, the number of sets turned on to television news is enormous—tens of millions. Even more significant for potential civic education are the vast masses who, fully equipped for television reception, do not yet tune in the news. For the 23,000,000 "functional illiterates," it is reasonable to suppose that television and radio are the only now-available links to national politics. What all this adds up to is the machinery, the broad public predisposition, and the resource to revolutionize popular civic education in the United States. What makes it all the more curious is that the television industry knows so little about how people relate to the news. Even those who are unwilling merely to humph away the topic with a professional shrug have to fall back on conventional wisdom, typically agreeing that the public is (a) dumb—the proverbial Kansas City milkman who moves his lips as he reads—and (b) shrewd—the proverbial old Yankee crinkleface who can tell a silk purse from a sow's ear. Typically these clashing images pop up when the quality of television news is questioned, the first to imply that the message suits the messagee and the second to imply that he can make sense of whatever he gets. The dumb public theme reinforces the prescription, "Give them what they want"; the shrewd public theme reinforces the caution, "The viewers won't stand for that."

Television market research churns out data on the number of sets tuned into a given channel at a given time, electrically recorded. There are numerous technical difficulties—high proportions of busted meters; rapid turnover; underrepresentation of poor, rich, away from home, and foreign language viewers. Neil Hickey in the May 8, 1976 *T. V. Guide* describes the fall of 1975 when the machinery seemed to show an unprecedented 6 percent drop in household viewing, "the news hit like a thunderbolt hurled down from Parnassus to wreak confusion on the innocents below." Just as the critics were gearing up their indignant explanations, centering on the supposedly abysmal quality of the programs, the Nielsen company explained that a handful of aberrant zero-viewing households had temporarily botched the findings; soon the sets-on figures were back to normal. Even more error-prone is the diary technique: viewers are asked to write down what programs they watch, a family novelty which soon wears off, tempting the diarists to put off the task till the end of the week or month, when, perhaps with the help of *T.V. Guide*, they struggle to remember what was flickering forth when. But even if these numbers were perfectly accurate (and they are, of course, taken very seriously by those who buy and sell the advertising), they give no help at all to program makers trying to understand what kind of connection, if any, they are establishing with the people at the other end of the tube. Like figures on enrollment in college courses, the numbers stand mute on the crucial question—the question of educational effect.

An implausible substitute for science in this research is casual acquaintance. Like other Americans, reporters and broadcasters tend strongly to party with their own class and race and neighborhood. Earnest forays across these boundaries can perhaps give the journalist some sense of how he is being received, but as a regular event, Harry Reasoner is not to be found incognito in a waterfront bar taking surreptitious notes as he watches himself with the dock workers. In the scale from mass to elite, the journalist's attention is focused upward, where the newsmakers are. On the campaign trail, the boys are isolated in the bus or outside experiencing the people as the candidate himself does, in crowds and momentary encounters. Even more restrictive are the peculiar schedules of the journalist's life which cut him off from the popular flow. Typically the *Washington Post* reporter is hard at it in the office with his typewriter as America settles down to watch the evening news—and the evening newscasters are at the studio. More bizarre yet is the life of the morning television journalists. Rising in the dead of night, whisked in their limousines to the studio, they labor away toward dawn—every weekday dawn—to compose and present a refreshing version of the news. According to Robert Metz in *The Today Show,* the performers "knew that theirs was a world apart. Working in the predawn hours and sleeping during the day meant that, except for the people they knew on the show, almost everyone else in their lives, including family, existed on a different planet." By 1976, Barbara Walters had been at that for almost sixteen years. This weird existence presses the sufferers together like combat soldiers. In *We're Going to Make You a Star,* Sally Quinn reports that she and Hughes Rudd, fellow fighters for the "CBS Morning News," meeting to ride to the studio, had a standard greeting: "Every day the first thing one of us asked the other was if he had gotten enough sleep. Sleep was everything. It was our major preoccupation. If I wasn't sleeping I was trying to sleep or worrying about whether or not I would be able to sleep." If they were lucky, sleep came in the afternoon light and deepened through America's dinner hour.

The professor's "eat-with-the-students" routine is rarely an option for the journalist. R. W. Apple gets his sanity bolstered by eating from time to time with a cellist friend, and *Newsweek's* Hal Bruno grabs at chances to pick bluegrass with his musical pals. But the normal rhythm of their life is abnormal. And when the journalist does manage to get together with a civilian friend, odds are the conversation centers on topics other than how they affect one another professionally.

There is a little shaky evidence that newsmen who imagine a friendly reader report good news more accurately than bad and that those who imagine a critical reader do bad news better. But former *New York Times* reporter Robert Darnton probably has it about right when he argues in the spring 1975 *Daedalus* that "whatever their subliminal 'images' and 'fantasies,' newspapermen have little contact with the general public and receive almost no feedback from it. . . . All too often, 'publishing a story can be like dropping a stone in a bottomless pit: you wait and wait, but you never hear the splash.' "

As always when information is lacking on a salient matter, supposition slips in. For instance, take the question of "media power." Early critics of television raised the Spectre Enormous—mass hypnotism by manipulative Svengalis at the controls. Dan Schorr in *Clearing the Air* worries about that today:

> By forging a magic electronic circle, coast to coast, television has created a national séance. Millions sit figuratively holding hands as they are exposed together to a stream of images and suggestions, mixed-up facts and fancies, playing more on their senses than their intellects. Television may be on its way to doing in America what religious mysticism has done in Asia—dulling the sense of the objective and tangible and making the perceived more important than the fact. There is at least a superficial similarity in the trancelike state that accompanies both experiences.

Schorr's speculation could be right, but the standard reasons for thinking so leap over some deep logical gaps. Exposure does not equal influence: if anything is known about human communication, that is known. Effort does not equal power: the fact that millions of dollars, millions of hours, millions of gallons of sweat and tears go pouring into the persuasive enterprise tells us nothing reliable about impact. One could raise the same questions about the nation's vast higher education business. In his darker moments, Robert Hutchins used to wonder whether it was not all just babysitting—keeping the adolescents safely off the streets while their limbs lengthened and their neurons synapsed.

What is known—and what we professors find hard to hold in mind—is that the audience for news is a *volunteer* audience. To cut me off, a student has to walk out in the middle of class, which can be kind of embarrassing for him and for me. The news reader has but to let his eye slide a little; the viewer has but to touch the switch. His particular teacher will never know that he was the particular one who tuned out. No examination looms ahead at the end of the term. He will not need a letter of recommendation from Walter Cronkite. If he attends, absorbs, believes, remembers, and acts on what he has learned, it is because he wants to. Like voting, political news is something the citizen can take or leave. Professors who approach television with what Anthony Smith in the winter 1978 *Daedulus* calls a "combination of disdain and social grief" might pause and remember that it is not for them as it is for us: rows of ready perceptors with nothing else to do.

There is evidence that the voluntary quality of television viewing is becoming more significant. Television sets are nearly universally available now, not only in homes but increasingly in motels, bars, airports, offices, schoolrooms, dormitories, hospitals, prisons, and even cars. Ninety-eight percent of homes wired for electricity have at least one television set, and the statistics on multitelevisioned homes are galloping upward. New technologies—UHF, cable, videodisc and casettes, videorecorder—increasingly make it possible for the viewer to get at many more broadcasting channels and to see what he wants when he wants it. The growth of public broadcasting and the adaptation of movies for television increase the range of *kinds* of programming. Radio, with an average of *four* sets per home plus seventy-four million in cars as early as 1969, broadens the range even farther.

What do the volunteers do with all this opportunity? That, too, appears to be in rapid change, though the evidence is shaky. Back in the early years of television, it seemed plausible to believe with Marshall McLuhan that television, in contrast to radio, was a highly involving, "participatory" medium. McLuhan in *Understanding Media* thought that "radio will serve as background-sound or as noise-level control, as when the ingenious teenager employs it as a means of privacy. TV will not work as background. It engages you. You have to be *with* it." But in the thirties, radio had been an engaging, with-it medium: one remembers the family gathered around the cathedral-style receiver, listening intently to the Mercury Theater of the Air or William L. Shirer, entranced, staring through the furniture. Early television was like that: the set was small, black and white, and the picture jiggly—you had to watch closely to see what those little people were doing. The family stared together over their warmed aluminum plates—a household communion, a séance of sorts. Now radio sound is everywhere, from the elevator to the sidewalk to the trees in Forest Lawn Cemetery; it is fed into the telephone to keep you calm while on hold. Increasingly, the same thing is happening to television. Today's "ingenious teenager" does his homework while "watching" television. In England, televiewing is becoming "a *secondary* activity"; in the United States, according to Michael Robinson in the summer 1977 *The Public Interest*, the audience for television news "is an *inadvertent* one—which, in large proportion, does not come purposely to television for news, but arrives almost accidentally, watching the news because it is 'on' or because it leads into or out of something else." Michael Arlen in *The View from Highway 1* catches the contemporary mode in a morning scene:

On the television screen, soldiers were now walking slowly down a country road. "Patrols fan out from the city, looking for insurgents," said a voice.

Mother said, "Joey, you finish the toast."

Joey said, "How come I have to do the toast when I don't eat toast?"

"Do you think it might be in the laundry?" Father said. "It might have fallen to the floor of the closet, and somebody might have put it in the laundry." Father passed by Clarice on his way out of the kitchen. "Don't talk all day on the phone, Clarice, " he said. Clarice rolled her eyes at the ceiling.

Frank Blair said, "Armored cars and Russian-made tanks broke up the disorder. A curfew and a state of national emergency have been proclaimed."

There was the sound of a crash from the back of the house.

"Eggs are ready, everyone!" Mother said. On the television screen, two tanks were firing into a brick wall. "Fix the set. That's too loud, Joey," she said. "Everyone! The eggs are getting cold . . . . "

Father and children left for work and school.

Outside the window, two robins padded on the snow. The rumble of the dishwasher filled the room. Mother sprayed the skillet with a jet of hot water. Charles Colson said, "There was certain information of that nature which was passed to us in the White House in 1972." The refrigerator clicked on. The dishwasher churned. The telephone began to ring. "Hi, Beth," Mother said. "Wait a minute while I turn the TV down. We were just listening to the morning news."

New and striking research by Robert L. Stevenson and Kathryn P. White is consistent with Arlen's impression. The standard question asking people "where you get most of your news about what's going on in the world today" (64 percent said television in 1976) is knockable on a number of counts, but the main knock is that most of nothing is still nothing. Stevenson and White cite a careful study by the Surgeon General's Scientific Advisory Committee on Television and Social Behavior—a national sample of 6,000 adults kept viewing diaries for two weeks. About half reported they did not watch one network evening news program in those fourteen days. About a fifth said they watched six or more times. By contrast, 90 percent said they had read yesterday's newspaper. But another ingenious study casts strong doubt not only on the meaningfulness of the Nielsen ratings but also on these diary and self-report estimates. Twenty Kansas City families let cameras be set up in their homes to videotape the watchers and what they watched for six days. On questionnaires asking how much viewing they did, yesterday and over the six days, the families inflated the actuality by 40 to 50 percent. And Nielsenites would be shocked to learn that almost half the time the evening news shows were blazing forth into these living rooms, no human eye at all was focused thereupon. Stevenson and White's own careful national research gives the same rough picture: half of America does not watch the evening news, one in four watch it occasionally (one to four times in two weeks), one in fifty watch it every night (thirteen or more times), one in a hundred confess to every-night viewing at "full attention."

In this light it is not too surprising that many a message misses. Thomas E. Patterson and Robert D. McClure in *The Unseeing Eye* note that a *majority* of viewers cannot remember two minutes later what was being advertised on the commercial they saw two minutes before. Similarly, of people who said they had recently watched the evening network news, two out of three could not recall accurately even one news story. And with respect to the 1972 presidential campaign, "if people only watched network news, they did not come to know more than people who ignored the news media"—print and broadcast—"during the fall of 1972." Plenty of other evidence supports Anthony Smith's view that "the gentle release from the embrace of television" is a real happening, if ever we were so embraced.

On a good old educational principle, these lessons bear repeating. Both the enthusiastic ad-seller and the indignant intellectual have let the facts slip by them. Television today is a gigantic enterprise. The prime time advertising rates waft ever higher, and the politicians pant after coverage. Frank Mankiewicz in *Remote Control* reports that the 1976 presidential race was "the first campaign in which both candidates virtually ignored other ways to reach the voter, and concentrated almost all of their time, energies, staff resources, and money on the ways in which they would be seen—and heard—on television." But three truths now stare us in the face. First, the impact of television news has been grossly overdrawn by the medium's friends and enemies. Second, for many millions of Americans, television is the *only* source of news about the candidates. And third, there are millions more out there—their right to vote in hand—who are not even being reached by television.

Before leaping to the professor's usual conclusion, that people don't watch because the stuff is not worth watching, we might pause to notice where these truths put all of us who think of ourselves as educators. It turns out that all our national smarts and all our sophisticated machinery have as yet made a pretty modest dent in persuasion's first obstacle: getting cognized. The call for volunteers goes begging. The rattle of the civic drum, out there in the town square, cannot be heard through the tavern door, and when Paul Revere hoots by, down slam the windows. To get the American mule's attention, we find, is harder than we thought. To put the matter positively, there is a job to be done and the tools at hand to do it.

The Ego Strategies

The dictionary says the archaic meaning of a "lecture" is something read aloud. In olden times when books were rare and literacy more so, the lecturer proclaimed from a script positioned on his lectern—a primitive teleprompter. If he was thought to believe in what he spoke, he was a professor (from *profiteri*, to declare publicly). Time passed and status passed to the professor who wrote his own material, collecting his thoughts and facts in an original composition—a sermon (from *serere*, to join, link together). Even more impressive came to be the professor who got out and did his own research (from *circare*, to travel through, traverse) and lectured on that. And added points accrued if the professor had so mastered his material that he could throw away the script and wing it (*ad libitum*, in accordance with one's wishes).

Like badges deck today's newsmen: the reader only, for all his acting embellishment, is an announcer, a town crier braying whatever is handed him. A notch above is the professing journalist, who attests to the truth of what he says. The writer frames the message he speaks, and the reporter fares out and carries back his own reports. The commentator and the interviewer appear, at least, as spontaneous thinkers-along-with, readers from the heart.

Whichever of these stances the viewer recognizes in the face of the newsspeaker, a plausible reason for attending is to get information. Education as essentially a conveyance affecting the student's knowledge is an old and wide theme in our culture. It links with the theory of democracy through the concept of informed consent. Normatively speaking, consent from ignorance can never be genuine, no more so than conversion by the sword. Pragmatically speaking, an ignorant citizenry is dangerously unready when the time comes for choice, the key citizen choice being election. Fanatics are always available, Lippmann in *Liberty and the News* saw, and

> both in war and revolution there seems to operate a kind of Gresham's Law of the emotions, in which leadership passes by a swift degeneration from a Mirabeau to a Robespierre; and in war, from a high-minded statesmanship to the depths of virulent, hating jingoism.

How does that happen?

> The cardinal fact always is the loss of contact with objective information. Public as well as private reason depends upon it. Not what somebody says, not what somebody wishes were true, but what is beyond all our opining, constitutes the touchstone of our sanity.

If political sanity depends on voters knowing facts, a great many Americans are political neurotics. Scattered polls over the years since World War II hint at the magnitude of the remaining educational opportunity, even allowing for the fact that some respondents may say they "don't know" just to get the quiz over with. Roughly *half* or more of The People don't know *how many* U. S. Senators there are from each state, don't know that U. S. Representatives come up for reelection every two years, don't know who their Congressman is, don't know who their Senators are, don't know that the United States is a member of NATO. Roughly two-thirds to three-fourths or more don't know what the three branches of the federal government are, don't know what the Bill of Rights is, don't know what important event happened in this country in 1776, don't know the name of the national anthem. A survey published in 1974 (done by "The National Assessment of Educational Progress") showed that of people twenty-six to thirty-five years old, less than half know how to vote or knew how presidential candidates are nominated. Half the seventeen-year-olds thought the President can appoint members of Congress. In 1976 nearly all young people knew who President Ford was—but two-thirds of the thirteen-year-olds and a quarter of the seventeen-year-olds didn't know that he was a Republican. Nor is the problem confined to wayward youth: back in the 1960s, a third of The People thought the John Birch Society was a leftist outfit. Many another survey shows that high fractions are ignorant of who the Vice President is, who the candidates are, what they stand for, what standard political concepts like tariffs or price supports mean.

Professional reporters, perpetually marinating in the brine of politics, keep getting shocked by public ignorance. In May 1976 David Broder took a brief respite from the campaign to reflect in the July-August *Democratic Review*:

> I think that the general public, those who will be voting in November, are just now beginning to tune in. The majority of them will not tune in until convention time. But that's nothing new. I can remember my absolute astonishment at a Gallup Poll that was taken immediately after the Democratic convention in 1960 which showed that, at that point, more than 50% of the voters knew for the first time that John Kennedy was a Roman Catholic. That fact had been the starting point for every political discussion among Democratic Party insiders, people who were attentive to politics, for four years, going back to the Bailey-Sorensen memo about why Kennedy should be the vice-presidential nominee. You cannot exaggerate the difference between the perceptions and awareness of those who are part of the attentive public and those who are ultimately going to make the decision in the general election.

Television news puts out some corrective input, with respect to presidential campaigning. About 40 percent of the evening news stories from September 18 to November 6, 1972 were campaign stories, according to Patterson and McClure in *The Unseeing Eye*. Earlier in the year, when voters were making their key nomination decisions, coverage was spread more thinly. But even at the fall apex, only little scraps of network time were devoted to what voters needed to know: information relevant to comparing future Presidents. Over all those nights, at about 22 minutes of news each program, ABC gave us a total of 19 minutes 30 seconds; CBS, 16 minutes 24 seconds; and NBC, 8 minutes and 5 seconds on "the candidates' key personal and leadership qualifications for office." There were more drops in the bucket on "key issues of the election": ABC, 35 minutes 19 seconds; CBS, 46 minutes 20 seconds; and NBC, 26 minutes 14 seconds. By contrast, each network broadcast more than two hours of news on the campaign as a horse race—rallies, motorcades, polls, strategies, and the like. At the height of the 1976 primary season—back when the race had a lot of hard runners—between the New Hampshire primary in February and the Pennsylvania primary in April, Jimmy Carter got several lions' shares of news attention: 43 percent of network coverage, according to a paper Patterson presented in 1977 to the American Political Science Association annual meeting. Jackson was next with 18 percent, and Harris, Bayh, and Shriver got 4, 3, and 2 percent, respectively. (Newspaper and magazine coverage was somewhat *more* out of balance.) Whatever the broadcasters' intentions, the predominant *operative* criteria were: winners and pictures.

The viewer tuning in for facts to guide his choice would, therefore, have to pick his political nuggets from a great gravel pile of political irrelevancy. Even then, most of what he would get would not be facts "beyond all our opining" but rather candidate opinions on issues—notoriously poor predictors of presidential action. And television's felt duty (imposed and voluntary) to give a "balanced" account means that a clear expression of one opinion impels presentation of at least one more, subtracting yet more time from the crucial questions: who are these guys, where are they coming from, what are they likely to do to us?

Why don't the people and their educators do better? A beginning explanation focuses on the *costs* of getting and giving information. Most people have a lot of demands on their time and, more significantly, on their attention. The old image of the dozing citizenry, dawdling away its leisure while Rome burns, waiting to be tickled and poked into political life, is, in modern America, a romantic myth. So is the idea that the rich new professionals, free at last from the chains of necessity, lie around in their lawn chairs between traipses on the golf course. So is the picture of youth hippiedom wallowing away the best years of its lives. Teenagers are entering the work force 2.5 times as fast as babies are entering the American world. Close to half the grownup women are working away from home. Men with a little time left over from their main jobs take on another one, and your average American worker changes jobs a dozen times in his career. Forty percent work overtime on the job, and, in more and more one-parent families, double-time at home (Rosabeth Moss Kanter, "Work in a New America" in *Daedalus*, Winter 1978).

In *Working* Studs Terkel quotes steelworker Mike LeFevre: "It isn't that the average working guy is dumb. He's tired, that's all." Here is how he relates to television:

When I get home, I argue with my wife a little bit. Turn on TV, get mad at the news. (laughs.) I don't even watch the news that much. I watch Jackie Gleason. I look for any alternative to the ten o'clock news. I don't want to go to bed angry. Don't hit a man with anything heavy at five o'clock. He just can't be bothered. This is his time to relax. The heaviest thing he wants is what his wife has to tell him.

"He just can't be bothered." The cost is too high. Scholar Anthony Downs in *An Economic Theory of Democracy* puts it this way:

> In general, it is irrational to be politically well-informed because the low returns from data simply do not justify their cost in time and other scarce resources. Therefore many voters do not bother to discover their true views before voting, and most citizens are not well enough informed to influence directly the formulation of those policies that affect them.

That is not true just for the steelworkers of the world. "Ironically," notes Ben Bagdikian in *The Information Machines*, "professionalization of occupations with its high income rewards has not produced a simple expansion of daily leisure time but an increasing intrusion of career into almost every available segment of waking hours." But the same thing happens at the other end of the communications connection. Leonard Woolf sees "great mental dangers in journalism," the "most virulent" of which affects editors (and, without a doubt, television producers):

> It creates a kaleidoscopic, chaotic, perpetual motion rhythm of the mind. As soon as you have produced one number of your paper, you have to begin thinking and planning the next. Your mind gets into the habit of opening and shutting at regular intervals of 24 hours or seven days like the shells of a mussel or the shutters of a camera . . . . (*Beginning Again*)

Busy, busy, busy. Broadcaster and broadcastee rein in the reach of their temporal and spatial imaginations as the immediacies thunder through their heads. To stand back from all that, and *think* about it, costs more than it turns out to be worth.

What that means for democracy today and tomorrow is pure and simple: we have to begin where we are. Democracy's virtue is realism. It is not the best form of government; it is the best real form of government. It makes itself up out of what it has got. Nothing is to be gained by lashing the public, the educators, or the televisors with the whips of scorn—at least we know that much about educating: scorn inhibits receptivity. Defensive posturing of the "we-know-our-business" variety does not work either. Nor does the romantic dream of the Wise People as stand-ins for God, capable of alchemizing whatever dross they are handed into civic gold. When democracy works, which is far from all the time, it is essentially a learning enterprise by which the society comes to see what government can and cannot do to make life better, happier, more just for more of us. It is a second-best business, edging toward second-best values like freedom and fairness, equality and rights. There can be health in it, but no perfection; it struggles to establish *conditions* for virtue.

Journalism has, I think, contributed to perfectionistic thinking about American politics in curious ways. Polls ask people their opinions (70 percent have an opinion on anything) and thus give the impression that knowledge stands therebehind. The television ratings wildly exaggerate popular cognition—it is so easy to slip over from "x" number of sets on to "x" number of people watching to "x" number obsessively glued to their tubes. But a profounder distortion may be an ironic consequence of journalism's skepticism. Network television is our first really national news facility, and it may not be accidental that public skepticism about national leaders grew up with television. But a supposition underlying the skeptical mode is that performance could be—and even usually is—much better than the individual lapse being reported. A myth of general competence is conveyed, reinforced by the apparently exceptional character of the immediate error.

Now, as anybody knows who has kicked around with professors and professionals and literati and politicians and administrators of one kind or another, the world gets by on much less competence than the innocent suppose. We have an interest in persuading clientelia that we know what we are about. They have an interest in believing that. But one has only to listen in when doctors or lawyers or journalists hold one of their hair-down humor sessions to perceive the thin ice under the snowbank. We have not read those things that we ought to have read. We subscribe to more than we can cognize. We are far less certain than we seem, all of us authorities. Insofar as it pretends otherwise—conveying a sense of competent, thoroughly-informed rationality as normal—journalism brittle-izes reputations, so that one crack shatters them. Thus also the reputation of the public flashes back and forth between dumb (the fear of George Wallace's popularity) and smart (the hope that Reagan's transfer plan would laugh him out of court). Perhaps the prime example is the anchorman himself, whose years of pithy practice make him such a good conversationalist, but whose calm and knowledgeable air probably produces in his audience the habituated conviction that the right way, the true way, the competent way is *known*.

Beginning where we are would start with acknowledging the extraordinary difficulties people experience in trying to teach one another. It would develop strategies based on the actualities of the teacher's knowledge and the student's capacity to learn. Most importantly, it would experiment and vigorously assess the results.

An example of experimental content on television could be coverage of busing for school integration. Frank Mankiewicz and Joel Swerdlow in *Remote Control* point out a fundamental change in our social knowledge about busing. A very few years ago, busing was a theory—a rather complex theory largely born by generalization from situations different in important respects from those its application would create. Since then, busing for integration has become an *experience* for millions of American children. The authors claim it works:

> Occasionally, newspapers will carry "round-up" accounts of busing, and when they do a close reading yields the information that, except for Boston—which has contributed its good "visual" television coverage every September as the school year begins—busing is accepted and "working" in every other city where it is going on.

If that is true (and a thorough report by the Department of Justice backs it up), television news could surely find ways to show and tell that story, including the uncertainties. For example, they could balance Boston with Rocky Mount, North Carolina, where a whole community worked through to integration in a drama featuring such highly-videoable phenomena as cheerleaders, school anthems, locker mates, and Boy's State delegations. Along a wider front, television journalists could learn to cover success without sentimentality, without romanticizing The People, without pretense of finality. Considering the enormous popularity of "how to" print publications and the myriads of Americans up against tough community problems, it might work—even in the ratings. The purpose need not be charity or encouragement or moralizing, but simply the accurate representation of realities highly salient to the viewer's round of life.

An example of experimental form is already in train: slightly longer and, more importantly, more factual and thematic pieces on the evening news. When in 1963 the networks shifted from fifteen to thirty minute news, it was plausible to suppose individual stories would get longer, but they did not; ninety seconds became standard. Part of the reason was the need to work in more commercials; part was the broadcasters' felt duty to cover as much as possible of the day's events. A rationale from science was that viewers have short attention spans. "What men who make the study of politics a vocation cannot do," wrote Lippmann in a slower time, "the man who has an hour a day for newspapers and talk cannot possibly hope to do. He must seize catchwords and headlines or nothing." Thus the concept of television news as a "headline service," though in fact standardized story length sacrifices the precise utility of headlining: differentiation. The barrel-bottom ratings of long programs featuring candidates or social issues seemed to confirm the traditional wisdom. Thus television got stuck, or stuck itself, in a lockstep tiptoe through one little ministory after another. Warren Mitofsky felt the constraint in 1976: "You can't put anything on the air that you have to sit there and explain. If the picture doesn't tell its own story, forget it. It's not there long enough." That tradition dies hard, but there are hints of change. Longer-story programs like "60 Minutes" have sustained popularity and spawned imitations, and it has dawned on the mind that people sit still and watch hard for many a sporting event and sitcom. The audience for "Roots" hung in there for eight straight evenings, opening to an estimated 77,868,000 pairs of eyes and closing with an all-time record-smashing 99,226,000. Conceivably the evening news might follow the development television comedy has taken: from shows jammed with one-liners, to the series of anecdotal funny stories, to Norman Lear's half-hour connected sagas.

There is nothing virtuous per se about longer news stories, but they at least open up a chance for experiment, as the "McNeil-Lehrer Report" shows. Television already has an advantage: "Television news is more *thematic* than other types of news; only the shortest items—those less than 30 seconds—lack a didactic conclusion or message. Especially since the development of the 30-minute newscast, television tends to offer us 'stories,' not news items." In *The View from Highway 1,* Michael Arlen suggests what the new wave might float into consciousness:

> Think of the advances in film or visual language over the past thirty years. Think of the ways that people found to tell stories, play dialogue, set scenes, handle motion—and think of the incredibly expanded vocabulary of the modern film audience. Think of what in the way of new visual language people are given, and expect, in TV advertising.

In fact there may be a special opportunity for imitation in television ads for presidential candidates: ordinary commercial ads are soon forgotten (though they probably have Chinese water torture effects), but, according to Patterson and McClure, presidential ads are much more widely and accurately attended and remembered—and the cognition centers on the information they convey rather than the style of conveyance.

Nor is it etched in stone that news interviewing has to be done as it has been done. According to Mindy Nix in "The Meet the Press Game," the press panel shows miss many an opportunity for winding out strings of information because the professional culture (fostered by the print reporters asking questions) has insisted on a narrow goal: "Their major corporate purpose is to produce a story, with appropriate credit for the network, in Monday's newspaper." The producers say they "love to make news on Sunday instead of just talking about it" and aim "to make headlines in the record-breaking interviews with national and international leaders." In better pre-game skull sessions, the reporters might think through sequences, beyond the single "follow-up question," that would delve into the candidate's train of thought to produce a headline perhaps, but maybe a running story.

Arlen points out that the little interviews on the regular news shows habitually concentrate on one question: "How do you feel?" Then because the person interviewed may have trouble articulating how he feels ("Fine." "Bad."), the interviewer steps in to help him, as in this question posed to "a perplexed but amiable Soviet scientist": "After the years of oppression and

danger in your homeland, and after the incredible danger and difficulty of
your escape, which carried you to England ten years ago—well, perhaps
you can tell us about the kind of hospitality you've met with here?" As spies
and psychiatrists learned long ago, there are better ways to elicit *his* story,
his feelings. On occasion, the interpretation can overwhelm the interpreted.
Michael Robinson reports on his study:

> The survey data show unambiguously that the public did not realize how serious
> and significant [Ford's 1976 debates slip] the "Polish blunder" was until network
> news told them. According to Robert Teeter, on the night of the second debate,
> Ford actually held an 11-percentage point lead over Carter [as measured by
> responses to the question about "who won"]. Twenty-four hours later, Ford was 45
> points behind Carter—a net loss of 56 percentage points!

Television on the San Francisco sidewalk asked the emerging "live"
audience how they felt, how they liked it, much as later interviewers
concentrated on the affective responses of Messrs. Sadat and Begin after
their historic encounter.

Education means leading out of; teachers from long ago until now have
struggled actively to guide their pupils to the right answers. H.S.N.
McFarland in *Psychological Theory and Educational Practice* gives an example.

Who can tell me about Shakespeare?
Sir, there's a Shakespeare Café in the High Street.
Yes, but this is not a lesson on cafés, is it?
Sir, he was the author of Romeo and Juliet.
Yes, and what is Romeo and Juliet?
Please sir, it's a film. I saw it on television.
Yes, but what was it before it was a film?

Here the teacher, with his "Yes, buts," is sacrificing chance after chance to
capitalize on the learner's preexisting perceptual set. McFarland says new
information is only likely to click into place in the learner's mind

1   if it fits into a context that he recognizes and that matters to him,
2.   if he has plenty of previous experience of the kind of thing perceived, or
3.   if he has received instructions which effectively direct his attention, even
     if the context or the thing to be perceived is unfamiliar.

Similarly with remembering: it depends on recognition, salience, experience,
and instruction. Unlike controlled laboratory contexts, "The contexts of
everyday life . . . . play the pianoforte of attitudes which they elicit or
rather interact with, thus *determining* and *organizing*—not merely *facilitating*
or *inhibiting* imprinting and recall" (David Rapaport, "The Dynamics of
Remembering" in *Reflexes to Intelligence*). Thus teachers are preached at to
supply contexts, to link them to those already in the students' heads, to
press outward toward a larger inclusiveness. For all our effort, we very

often fail, and McFarland's obstacles to success will not seem strange to the televisor:

1. Teachers and students become so obsessed with "covering the ground" that they do not take enough time to formulate clearly what the principles of observation are. There is a reluctance to sacrifice coverage in the hope of strengthening principle. And there can be failure to distinguish even which principles are relevant to a particular group of learners—as when a young scholar obsessed by his personal research fails to present the broader perspective that a junior student needs to begin with.
2. Most teachers try to organize their material intelligibly, but, just as they may be reluctant to sacrifice detail to principle in terms of the subject itself, so they may be reluctant to sacrifice any of the subject to the psychological perspective and capacity of the learners. It may seem easier to bemoan the learners' defects than to make concessions to them—for example, by going more slowly (or quickly), recapitulating if necessary, or sacrificing expository to discussion time.
3. The time-tabling of courses must often put organizational feasibility before ideal patterns of learning practice. Solving the routine problems of the time-table can be such a major achievement that no provision is made to confirm or link the larger units of learning. It is hoped that everything will fall into place in due course. But few learners establish broader perspectives so readily. They have to be helped towards them by special discussions and exercises.

Food for thought, there. Possible experiments. A start in recognizing why we find it so hard to do it otherwise than it is done—not because we are forced by ineluctable constraints, but because we have, too often, let habit cast its wet blanket over the reflective imagination.

Unless we are going to give up on the nation's slower students, news of presidential campaigning must be made appealing enough to convince them to volunteer attention. Normally that will need more than links to the past; motivation points ahead. The human ego deliberates when it can see some use for it. Citizens who can be brought to see some connection between the Presidency and their lives face forward toward a vote choice. They want information they can use in vicarious experimentation before their hands are on the levers. "Deliberation," saith John Dewey "is a dramatic rehearsal (in imagination) of various competing possible lines of action"—exactly what the expectant voter is about. He is awake already, feeling already, preferring already. Dewey puts his problem in a nutshell:

> It is a great error to suppose that we have no preferences until there is a choice. We are always biased beings, tending in one direction rather than another. The occasion of deliberation is an *excess* of preferences, not natural apathy or indifference. We want things that are incompatible with one another; therefore we have to make a choice of what we *really* want, of the course of action, that is, which most fully releases activities. Choice is not the emergence of preference out of indifference. It is the emergence of a unified preference out of competing preferences.

Television news, which moved beyond telling the citizens what their momentary collective preferences are as the next primary approaches, to telling them what they need to know—precisely on the issue of President choosing—might yet enlist intellectual apparatus.

Superego and Id Strategies

The evening news is like a ritual. John Chancellor says, "Good evening," in a pastoral tone, inviting the faithful to the ceremony.There follows a train of abuses and cautionary tales; we experience the minihorrors and anxious perils, but are comforted the while: nothing is so bad that the commercials are canceled or the anchormen cast emotionally adrift. The steady, regular rhythm of the liturgy lulls along. Then Howard K. Smith appears, barely restraining his ministerial rage às he Jeremiahs various distant miscreants, a spoon of bile to spice the blandness. And then at last Walter Cronkite sighs his ambiguous benediction, that all of the above has now passed away; we should go, and sin no more.

Much news consumption is that way—a familiar little arc in the round of life. Father picks up the newspaper from the stoop, brings it in, sits in his chair, opens it, and makes a quiet, private place for himself. The radio helps Mother cook; the television light colors the children's homework. Deprived of these easing events, as when the power fails, one feels vaguely anxious, like discovering at the office that you have left your belt at home.

The news ritual plugs in America's civic religion, reinforcing values thought essential to democracy. The duty to vote—the main motivator for voting, the studies show—is a prime example: anticipations of apathy are always announced in grievous accents. Attacks on free speech are satisfyingly deplored. Progressivism, liberalism, pragmatism, egalitarianism, and Constitutionalism get their licks in. In a steadily bourgeoisifying society, demographically aging, homing, and "rising," barely diverted, in our behavior, by a few literarily renascent bohemian flashers, the media tutor us in the political proprieties as they take exception to deviations therefrom. Mostly mild, on rare occasions the anchormen let us know, not only by their words, but by their demeanors, how revolting they find the rule-breakers. That happened late one Saturday night: John Chancellor broke out in indignation when the President had the FBI surround the Justice Department. "I heard boots!" Chancellor explains, "The Constitution was being ripped up!"

The duty to watch the news probably works among the less educated as the duty to read the *New York Times* works among the more. The utile payoffs for most are conversational. We being an opinionated people, the news helps us with the one most critical evaluative problem democrats face: linking political ethics with political experience. Much of our talk centers on that; many of our failures trace to missing that link. Gunnar Myrdahl taught us that. Decade after decade, we went along believing in justice for black people and acting as if they were another, lesser species.

Political values in America stay remarkably steady. From 1956 to 1972, years of formerly unbelievable change in public policy and practice in civil rights, support for school integration perked along, year by year, at about 40 percent. Everett Ladd in *Public Opinion*, March-April, 1978 marshals data to show that "continuity, not change, is the most striking feature of American values today. As a society, we are being propelled by old beliefs, not by the new ones, and it is the survival of those old beliefs that is the distinguishing feature of our time." Sensitive to change, we repeatedly overestimate the degree to which party loyalties have eroded. Possibly voters are becoming somewhat more consistent in bundling issues together, but the evidence is mushy because the questions asked in the relevant polls have been changed in ways encouraging more consistent answers. So we are not in the middle of any ethical revolution, at least as far as politics is concerned. The galling old problem is not that people believe wrongly, but that they apply uncertainly. There are many examples like this one in Flanigan and Zingale's *Political Behavior of the American Electorate*: in 1971, 95 percent said they were willing to support the right of their neighbors to circulate a petition—but when it is specified that the petition favors legalizing marijuana, support drops to 52 percent.

Television news has the format to address this challenge, in the sermonette and in the little hooker the reporter is supposed to attach at the end of his story. Mostly, though, those value-event connectors are far too elegant and enigmatic to get through and take hold. Years of research on such topics as anti-antisemitism education shows how wonderfully adroit we are at missing the point when it sticks too close to the heart. Television's devotion to balance and diverse appeal and perhaps the reporter's inhibition against sounding naive make it hard for him to say, flat out, what democratic goods and bads are tied to this and that happening. It could be tried. Tomorrow's twenty-two minutes await the attempt.

The newsmen might even find friends for this ethical adventure among their neighbors in the network—the soap opera makers. Popular romances like "As The World Turns" plod along from one sodden tragedy to another, but they do express and reinforce the value of the human care of human beings. People are portrayed as committed to one another, locked together for better or for worse in an endless round of betrayals and reconciliations. Love wins out over sex (Nancy beats Lisa), at least eventually. There is violence aplenty, but it is dramatized as awful, not easy, as in the shoot-'em-up shows. Unlike the evening comedies, the soaps do not wrap it all up at the end in a happy package; rather, this tragedy's denouement coincides with the next one's rising action. The characters are relatively complex and individualized compared to Kojak or Hawkeye or Charlie's Angels; they are moral mixtures. Children exist and are worried over. The broad human image is of flawed people struggling to cope with one damned thing after another, drawing on such faith and strength as they can muster, hoping for some happy times, discovering, now and then, a little lightening charity. In *these* respects, soap opera faces life more honestly than much "real world" political portrayal, in which slick know-it-alls prance around displaying their certainties.

There are other powerful friends of evaluative education. The *New York Times* editorial page, says its editor John Oaks, is "the soul of the newspaper," and its "guiding principle" is "to provide leadership in what we hope and believe and consider to be the public good" *(New York,* November 3, 1975). The *Times'* cramping sense of responsibility and restraint may occasionally restrict publication of all the fit news, but the paper is the country's preeminent chaired professor of political ethics. Yet in its direct influence, it passes right over the heads of the great national student body. If *they* are to be reached—their life-linked superegos activated—television must do it.

There are those who think that television news *is* soap opera and is on the way to becoming a heehaw laugh show. If the public ego is otherwise occupied and the public conscience disconnected from concrete public choices, the way to get at them is Barnum's way—through the id.

Nowadays the public is pictured as bored and alienated—58 percent "alienated" in 1977, according to the Harris poll. Back in 1966, 37 percent said "yes" when asked whether or not they felt that "what you think doesn't count much anymore." By 1973 that feeling was with 61 percent. The angry alienated were far outweighed by the passive alienated, the shruggers and turners-away.

Political journalists in 1975 and 1976 largely agreed with David Brinkley (quoted by Amitai Etzioni in *Psychology Today,* April 1978): the people are "bored, sick of a government which is remote, arrogant, pushy, costly, and self-serving." In our interviews, Wallace Westfeldt had them "bored with a lot of bullshit." Lou Cannon saw the people "retreating to the joys of the private garden," like Epicurus, and the candidate managers, from Reagan's Nofziger (people are "sick to death of politicians who want to be all things to all people") to Carter's Powell (people are "tired of constant yapping") agreed. The *Wall Street Journal*'s Allan Otten says, "I just have a feeling of a huge iron screen between me and everybody out there. And they are not listening or looking."

A strong old deep theme in the journalism culture is that you had better not be bored. When reportorial boredom is unavoidable, the reporters strike back; for example, by chanting along in unison with the candidate as he intones some shopworn sobriquet. But normally reporters are professionally unbored; perhaps the main journalistic more is "Thou shalt not be bored." One says "We *can't* be bored," another says "Reporters shouldn't be bored. They are not to get bored." If in fact boredom starts to infect his mind, the reporter keeps it to himself. "Dull?," says one, "Relative to what? You don't report it as 'dull today' because that's a subjective judgment." Stan Cloud expresses precisely the journalist's internalization of the antiboredom rule: "I don't think journalists ought to ever say anything is boring. I just don't think things are boring, especially any story I'm working on. If I'm on it, it ain't boring!" As the national conventions approached, journalists worried that they were up against yet another "lull before the lull." When John Lindsay begins to sense the candidates as "a drab lot, slate gray, like a flotilla of United States destroyers," he can remind himself pridefully that he is "the only reporter left who is not bored by Hubert Humphrey." The norm is to see the campaign as a "great mystery," "lots of fun," "terribly exciting," "fascinating—a helluva good story."

Eleanor Roosevelt once fell asleep while being interviewed on the "Today Show." Ron Rosenbaum in *More,* March 1978, says the network evening news audience trends older, and the oldness of it gets reinforced by the extraordinary frequency of ads for Dentu-Creme, Ex-Lax, Arthritis Pain Formula, Preparation H, Sominex, Nytol, Geritol, Tums, Polident, and Pepto-Bismol. The wisdom of the 1960s was to low-key the television experience, as in NBC's principle of "Least Objectionable Programing." The rule was not to dwell unnecessarily on anything too upsetting or annoying, which is why, Ron Powers says, "Television has had to be dragged screaming by the hair into every important 'investigative' story of the past ten years." News designers worried when an authority like Jacques Ellul warned that, by always raising problems without offering solutions, the newscasters were threatening their audiences with what another critic called "psychic overload." The candidates in 1976 put their hardhitting commercial messages back in the cans, opting instead for "Feelin' Good"(Ford) and "Down Home" (Carter) strategies.

Obviously least-objectionalism risks boredom. These days, particularly in local news broadcasts, experiments are underway to make newswatching fun. Apparently it pays. Professional consultants are felicitously feed for this kind of advice:

> Many journalists make the error of assuming that good factual reporting alone will involve typical "concerned" citizens. The truth is that there aren't too many "concerned" listeners out there . . . .

> First, we suggest that the writers avoid starting a newscast with a stark fact. Begin instead with an evocative line which will catch the ear of the listener, arouse his curiosity, and begin to "pull" him into the newscast . . . .

> For example, instead of beginning with the words, "Ralph Botts has been fined

$10,000 for his part in an alleged . . .", you might begin with, "Is the FBI nosing in on Chicago?" or, "He'll have to cough it up . . ." or, *"Ten thousand dollars* and the poor guy is penniless . . . ."

The whole idea is to set the listener up so he becomes interested and must listen for more. (Frank Magid, quoted in *The Newscasters)*

Television did not invent the hyped lead. "You've got to lure them into it," says a print man, "get them to read the story. Give them controversy, a circus, make it funny. You're like a circus barker – 'Get 'em in! Get 'em in!' " In his 1920s novel *Scoop,* Evelyn Waugh had defined news as "what a chap who doesn't care much about anything wants to read," and in *Ballyhoo* (1927), Silas Bent worried over "the inflation of matter appealing to unconscious passions and hungers . . . . The news which startles, thrills and entertains . . . ."

Today we have Kelly Lange, formerly known as Dawn O'Day, anchoring newsonality for the top-rated NBC-owned television station in Los Angeles. "Look," says Lange in the *Washington Post,* December 28, 1977, "you've got your boredom. You've got your misery. You've got your tragedy. You've got to have your laughs, too. You've got to have your chuckles. Otherwise you're just asking too much of viewers who've been hassled all day long." She thinks that unlike in Washington, the newscasting "people out there [in California] really care. It's a known fact that the guys and gals out there seem to be more together as far as putting things together . . . . I *care*. I care, you know? Maybe that's silly but that's the way I am." Lange credits Tom Snyder with inventing "interplay" – bits of conversation among the newsies themselves.

"In 1976," videoanalyst Ron Powers writes in *The Newscasters,* Snyder's "News Center 4" [in New York] was quite likely the best local newscast on television: the *New York Times* of TV news." In *T.V. Guide,* May 8, 1976, Gerry Nadel says Snyder was discovered in Los Angeles by an NBC senior vice president whose evaluation is, "You'll believe *anything* he says. A *great* piece of talent! . . . a guy who's sooner or later going to be the biggest star we've got!" The president of NBC thinks he's "unique . . . the kind of guy you can't help noticing." Another television executive explains Snyder's appeal, his "magic": "Because he can be so abrasive, when he suddenly turns on that boyish charm of his, you're so surprised, you just fall in love with him." The president of NBC News says, "Tom has a big future with this network." Snyder's orientation toward his profession lacks ambiguity:

I want to be *first!* I mean, when they sit down to write the history of television and they ask, "Who did the first late-late network talk show?" – it's going to be *me.* When they write about the guy who turned around the Los Angeles and New York local-news ratings, it's going to be *me.* When they write about who did the first one-minute prime time news, it's going to be *me!* Give me the firsts, please, not some 24-year old show . . . .

If Tom Wolfe is right—that ours is "The 'Me' Decade"—Snyder's projection must ring a bell with contemporary viewers. But Snyder, brushing his long, dark hair out of his eyes, recognizes "it could all be over tomorrow. Guys like me, we're like football players or home-run hitters. We're loved for our bodies, our attractiveness. When that wears out, you're assigned to the ash heap."

Here is Tom Snyder (with anchorman Chuck Scarborough) handling the crucial news transition at 5:59 one evening:

SNYDER: You know, it's a funny thing, and we could probably spend the rest of the hour just *talking* about this and let people come in and talk about it with us. And I understand how people don't want their children to see naked bodies on television. I-I-I *guess* I understand that, a person's home is their castle. *(Pause)* But yet they go down to Forty-second Street and see it *there,* and they complain about seeing it *here,* and last night we had a picture which I thought was a little extreme, a guy in a car with five bullet holes in his *head*—and-and nobody complained about that, but they complained about seeing a woman's *breasts* on television.

SCARBOROUGH: Well, it's . . .

SNYDER: (Snappishly) It's *confusing!*

SCARBOROUGH: I think we should just give 'em the option, that's all. They have the option of going to Forty-second Street.

SNYDER: Exactly. Anyway, it comes on at 6:45 and, uh—that's it. It's called Sex Fantasies. *(The Newscasters)*

Kelly Lange's caring, Tom Snyder's air of barely restrained animal energy, are two modes of pitching for the youth audience. Another is the sporty bite of Howard Cosell at ABC. The leap to fiction happens with Chevy Chase whose news spoofs on "Saturday Night" were immensely popular. Here's Chevy:

. . . and President Ford's regular weekly accident took place this week in Hartford, Connecticut, where Ford's Lincoln was hit by a Buick. Alert Secret Service agents seized the Buick and wrestled it to the ground. No one was injured in the accident, but when the President got out to see what happened, he tore his jacket sleeve on the door handle, bumped his head, and stuck his thumb in his right eye. Alert Secret Service agents seized the thumb and wrestled it to the ground. Said Mr. Ford, quote: "I just assumed that my thumb was in my pocket with the rest of my fingers . . . ." *(New York,* December 22, 1975)

The print analogue to this hard and happy talk on television is the growing fashion of gossip news. The grocery store press (e.g., *National Enquirer)* lure the pruriently curious with the endless sagas of assassination detection and Mrs. Onassis' affectional life. Great Britian's greatest gossipist, Nigel Dempster (whose byline is "Grovel"), explains the philosophy behind his line of work to Alexander Cockburn (*New York*, May 3, 1976):

I think human beings are unpleasant and they should be shown as such. In my view we live in a banana-peel society, where people are having a rotten, miserable life—as 99.9 percent of the world is—can only gain enjoyment by seeing the decline and fall of others. They only enjoy people's sordidness . . . which—but for me and other journalists around—they would not know about. They see that those who obtain riches or fame or high position are no happier than they are. It helps them get along, and frankly that is what I give them.

A milder, friendlier gossip appeal comes through in *People* magazine (circulation 1.8 million in 1976) and *Parade* (about 20 million).

What is one to make of all this? It is easy, and perhaps correct, to dismiss it as a torrent of trash, a bubbly mash of prurient indignation, secondhand licentiousness, pseudomotherly sympathy, and soul-wearing chatter, all destined, one hopes, to be washed out of public discourse by the waters of rationality. That has not happened, despite revolutionary rises in educational levels and broadcast information. Its popularity goes way back, at least to J. Fred Muggs, the dressed-up little ape on Dave Garroway's "Today Show," who won and held énormous audiences for four and a half years in the early 1950s. The realistic question then is not whether caring and bite and fun and curiosity should be walled away from the news, but rather how they might be turned to educational advantage.

We teachers have also tried to enlist student ids. In universities, one of the reasons we keep insisting that professorial advancement depend on research as well as teaching ability is that the former tends to excite and enhance the latter. Simply conveying information, year after year, can make Professor Jack a dull boy, even to himself, however inventive an actor he is. But if he is engrossed in some hot truth pursuit of his own, that shows and can heat up his presentation in adjacent subject areas. The showman only, whose mind is taken up with his own act, has a comparatively short intellectual half-life and is likely to flame out as the joys of entertaining pall. More importantly, the researcher-teacher in his ideal incarnation communicates excitement about his *subject*, not just about himself. His affect and his intellect are coupled in tight embrace. His students see and hear his mind at work on a matter beyond himself, are lured to *it*, not to him. Alumni who will never forget old What's-his-name—that marvelous fellow who taught them chemistry (or was it English?); anyway, he was one hombre of a teacher—have missed connection with the heart of the enterprise. The Socrateses teach because they cannot help themselves; their fascination with truth-loving makes it impossible for them not to tell about it.

That analogy is useful, I think, in considering id strategies for the news. The cool commentator and the temporally-undifferentiated lock step evening news' tramp through the standard story categories deprive the viewer of an educationally effective stimulus—the speaker's own reactions.

In ordinary life, a very large element of communication is emotional: how important does this seem to him? Does it pain or please him? Is he casual or engaged? Afraid or confident? Much of that communication is nonverbal—as in face and body language—and even more is nonliteral—as in tone of voice, accented expletives, etc. In the classroom, students are very quick to pick up signals that teacher is "really into" his subject or is "covering material" he "could care less" about. On television news, cool modes of presentation, appropriate for an earlier time when audiences were cognizing the newscaster's reactions closely and continuously and were thus more vulnerable to overreacting to his emotive twitches, are out of sync with a generation gone cool to television. Struggling against hysteria, the cool newshawk may contribute to "psychic numbing"—further narcotizing an already nodding viewership, routinizing real horrors and glories into a pallid and uniform flow of current events.

The solution is not chimpanzees jumping up and down in their studio blazers. With respect to political news, what is needed are newspeople who are themselves genuinely interested in politics and who know instinctively or can learn how to get that caring curiosity through the tube. If that genuine concern is just not there, if the performer is enlivened by something short of that (such as his own ambition), over the long run it will be hard for him to fake it. The ratings may blip up for the moment with most any novelty, but it is the excitement of politics itself which will sustain. The reporter whose fascination is so fastened to the news that he will on occasion step aside and let us see it understands that.

Anchors Aweigh?

For Jimmy Carter, says his television advisor Barry Jagoda, "Television has become a regular part of his life, as natural as anything else in his life. It's not a big deal." And thus it has become for the American millions. Its educational potential and problem is summed up in just those phrases: "a regular part of life" and "no big deal." We know far less than we might about how people connect those concepts. We do know that the trickle-out or two-step-flow idea—that highly attentive viewers will clue in the casual ones—does not work for television. The really intense electronic freaks are not widely plugged in socially and may use the medium for self-hypnosis, as does one who reports that "When I am hyper and need something to bring me down, TV is my tranquilizer. One half-hour of TV is better than a handful of Seconals." A psychological study of "heavy" television viewers found them people who "see the real world as more dangerous and more frightening than those who watch very little," and are "less trustful of their fellow citizens and more fearful of the real world"(George Gerbner and Larry Gross, "The Scary World of TV's Heavy Viewer" *Psychology Today*,

April 1976)—folks hardly likely to have circles of friends or to relate to them as a source. "Television's Four Highly Attracted Audiences," by another report, are women, blacks, the poor, and the elderly—the discriminated against, not on the average those turned to for discriminating political judgments (George Comstock, "Television's Four Highly Attracted Audiences," *New York University Education Quarterly,* Winter 1978). Like every new mass medium, television cuts ground out from under extant elites, an important part of whose authority was in knowing first.

For the typical television viewer—a citizen, a voter—television news is as it is for Jimmy Carter, as natural as anything else in his life. He pays attention to the weather because he will have to cope with it tomorrow. The rest of it he can take or leave. But if Walter Cronkite says clearly and forcefully that he ought to take, he probably will, for a few minutes anyway—particularly if he can hear in the message some of the sound of the life he knows, the faith he believes, the song his heart sings.

What we have left in this country is a new elite, like it or not. They now occupy Jefferson's "higher degrees of genius," and they have a chance to impart to general America a new education, fit for the new time, a modern curriculum in the capacity for "vigilant and distrustful superintendence." They stand by at the anchor, watching and calling, lest the rest of us suddenly discover that some rogue of a pilot has run us into an enemy's port.

Like today's generation of journalist anchormen, Thomas Jefferson felt a little worn in 1795, penning that letter in Monticello; he saw himself "but as a passenger, leaving the world and its government to those who are likely to live longer in it." In 1800, he ran for President and he won.

Index

The American Assembly
COLUMBIA UNIVERSITY

About the American Assembly

The American Assembly was established by Dwight D. Eisenhower at Columbia University in 1950. It holds nonpartisan meetings and publishes authoritative books to illuminate issues of United States policy.

An affiliate of Columbia, with offices in the Graduate School of Business, the Assembly is a national educational institution incorporated in the State of New York.

The Assembly seeks to provide information, stimulate discussion, and evoke independent conclusions in matters of vital public interest.

AMERICAN ASSEMBLY SESSIONS

At least two national programs are initiated each year. Authorities are retained to write background papers presenting essential data and defining the main issues in each subject.

A group of men and women representing a broad range of experience, competence, and American leadership meet for several days to discuss the Assembly topic and consider alternatives for national policy.

All Assemblies follow the same procedure. The background papers are sent to participants in advance of the Assembly. The Assembly meets in small groups for four or five lengthy periods. All groups use the same agenda. At the close of these informal sessions, participants adopt in plenary sessions a final report of findings and recommendations.

Regional, state, and local Assemblies are held following the national session at Arden House. Assemblies have also been held in England, Switzerland, Malaysia, Canada, the Caribbean, South America, Central America, the Philippines, and Japan. Over one hundred thirty institutions have co-sponsored one or more Assemblies.

ARDEN HOUSE

Home of the American Assembly and scene of the national sessions is Arden House, which was given to Columbia University in 1950 by W. Averell Harriman. E. Roland Harriman joined his brother in contributing toward adaptation of the property for conference purposes. The buildings and surrounding land, known as the Harriman Campus of Columbia University, are 50 miles noth of New York City.

Arden House is a distinguished conference center. It is self-supporting and operates throughout the year for use by organizations with educational objectives.

The background papers for each Assembly are published in cloth and paperbound editions for use by individuals, libraries, businesses, public agencies, nongovernmental organizations, educational institutions, discussion and service groups. In this way the deliberations of Assembly sessions are continued and extended.

The subject of Assembly programs to date are:

1951____United States-Western Europe Relationships
1952____Inflation
1953____Economic Security for Americans
1954____The United States' Stake in the United Nations
____The Federal Government Service
1955____United States Agriculture
____The Forty-Eight States
1956____The Representation of the United States Abroad
____The United States and the Far East
1957____International Stability and Progress
____Atoms for Power
1958____The United States and Africa
____United States Monetary Policy
1959____Wages, Prices, Profits, and Productivity
____The United States and Latin America
1960____The Federal Government and Higher Education
____The Secretary of State
____Goals for Americans
1961____Arms Control: Issues for the Public
____Outer Space: Prospects for Man and Society
1962____Automation and Technological Change
____Cultural Affairs and Foreign Relations
1963____The Population Dilemma
____The United States and the Middle East
1964____The United States and Canada
____The Congress and America's Future
1965____The Courts, the Public, and the Law Explosion
____The United States and Japan
1966____State Legislatures in American Politics
____A World of Nuclear Powers?
____The United States and the Philippines
____Challenges to Collective Bargaining